W9-DAX-853

Javanese Lives

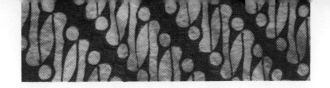

Javanese Lives

Women and Men
in Modern Indonesian Society

BY WALTER L. WILLIAMS

with
Claire Siverson
F. X. Andrianto
Hazairin Eko Prasetyo
Hernie
Kedah
Martha Pardede
Priyanto
Ratna Indriani
Robertus Widjojo
S. M. Darmastuti
Sindhu Suyana

with an introduction by
James Peacock

RUTGERS UNIVERSITY PRESS
New Brunswick and London

Portions of "A Market Woman," "A Seamstress," and "A Cake Seller" have been previously published, in a different form, in the *Journal of Women's History* (1990), and are reprinted by permission.

Design element: Lost-wax Batik cloth in the pattern for members of the Sultan's family, Yogyakarta, Java. *Photo: Walter L. Williams*

Williams, Walter L., 1948–
    Javanese lives : women and men in modern Indonesian society / by
Walter L. Williams with Claire Siverson . . . [et al.] ; with an
introduction by James Peacock.
        p.   cm.
    Includes bibliographical references.
    ISBN 0-8135-1648-X (cloth)   ISBN 0-8135-1649-8 (pbk.)
    1. Java (Indonesia)—Social conditions.   2. Java (Indonesia)—
Social life and customs.   3. Women—Indonesia—Java—Interviews.
4. Men—Indonesia—Java—Interviews.   5. Java (Indonesia)—
Biography.   I. Title.
HN710.J3W55   1990
959.8'2—dc20   90-45113
                                                                  CIP

British Cataloging-in-Publication information available

Copyright © 1991 by Rutgers, The State University
All Rights Reserved
Manufactured in the United States of America

"We should make every effort to overcome obstacles, to go out and record the memories of people whose ways of life often are preserved only in those memories. And we should do it urgently, before they disappear. No more elegant tool exists to describe the human condition than the personal narrative. Ordinary people living ordinary and not-so-ordinary lives weave from their memories and experiences the meaning life has for them. . . . The spectrum of voices from otherwise obscure individuals helps us learn tolerance for differences as well as for similarities. What better place to begin our dialogue about human nature and the nature of human possibilities?"

—MARJORIE SHOSTAK, in *Interpreting Women's Lives:*
Feminist Theory and Personal Narratives (1989)

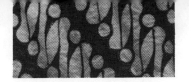

Contents

CONTENTS

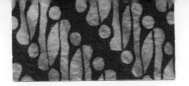

List of Illustrations

Preface

The island of Java, located between the Indian Ocean and the Pacific Ocean, is the site of an ancient Southeast Asian civilization. Even today, its people hold onto their traditions, chiefly in terms of their emphasis on artistic and spiritual traditions. Yet, the Javanese people now reaching old age have seen incredibly drastic changes in their lifetimes, probably more than any other single generation in human history. They were born in the era of European colonialism, when the Netherlands still firmly controlled Java. During World War II, the Dutch East Indies was taken over by the Empire of Japan, and a European occupying force was replaced by an Asian one. After the Japanese surrender in 1945, the Dutch returned, eager to reestablish their colonial empire.

But the winds of change were hitting the Third World, and in 1945 the independence of the new nation of Indonesia was proclaimed by the nationalist leader Sukarno. The nationalists were able, after years of armed struggle, to overthrow their Dutch colonial masters and to unite the many islands of the Indies into one nation. With Java by far the most populated island of the Indonesia archipelago, Javanese have been the main leaders in the national government, in both the Sukarno regime and the following years. Besides its bloody political revolution in the late 1940s, in 1965 Java was convulsed by a massive extermination of leftists, which resulted in the removal of the left-leaning Sukarno and the establishment of a new regime under General Suharto. Since the inauguration of a "New Order" under Suharto, Indonesia has experienced an economic revolution as well. Especially notable in recent decades is the increasing urbanization and modernization of Java. There have been many paths to the present, as people adjust to the transition from an agricultural to an urban industrial economy.[1]

In the context of great change, Indonesian people today are quite concerned about their nation's future, as the new generation struggles to merge both the traditional and the modern aspects of its way of life. In a book devoted to modern Javanese women's and men's perspectives on their lives, it is not surprising that the themes of past traditions, recent changes, and future hopes and concerns should be dominant in their minds. The purpose of this book is to let Javanese people speak for themselves. While some good anthropological studies have been written about Java, there is surprisingly little written in English about modern Indonesia. Because this is an increasingly important trading partner in the Pacific Rim economic sphere, such an oversight is regrettable.

In an attempt to collect more information about the lives of Javanese people in modern Indonesia, in 1987 the Council for the International Exchange of Scholars, sponsored by the United States government, awarded me a Fulbright research grant. For the thirteen months while I resided in Java, I was affiliated with Universitas Gadjah Mada, Indonesia's oldest university. Gadjah Mada is located in the city of Yogyakarta, a major center of Javanese culture. The juxtaposition of the sultan's court, centers for music and dance, leading art institutes, and several universities make Yogyakarta a fascinating place to live and a captivating blend of old and new.

Although I had previously interviewed some people during trips to Thailand and the Philippines, I had never before been to Indonesia. My previously published books have mostly dealt with American Indians, but my work has been based largely on life-history oral interviews. American Indians were the earliest subjects of anthropological life histories, and personal narratives have continued to exert a larger influence in American Indian studies than in other areas of anthropology. Thus, I as an American Indianist was brought in to apply this research approach to Java. I decided not only to conduct my own life-history research but also to train Indonesians to assist me.

Personal narratives are particularly valuable for allowing a reader to perceive a foreign culture from *within*. Although the act of compiling a narrative is necessarily a collaborative venture and the translation and editing necessarily reflect the researcher's cultural background and personality, life histories remain an excellent way of understanding an unfamiliar society from the perspective of a participant in that society. This is not to deny that persons might distort or idealize what they say about their lives and might avoid mentioning certain topics. A life story is not *the* truth, but it is that person's understanding of what has happened. The strength of the personal narrative is that the native person, not the researcher, is reflecting and choosing which things are most significant. We see the topics most important to that person by the amount of attention the person devotes to those topics.[2]

For example, social trends may be deduced from life histories; it became evident when conducting these interviews that the more traditional Javanese people do not talk much about their spouses, in contrast to those more Westernized individuals in nuclear families who do focus on their spouses. This denotes the traditionally less intimate relations between married partners. In Javanese culture, people marry primarily for the purposes of having children and providing stable economic units in which to raise those children. Traditional women thus tend to talk more about their children and their work, than about their husbands.

Because I regularly teach in a gender studies program at the University of Southern California, I have a particular interest in women's roles. As is the case of many areas of scholarship, there has been too much ignorance of the important roles and perspectives of women in cross-cultural studies. Therefore, I have attempted to pay particular attention to women's lives in Indonesia. This book provides an approximate balance between the number of men and women interviewed.

This focus on women is appropriate in a book of life histories because feminist scholarship has been responsible for helping to revive interest in personal narratives. By the 1970s, a new self-critical viewpoint began to emerge within the discipline of anthropology. Younger anthropologists began to question the absence of individual personalities in modern ethnographies, as well as an ahistorical presentation of "cultural systems" that seldom allowed for focus on change over time. They likewise began to examine the significance of the interaction between ethnographer and informant, itself a factor influencing the interpretation of facts. Rather than seeing ethnography as "objective scientific fact," they began to question whether that outsider's (etic) viewpoint was any more valuable than an insider's (emic) viewpoint. In reacting against "modern science," they labeled themselves "postmodern."[3]

At the same time, feminist scholarship made its point that human experience is first and foremost *gendered*, and thus for both the anthropologist and the subject of study the gender of those persons would influence what is spoken and what is written down. For most male anthropologists, especially when they directed their research to the words and actions of male informants, the masculine gender role of both the researcher and the informants was unmarked and unexamined. In contrast, feminist theory explicitly rejected a "science of man" that postulated theories for humanity based largely on the perspectives of males alone. Many female anthropologists began to look to women's experiences as a better indicator of reality for women than the androcentric theories of modern anthropology. Feminist thought emerged from and responded to the realities of the lives of women; it stressed the need to listen to women's voices and learn from women's experiences. With this critical perspective, feminist researchers turned their attention away from androcentric concepts that ignored women and began to listen to women's voices. Personal narratives of women talking about their own lives and structuring their experiences as conscious social actors became essential primary documents for a new feminist perspective.[4]

For both these reasons, the postmodern self-critical ethnographers and the feminist scholars have revived the life-history method as a means of capturing a more varied perspective than just depending on the Western (usually white male) academic to explain through Western theory. With life histories, perspectives from within the culture may be obtained, even if only imperfectly. The researcher implicitly takes a position that the perspective of the native person should be a priority in anthropology. In fact, the life-history interviewer-interpreter-editor may be the means by which Third World peoples are given a voice and thus empowered vis-à-vis the West. As these narratives demonstrate, life histories can show colonialism from the colonial subject's point of view. In these pages the expressed unanimity of opposition to both Dutch and Japanese occupations, even when the person was individually treated well by the colonialists, cannot fail to impress the reader.

Moreover, the viewpoints presented are not just a faceless Third World reaction, or even a Javanese reaction, but multiple actions and reactions by real persons. Life histories show that people are neither merely passive reactors nor inert recipients of their culture.

Individuals cope creatively with life and are actively involved in the creation of historical change. Anthropologists often have a tendency to homogenize a sociey, as if "a culture" were a single unitary whole, an exotic "other." Personal narratives, even while showing the commonalities among people who are socialized in the same society, demonstrate above all our common humanity.

At the same time, life histories show that humans—of whatever culture—are varied and diverse. Personalities and inclinations differ with any group. Not a deterministic formula, culture would be better seen as the dynamic interaction between the individual and the larger social setting, between intentional direction and historical accident. Individuals absorb the culture they have inherited, but they also innovate (to varying degrees, depending on the individual) from what they have been given. At each stage of life and at major turning points, a person takes on new roles and social relations and adds new capacities that integrate into an evolving state of being.[5]

I make no claim that these people are "typical" Javanese. Instead, because I was immediately struck by the diversity of contemporary Indonesia, my intent was to interview persons who represented various aspects of that diversity. Religious diversity is represented here, reflecting Java's traditional animist religions and the later South Asian imports of Hinduism and Buddhism, which still continue to affect the spiritual viewpoint of many people who label themselves Muslim or Christian. The more recent religions to spread to Java, including the now-dominant Islamic religion and the minority Christian religion, also are represented here. Ethnic diversity is represented by several Chinese life histories. I have endeavored to include all economic levels of both rural and urban society, from the poorest pedicab driver to wealthy businesswomen, from village market women to royal members of the sultan's court. Especially notable in these interviews is the range of people's responses to Indonesia's current rapidly changing conditions. Rather than a stereotype, I hope that these life stories, in all their fascinating diversity, can show the range of opinions and outlooks contemporary Indonesians express.

Differences not only in social position and gender but also in age must be explicitly recognized. The ages of the women and men intereviewed here range from their fifties to their eighties. For life-history research, the aged are often the best informants simply because they have longer lives to report. But beyond that, I have often found in my oral history research that elderly people have a larger perspective on life and on what they have tried to accomplish than is usually the case with younger persons. As with American Indian culture, Javanese culture gives high status to the elderly. Unlike modern capitalist countries, where the aged are often superfluous "senior citizens," Javanese elders are active, useful members of society. They serve as sage advisers, spiritual intermediaries, and child-care providers. Because they are treated as important authorities by society, the elders have much advice to offer.

This particular generation has experienced such great change, thus I decided to focus my life-history interviewing on the elders. Certainly younger Indonesians offer their own unique perspective for understanding modern Indonesia, but when this generation of elders is gone much will be lost if it is not soon gathered by social scientists. With that urgency in mind I decided to focus my research on the unique insights of the elderly Javanese. The people I interviewed live in Yogyakarta or its nearby twin court city Surakarta (Solo) and the towns and villages in neighboring areas of central Java.

These people have lived through four eras: under governments directed by the Netherlands, Japan, the revolutionary independence movement, and now the modernizing New Order. What these elders can tell about their life experiences, and the lessons they have learned can be of great value as younger generations of Indonesians strive to bring about a better life for their country in the future. As they adjust to the new order, however, it is good that they not forget the older values that can continue to help people deal with the future and give meaning to their lives. As an outsider who has lived in Indonesia for more than a year, I feel that some traditional Javanese values are worthwhile to anyone, regardless of cultural background.

It is fitting that these elderly men and women, in telling their stories of their lives, have themselves focused on the implications of their insights for the young. Some are teachers, and others are concerned about imparting knowledge and education to the next generation. Others are traditionalists, concerned about the continuation of Java's ancient heritage—especially its philosophical and spiritual aspects—into the modern age.

This book is genuinely a collaborative effort. After I began this project, I became aware of my limitations as the sole interviewer. Although I speak some Bahasa Indonesia, I feel more comfortable with a native speaker present to make sure I do not misunderstand the nuances of communication in a different language. Some people I interviewed speak excellent English, and I felt confident to conduct these interviews myself. However, most people interviewed do not speak English; a substantial number do not even feel comfortable speaking in Bahasa Indonesia, the new national language that has only become common in the last few decades.

Many elderly people prefer to speak in their native Javanese language. Javanese is a complex language, with much attention to politeness. "High" and "low" forms of words should be used depending on the relative level of the speakers in the social hierarchy. By using the incorrect form, especially with the status-conscious older generation, it is easy to offend someone inadvertantly. Also, Javanese people have a roundabout way of speaking, and an American-formulated question is often considered too direct. Such directness might be best for publication in English, but it could be detrimental to the interviewing process. For these reasons, it became obvious that using an Indonesian as interpreter would be better than having me, an outsider, try to conduct the interviews by myself.

Outsiders, and even non-Javanese Indonesians, find the indirect Javanese responses boring and long-winded; Javanese find them polite and politic. Because I wish this volume to find a wider readership, I have made an editorial decision to condense the interviews into a more direct format. Although this makes the reading more "interesting" to a non-Javanese, the reader must be forewarned that something of the Javanese style is lost in this translation.[6] Perhaps we outsiders are not as patient as we should be.

Besides all this, there is the question of Javanese people speaking intimately about their lives to a person of a different gender. Feminist scholarship has demonstrated that many women research subjects will not open up to a male researcher the way they do with a female researcher. I suspected that this tendency would also be true in Java, so I was hesitant about the value of a male researcher interviewing elderly women.

Given my limitations as a foreign, non-Javanese speaker and a male, I decided to bring into the project a number of native speakers. I organized a research seminar, consisting of equal numbers of women and men, in the Fakultas Pasca Sarjana (graduate school) of Universitas Gadjah Mada. With the exception of Claire Siverson, an American sociologist then resident in Yogyakarta who conducted the interview of the feminist psychologist in Part I, all the participants are Indonesians. Most of them are English teachers, and their translating abilities are quite good.

They did not, however, know interviewing techniques and research methodologies. For a period of several months, we met at least once a week for me to teach them how to do these interviews. In preparation, I had them read everything from classical ethnographic methods and oral histories to Studs Terkel's books of interviews. I began my interviewing in July 1987, and the research team conducted interviews between January and July 1988. Interviewing of a person was often done over a period of several days, and the most interesting parts are published here. In some interviews, I did everything myself; in other cases, I accompanied a native speaker. Later, after the female native speakers had gained experience, I sent them to do their own interviewing of some of the elderly women.

To my surprise, the interviews done by the women alone do not seem any more intimate than those conducted by me or a couple male Indonesians. After discussing this finding with the participant interviewers, I concluded that elder people of both sexes are so highly respected in Java that an elder woman does not feel threatened by a young man. Because all of us doing the interviews were relatively young (aged 27 to 39), we were in the positions of lower-status listeners in the presence of the respected elder speaker. With many Javanese women, having a respectful, interested, and empathetic attitude seems more important than the gender of the interviewer.

These elders were amazingly open about their lives, but every one of them—even those from the uneducated laboring class—displayed a certain dignity that only age can bring. For many reasons elderly persons would agree to present their life histories. In probably all cultures, many elderly persons see themselves as "memory bearers." They get meaning in their old age by offering something that the younger generation needs: information for living a life. Simply by having the ability to tell an interesting story, they may demonstrate their mental alertness to themselves and others. Particularly if someone feels that they may not have much longer to live, then the mere telling of their lives—with the pleasure of the good memories and the knowledge that their lives will not be forgotten—can make them feel better. They may gain a feeling of importance by having an academic scholar express interest in them. They may tell their stories to connect themselves to a particular group, to establish their social status as members of a select elite, or to reinforce their feelings of connectedness to the land and the people where they have lived. In the case of this study, a major motivation for many narrators was their desire to help preserve their culture and traditional values.[7]

With all this in mind, the interviews were conducted and the translations completed. Then the Indonesian interviewer and I went over the translations together, line by line. In some cases, unclear phrases in the translation required returning to the elder for clarification. Because information was gathered at different times some insertion and narrative detail was rearranged. I did this to make the life history topically related and generally chronological. This rearranging, it might be argued, may distort part of the personal meaning. Rearranging according to the tastes of a Western readership—imposing a chronological framework—is inevitably culture-bound.

Yet, after thinking about these problems, I decided it was more important to make each life story a smoothly flowing narrative, not just a raw transcript interview. There is something to be said for exactness of a person's literal words, but that is difficult to accomplish in a translation. Such literal efforts are often quite boring and difficult to follow. Spoken communication forms are often repetitive and do not always translate well into written form, even in the same language. If I had attempted such an approach with these interviews, given the indirect Javanese style, few readers would complete this entire volume. Accordingly, I decided which interviews should be published and then further edited those interviews. The revised life histories were approved by the original interviewer for accuracy.

One purpose of this book is to provide a more complete understanding of Indonesia to outsiders. The very fact of its English publication indicates this purpose. I take the position that my editing and rearrangement is justified if it makes the text more readable without distorting the meaning of the person's statements. As these lives are presented, I have aimed to bring out the fascinating stories that they have to tell. Every reader of a book must, to some extent, accept the author's assurance that the words contained therein are accurate. I can only declare that these life histories reflect the meaning of the people's lives as accurately as possible, even if the style of expression differs between the Javanese and English languages.

The approach I used in this book, and the approach I asked the seminar participants to use in their translations, is to try to capture the overall flavor of the person's ideas and personality, rather than to reproduce exactly a word-by-word translation. As a result, I think this book is much more readable, and its ideas will reach a larger number of readers. One of my professors told me, "The writer must take pains so that the reader does not have to." That has been my guiding light as I have transformed the words of these people into their final written form. In the case of uneducated people, we have translated their thoughts into a readable style of standard English, rather than trying to reproduce a crude style that only denigrates the quality of their ideas. These lower-class people have little or no education; it is not surprising that they do not speak like members of the elite. The reader should keep this in mind when reading those interviews. While such persons may be less verbally articulate than educated persons, we must not underestimate their knowledge of life.

Although my role in this project is much more than editor and compiler, I take sole responsibility for editing and organizing this volume. I am grateful to Marlie Wasserman of Rutgers University Press for her suggestions on editorial matters and also to Robert Jay and James Peacock for their careful reading and critique of the manuscript. James Peacock's lucid introduction to the volume explains and sets the stage for the narratives that follow. I am also grateful to the Indonesians who participated in my research seminar and who gathered and translated these narratives with me. Rather than passing off these Indonesians as simply my research assistants or interpreters, as is too often done by anthropologists, I wish explicitly to honor the important contributions they have made. Despite dangers of misunderstanding in any multiperson scholarly effort, the participation of several people allowed us to conduct more interviews and to acquire more information than I, as a single researcher, would have been able to do. I hope that this kind of project can serve as a model for more collaborations in publishing in the future, between Western social scientists and native-speaking scholars.

Reflecting my regard for them, I dedicate this book to the participants in my seminar. They were the persons to whom I felt closest while I was in Java, and they helped make my time there both enjoyable and fulfilling. I am hopeful that they will make significant contributions to research about Indonesia in the future. Moreover, I hope this book will inspire them and other Indonesian writers to pursue more research on their rapidly changing society. The educational benefits that I was able to offer the Indonesian scholars and students, plus the work that I did in establishing an American Studies Center at Gadjah Mada University Library, as well as the scholarly contributions of this book, more than justifies the costs of my Fulbright grant. As a result of my experience, I firmly believe that the Fulbright program is a valuable contribution to American foreign relations. I thank the Council for the International Exchange of Scholars for awarding me the grant to conduct this research.

Lastly, I wish to express my gratitude to all the Javanese women and men who contributed their fascinating stories and allowed us to hear their lessons of life. Part I of this volume focuses on the drama of lived experience—the massive changes that have affected people's lives and how those people have adapted to those changes. Part II features the representatives of the traditional values of old Java. And Part III consists of interviews of educators and parents who address their concerns for Indonesian youth and their country's future. Each woman and man who consented to be interviewed had her or his own agenda, and they focused their comments on the most important messages they wished to leave as their legacy to the future. To promote their candor, I promised them anonymity; although their names are not included here I express my gratitude and admiration to them. Only the feminist psychologist had ever been interviewed before, but all the individuals approached the task with a serious appreciation for the opportunity that this interview gave them to pass down their wisdom for the next generation. Some of these people are ardent individualists with their own unique perspectives; others faithfully repeat the conventional remarks of their Javanese value system. We have something to learn from them all. No matter what our culture, their words have much to teach us.

Los Angeles, 1990   Walter L. Williams

Javanese Lives

Indonesia

Java

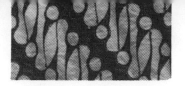

Introduction
James Peacock

Which are the world's five largest nations? India, China, the Soviet Union, and the United States are names that come readily to mind. Few people immediately name Indonesia. Yet Indonesia almost equals and may soon surpass the United States in population. Still less well known is Indonesia's most populous island, Java, which squeezes into an area the size of New York State a population approaching one hundred million. If the population of Indonesia, much less that of Java, is not widely known, still less known is its culture. Superficially, at least, most people have some sense of the way of life of the other four largest nations; but who knows much about the culture of Indonesia, the largest Muslim nation in the world, or of the refined Buddhist and Hinduist civilization of Java?

If we admit our ignorance of Indonesia, how best to learn about it? Certainly we should locate it on the map, more or less equidistant from China and Australia. And we can fairly quickly sum up its basic politics and economics. But what about the people and the culture? Most striking to many is the very diversity of Indonesia: "Unity in diversity" is the national motto. And even Java, despite cherished central values, shows enormous complexities reflecting influences from East Asia, South Asia, the Near East, and Europe. An effective way to discern at once something of both diversity and guiding themes of a culture is through life stories, the autobiographies of its individual members. That is what this volume offers. Here you have, simply told, the stories of individual Javanese lives, reflecting social types, varied yet unified by common experiences rooted in shared history and culture.

On the whole, these stories speak for themselves. Still, the tellers take for granted some knowledge of their history and milieu. Walter L. Williams sketches something of this context in his introductions to each life history. Obviously, a story of a life is not a carbon copy of history—whether of a society or of the individual narrating. Deep analysis of these stories would probe the structure of the narrative, the nature of the text. For an introduction to lives, this is not essential; given the somewhat streamlined character of the texts themselves, it is not even possible. But it is possible to sketch broad contours of the historical, social, and cultural milieux reflected in the stories and thus to alert the reader to some themes they manifest.

COMPRESSED CHANGE

These narrations are all by residents of central Java who are at least fifty years old. Their narrated memories therefore span a period reaching back to the end of Java's history as a Dutch colony and the beginning of its experience as a new nation. Although this is not the place to tell the history of either Indonesia or Java, a brief sketch of the history the narrators have lived and before that, older histories glowing in their collective memories, is essential.

Because this is central Java, their revered history extends significantly to the eighth and ninth centuries C.E. Within the region sampled by these narratives are two great monuments built during these periods: Borobudur and Loro Janggrang at Prambanan. Borobudur is a massive replication of the universe conceived by Buddhism. Loro Janggrang is a towering symbol of the pantheon of Hinduism. Together they represent the heritage of the great Hindu-Buddhist empires that dominated Java from the eighth until the fourteenth centuries C.E. Capping this central Javanese Hindu-Buddhist heritage, a third kingdom, the new Mataram, was created in the early seventeenth century, synthesizing Hindu-Buddhist and Islamic themes, framed within a Javanese cosmology centered around a divinized ruler.

In 1629, Mataram was defeated by the Dutch. Stripped of its political and military force by the colonial government, Mataram nevertheless remained, and remains today, a cultural empire, a kingdom within a state. It boasts two major sultanates, one at Yogyakarta and one at Surakarta. Each of these central Javanese cities still sustains a court centered around a palace ruled by a sultan, Hamungkubuwono at Yogya and Mangkunegara at Surakarta. Around each court continues to flourish—now flourishing for three centuries—a cultural life encompassing the arts of dance, theater, and music as well as special languages, ritualized politics, religious ceremonials and customs, mystical societies, and high manners. Within this court's cultural arena has originated the full spectrum of movements that define the polarities of Indonesian life: Islamic orthodoxy versus Hindu-Buddhist syncretism, manifested in revolutions, wars, and educational or religious organizations.

After the defeat of Mataram by the Dutch, the colonial government imposed itself on top of this cultural center of Javanism. This situation of colonial "Rust en Orde" (peace and order) endured for two centuries, only disrupted by periodic rebellions, notably the Java War led by Prince Diponegoro against the Dutch and the sultanate, lasting from 1825 to 1830.

Beginning in 1908 with a Javanese-led cultural movement known as Budi Utomo and continuing until 1940, nationalist movements agitated for independence. That event was delayed by World War II, when the Japanese occupied Indonesia. After the Japanese were conquered by the Allies, Sukarno and other Indonesians declared their independence on August 17, 1945.

Thus began the revolution, a five-year struggle against the Dutch who returned to reoccupy their former colony. Indonesia finally gained independence in 1950 and established a new nation with Sukarno as president.

After promising beginnings, Indonesia in the mid-1950s was divided by civil war between outer islands and the capital on Java. As a solution to such dissension, Sukarno instituted Guided Democracy, a semisocialistic state created after values of family and village but led by Sukarno flanked by communists and the army.

As inflation, corruption, and disorder grew, the Communist party attempted a coup in 1965. The Army, supported by Muslims, responded by massacring about half-million persons, either communists or accused communists. When the months of massacre (called Gestapu) ended, General Suharto, who had assumed leadership of the army, became president and instituted the "New Order."

The New Order is still in place, still headed by Suharto. The Suharto period has been a time of relative peace and prosperity, though with some limitations on political freedom. The multiplicity of parties under Sukarno has been reduced essentially to one domi-nant party, Golkar, representing the central government, and various Muslim parties, representing an opposition.

All these periods and heritages glow through the accounts of these narrators. They have lived through the colonial period, the Japanese period, the Revolution, the creation of a new nation, Guided Democracy, Gestapu, and now the New Order. From the standpoint of changes in one's collective and personal life, it is as though Americans had experienced their Revolutionary War, the War between the States, and the two world wars all in the space of fifty years instead of two hundred. Whatever else one may take away from these stories, they vividly depict ways resourceful indi-viduals live through periods of upheaval.

THE SOCIAL UNIVERSE

These narrators are situated in a special place—so special it is even labeled as such officially by the state. This place is the "daerah istemewah" (Special Province) of Yogyakarta. "Special" is awarded because this region is one of the surviving kingdoms of Java; the sultanates survived from the empire of Mataram after the Dutch partitioned it in the mid-eighteenth century into the courts at Yogya and Surakarta. The sultan, palace, and court still exist here, so there is a royal family—represented in these narrations by the "princess"—and there are officials and performers and teachers—represented here by the dance teacher. The presence of these fig-ures gives a special tone that would be lacking in ordinary Javanese communities. From narrations such as those of the princess, we are privileged to glimpse a bit of the lives of the contemporary Javanese royalty; she even expresses emotions, such as the "loneliness" of the princess.

Such special figures aside, the types represented in this collection provide a good sample of the Javanese social universe. The spread of class includes aristocrats to bourgeois to farmers and pedicab driv-ers. Ethnic Chinese are represented more or less in proportion to their numbers vis-à-vis the Javanese, who constitute the majority. Male and female are both well represented. We do not know exactly what political spectrum is represented, for narrators are not forth-coming about their party affiliations or preferences—a fact that might be less true in a place more politically preoccupied, such as the capital, Jakarta, but would probably be the case for Indonesians everywhere else. Given the objective of tapping narrators to describe full lives, no one below the age of fifty is interviewed, but of course experiences from the entire lifespan are narrated.

These accounts teach us about a number of values the Javanese cherish. Of particular interest are those that differ somewhat from cultures we customarily term Western, for we can learn most from alternatives to our own ways; many Javanese values, though, seem familiar.

Acceptance and Struggle

Javanese say that they "accept" (*nrima* or *terima*) what comes and that this attitude helps avoid too much disappointment or other emotional upset when things do not work out. In fact, many Javanese elaborate philosophical or theological explanations to justify and explain such a value. The narrators do not do this much, but many of them express such an attitude in reflecting on their own lives; they speak with resignation about their past. They seem content to await death, perhaps noting some condition that enhances their contentment—for example, they are surrounded by children and grandchildren.

Lest we stereotype our narrators as fatalistic or worse, simply passive, note also how they struggle and strive, often against heavy obstacles. The market woman tells of leaving home at 1:00 a.m. to walk twenty-five kilometers to reach the market by 5:30 a.m. Her account is doubtless true; one sees market women doing this all the time, all their lives. Similarly, the pedicab driver, now in his mid-fifties, labors at this hard, uncertain, barely-subsistence job, expecting nothing better than possibly a peaceable retirement to his village; but he has not become a beggar or thief. The women, especially, display a particularly enterprising spirit—in business, the arts, even in a career as a psychological counsellor.

Courtesy and Civic Virtue

Hormat (manners) are highly valued in Java, and manners are usually exquisite. Such etiquette is displayed in the courteous style of the narrations themselves. Perhaps that is not surprising among the aristocratic narrators, but note, too, the style of persons in occupations not ordinarily noted for their courtesy, for example, the policeman; his way of narrating is hardly like the stereotyped hard-bitten American cop, which is not to say that Javanese police are not tough when the situation demands.

Note, also, the language of the former soldier, who is now a village official. He describes himself as "a caretaker of society." The language is more ideological, more idealized than that one might hear from an American mayor or ward boss. Do we hear the ghosts of Sukarnoist Guided Democracy, of the Suhartoist New Order, or of the communalistic rhetorics of early Javanese philosophies mixed with influences of socialism?

Education, Aesthetics, and Civilization

The dalang, the shadow-play puppeteer, seems boastful about his vocation, the business people (with the exception of the Chinese) apologetic about theirs. One might expect the reverse in our society whose "business is business," whereas artists are marginalized. Indeed, Java does revere aesthetics. The *alus*, the refined and beautiful, is a moral value of the highest order. A Javanese town hall depicts forms of Javanese dance; compare this to the gold miners or steel millers one is more likely to see in American town halls. According to one count, there are many more theatre groups per capita in Java than in the United States, and one must also consider the great variety and accomplishment of classical Javanese dance groups and orchestras and other arts, ranging from batik printing to the revered *wayang Kulilt*, the shadow play. The language of the arts, especially that of the wayang Kulit tales and characters, penetrates the political culture of Java, perhaps comparable to the salience of biblical images in earlier American and British political culture; the late President Sukarno identified with certain shadow-play characters as with the dalang himself, which has led some to term Javanist governments of Indonesia "theater states." In any case, several narrators draw on the wayang figures, such as Semar the clown who is a god (a telling equation of the theatrical and the sacred), to depict their own lives. No wonder the dalang is proud!

If the arts boast a high valuation, so too does education, and for a similar reason: it emphasizes what the Germans would term *bil dung*, a cultivation of the spirit. A similar equation of spiritual and cultural is suggested by the Indonesian *buda*, spiritual culture, as in the term "Kebudajaan," meaning culture. From German/Dutch traditions valuing academia as well as Hindu/Muslim sacralization of the teacher, the Javanese accord teachers high status and respect, as several narrators attest. Teachers were called "father," for example, and addressed in high language. This tradition is examplified in the story by the principal. Though he is perhaps somewhat stigmatized as gay and Chinese, he is apparently respected and respectable, presumably reflecting in part the esteem accorded the educator. Although erosion of the teacher's status, especially based on income, is noted by one narrator, this value of education and educators is still manifest.

The Place and Potential of Women

Because Indonesia is the largest Muslim nation in the world, one might expect women to be subjugated to a patriarchal Islamic order. Yet, here some women describe the unexpected: a feminist psychologist is so emancipated that she finds organizations of wives tedious; a businesswoman is so successful that she must struggle to divert some of her children's respect from herself to her husband, a police inspector; and a "mother and revolutionary" begins her story stating "I am always lonely on Friday afternoon" because she must then face a day deprived of her absorbing weekday work.

It is true, some women tell sad tales of being exploited and commoditized by men; for example, the singer, was happily "teased," connoting her popularity and desirability, by men. Once rich and desired, now she is poor and ignored—a Javanese "Nana." Other women simply tell of dreary lives of never-ending work.

But because such lives are unfortunately typical of women in many cultures, the exceptionally bright and active side of the Javanese women's narrations deserves comment. How should we explain their independence and drive? The simplest explanation is that women in Java share with those in the wider Southeast Asian region relatively high status and independence. This pattern is apparent in the most pervasive Southeast Asian kinship system, which is bilateral; that is, it traces descent through both male and female lines rather than through only one, so that father and mother both count in the jural sphere. In Java, the mother has a special central position in the household because she manages the money, a skill that she often extends to the marketplace. In the case of the feminist psychologist, power is tilted even further in the female direction because she comes from the Minangkabau area of Sumatra, where kinship is matrilineal, so that property and status pass through the female line.

On Language, Narration, and Translation

Walter L. Williams describes the steps through which these stories passed: from Javanese or Indonesian to English, entailing not only translation but also condensation to streamline complex modes of Javanese narration.

What is lost? One can speculate. Javanese narration can indeed be baroque, rich in ornamentation—nuanced allusions to status, for example. The notion of life story—a factual account of one's life—is itself foreign to old Java, probably introduced by Islam, again by Western cultures and literature, and now spread as part of Indonesian language. So to tell one's life story (*riwayat hidup*) is to tap an Islamic-Western-Indonesian part of one's self, perhaps to leave behind some Javanese parts. But then these Islamic-Western-Indonesian aspects are today part of the lives and consciousness of these narrators. They have many ways to tell their tales. What would one's story be if told in Javanese language as part of a discussion at a meditation club, for example, or as part of a moralizing reflection for one's grandchildren?

Readers must take what is presented in these narrations—one aspect of the Javanese consciousness. The relatively streamlined approach is rendered even more so by the translation; perhaps these stories are more like the revised standard version of the Bible rather than the King James version. But it is important to realize that there is no *one* authentic story of a person's life by anyone.

What we see here in these stories are the contrasting aspirations of the narrators: dismay about the decline of educational standards, but excitement about the achievements of their children; resignation about the changes of modernization, but pleasure about the revitalization of aspects of the traditional culture. Such images, happy and sad, ironic and wise, historically grounded yet forward looking, hint at these individuals' complex and intriguing notions of time, death, future, and existence. Simply stated, they reflect complex philosophies of life.

Walter L. Williams has done fine scholarship in allowing these Javanese people to tell us something about their lives and experiences. When we open this volume, most of us know nothing about Javanese lives, culture, and history. When we close, we have taken a firm step toward such knowledge. And we acquire it through acquaintance with engaging and admirable individuals, whose poignant memories we are privileged to share.

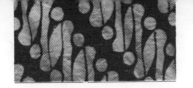

PART I

Paths to the Present

Village Life and Urban Development

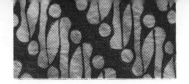

A Market Woman

This typical village elder looks to be about seventy years old. Her life has been characterized by long hours of hard work, laboring in the rice paddies and taking the crops to sell at the market. Today looking back on the poverty of her early life, she is grateful for material improvements like having a radio and living in a house with a floor of concrete instead of dirt. More important, she is grateful for the government-sponsored public bus system that allows her to get to market more easily and for the public schooling available for her grandchildren.

She lives in a small tile-roofed bamboo thatch house with her third husband, also in his seventies, and her sister's unmarried son (age forty-eight). Her daughter lives a few blocks away with the daughter's son and his wife and children. Her other son married into another village and lives there on land provided by his wife's family. Her unmarried twenty-seven-year-old grandson, who has a job in the city as a driver, is now able to visit his grandparents more often since he bought a motorcycle. The grandchildren treat their grandparents with the polite deference due to elders in traditional Javanese society.

Walter L. Williams conducted this interview in the living room of the woman's house; Kedah (male, age twenty-seven) translated it from the Javanese. Other relatives were not present at the time.

I don't know what year I was born or how old I am. I just know it was a long time ago. I was born into a traditional Javanese family with twelve children in this same village south of Surakarta where I have lived my entire life. Nine of the children are still alive today. My mother sold coconut drinks in the marketplace; she also bought

1. Women weeding rice paddy in front of the ancient Hindu temple at Prambanan. *Photo: Walter L. Williams*

wood in one market and carried it on her back to sell in another market. She worked in the rice paddies, doing the work typical for a woman: planting the sprouts, spreading decayed leaves and animal wastes as fertilizer, weeding, harvesting the mature rice, and carrying the rice home. We would eat the rice, and what was left over we would sell in the market.

My father did the man's work: plowing with the cows, irrigating the fields, and building houses. At that time, all the houses in the village were made of bamboo, and they had to be rebuilt every five years. The men also weeded, gathered wood, and harvested peanuts, cassava, and vegetables, along with the women. But the men do not harvest rice. After harvest, the people ate the rice, they fed the stalks to the cows, and the men would burn the rest down to the roots to fertilize the fields with the ashes. Nothing was wasted.

When I was a young girl, during the Dutch colonial era, it was very difficult to get enough food. We children would comb through the fields after the adults had harvested, to see if we could find any more grains of rice left. We would often walk far away from our village on these rice-gathering trips, sometimes more than five kilometers away. My parents were poor, so I never went to school. I needed to be working to help the family bring in food. Life at that time was just to get food. I never had time to think about school. Back then only a few went to school, not like the many people who go to school today.[1]

When I was a teenager I started going with my mother to the market to sell vegetables and fruit. Besides rice, we also raised and sold cassava, sweet potatoes, chili, peanuts, eggplant, cabbage and beans. We had banana, rambutan, durian, and coconut trees around the houses, as well as bamboo groves to use for building the houses.

I got married when I was about twenty years old because my mother told me I must get married to continue the family. I must have children so that when I die they will continue my life through my descendents. I wanted to have children, but at first I could not. There is happiness in children, and I still wanted some, so I raised one of my sister's sons. He still lives with me today, and I consider him my own son. Later, I became pregnant, and I had two more children.

I was so busy in my work that I did not have time to have any more children after that. Because I am now too old to worry about having children anymore, I don't know much about the government's family planning program.[2] But I think it is good not to have so many children. If someone has too many children, they are too busy to live. With small families, there is enough food and money to raise the children properly. But the bad thing about family planning is that there cannot be freedom in sex. Sex is a gift from God, which should be used whenever married people want.

Marriage has really changed over the years. When I was young, children always had to follow the wishes of their parents. Not like nowadays, when children can follow their own desires about who they want to marry. My parents chose the man that I was to marry. I did not even know him. The wedding was the first time I ever saw him. For the first several days after we were married, I was so shy I did not even talk to him. We were married a few years, but later separated. I later got married two more times. I now live with my third husband.

Since I was a girl I have worked in the market. When I was younger the economic situation was very bad. Later, I inherited some land from my parents. As a result, I and my husband and children have farmed my own fields. Still, we were not like the rich Javanese people in the village. They had more land, and they could get more money by selling food in bigger markets farther away from the village. They hired other people to work for them and sometimes had a store to sell things.

We never had that opportunity and always did our own labor. For many years I worked in the market, buying vegetables and fruit from a market near the farming area and selling them in the city of Surakarta. I would carry that food in a basket on my back. There were no buses then, so I had to walk over twenty-five kilometers each day. To get to the market by 5:30 when it opened I would leave home at 1:00 a.m.; I would leave the market between 8 and 9 a.m. and arrive back home after noon. Then I would keep the food I had bought until that night, when I would begin the walk to the city market. Each day I would alternate, buying in the farming market one day and selling in the city the next.

When I got home in the afternoon I would cook for the children and my husband, who had been working in the fields every day. One day each week I would stay home to do the washing and help in the fields.[3] Depending on the need, we would often work in the fields in the afternoon. My husband and I could only take short rests. We both had to take care of the children, but some of our relatives helped in this. Later, the older children took care of the younger ones.

Because my daily hours of work did not allow it, I could not devote as much time to my children as I would have liked. But at least I am glad to be able to say that I always made sure my children went to the mosque and did their daily prayers. There are many followers of Islam in this village, but many do not do the prayers. I have been Islamic since I was a child, and I used to pray often. I could not do that when I was so busy every day going to the market, but since my children have been working I have more time and can do the daily prayers again. Islam is very important to me. I think the most important thing about it is the prayers; doing them five times a day gives me a relaxing little break and makes me feel happy. Praying got me through some bad times years ago.

Back in the old days it was the colonial time, but the Dutch never came into my village so they did not disturb us. I never knew anything about colonialism directly. Still, I was afraid of the Dutch. If I was in Solo and heard a Dutchman was coming, I ran away. In our village, we dug holes in the ground to hide from them. I heard that the Dutch had taken some people from around Yogyakarta and killed them. Sometimes the Dutch would go into neighboring areas and take the food products from the farmers. This made it very bad because there was not enough food left for the people. In other villages, the Dutch would force a farmer to plant only one kind of crop, like sugar cane. After doing that, there was not much time or land to grow food to eat. Many people were killed by the Dutch. Fortunately, the Dutch did not do any of this to our village.

Things got even worse for Java during the time the Japanese came here [during World War II]. They bombed Yogyakarta, which made us very frightened of them. There was even less food than before. During the hard times, like during the World War, when we did not have enough food to eat, we would mix bush and tree leaves with the rice. We had to eat roots and whatever we could find. We could not afford to buy clothes, so we only had a little bit. It was poor quality cloth, and it often got infested by bugs. It was very itchy. Still, we were lucky because the Japanese never came to this village. We have been fortunate that our village was always peaceful and undisturbed.

The big thing that happened to Indonesia in 1945 was the revolution, but I did not know anything about it. Nothing ever occurred here. The Dutch just fought the soldiers, not the villagers. People told stories about the fighting in other areas, and sometimes I heard airplanes in their bombing. The first thing I knew about it was when independence was proclaimed after the Dutch left. I was glad to hear that, even though they had never bothered me.

After independence, everything became easier to get. We usually had enough food after that. The only bad thing to happen since then was in 1965, after the communist disturbance. There was not much food then because everything was in such an uproar. I did not know anything about communism, but in 1965 many people in this village were arrested by the government. Thankfully, within a year they were all released.[4]

Since then, things have gotten much better. Formerly, almost everyone was so poor, but today people have more money. My grandson could even afford to buy a motorcycle, so he can come visit me more often. Nowadays there is a public bus system, and I do not have to walk so far when I go to market. I only have to carry my things two kilometers to get to the main road, where the bus stop is located. I wear a big bamboo hat when it rains. Today, people can afford to live in better houses with electricity, and some even have televisions. My husband and I enjoy listening to the wayang music on the radio.[5] We now have a house with a cement floor instead of just dirt. And, most important, the young people can go to school to become educated. Things have definitely improved. Today, life is very peaceful and lovely.

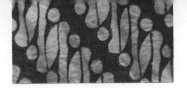

A Farmer and Village Leader

This well-respected elder represents a typical man's leadership role in a traditional Javanese agrarian village. He is about sixty years old and lives with his wife at the home of their eldest daughter. He chain-smokes the Indonesian-style clove cigarettes that are so popular among men of his generation.

This man is one of the revolutionary heroes, who have been honored but who are rapidly being forgotten as Indonesia quickly becomes more urban and industrial. He is grateful for the establishment of independence, the suppression of communism, and political stability under the Suharto government, yet he is apprehensive about the increasingly rapid changes in modern society. This village leader, like many people in other fast changing societies, finds it difficult to understand the multitude of outside influences entering his country. As with many other such individuals (in the United States as well as in the Muslim world), this man turns to fundamentalist religion as a way of addressing both the economic dislocations and the social changes around him. He both begins and ends his personal narrative by talking about children's roles in the family and the necessity of religious indoctrination.

Despite his uncertainties about the future, this village leader expresses pride about his past contributions to independence. He is typical of patriots who have put their lives on the line for the establishment of nation states throughout the Third World. It is clear that he had his position in history in mind when he spoke. The interviews were conducted on the front porch of his house, by Hazairin Eko Prasetyo (male, age twenty-nine) and Walter L. Williams, while other men of the village listened quietly. The women stayed demurely inside the house, as is typical in strict Muslim families. This leader was obviously recalling his accomplishments and addressing his remarks to both the younger men of his village and the interviewers. This interview, more like a speech than the other narratives included in this book, thus has become part of the oral tradition of that village as well as a written narrative in this book.

The Dutch were still in power here when I was born. It was about sixty years ago, and I was the only child of my mother and father's second and last marriage. From his first marriage, my father had one daughter and one son; my mother had two daughters from her previous husband.[1] My parents' last marriage was very successful, and they were able to bequeath a large tract of land to each of their children. All of us got almost the same size piece of land. All my life I have been a traditional farmer. I have one hectare of wet land, where I grow rice, and another hectare of dry land, where I keep hard crops like cloves, coconut trees, and coffee. I have been trying to follow my parents' example in providing my seven children with sufficient farm land. Yet, in today's unfavorable situation for farmers, it is impossible for me to give each of my children a one-hectare piece of land as their heritage. About ten years ago, several neighboring families moved to Kalimantan and Sumatra as a part of the government program of transmigration.[2] I could only afford to buy about one hectare of rice field they sold.

My mother was a small trader. She sold tobacco and some sorts of kitchen needs. Her customers were our neighbors. I was very glad when my mother asked me to bring her merchandise to the marketplace because I could stroll around the market and enjoy the situation. Market sightseeing was a kind of entertainment for rural boys and girls back them. And more important, my mother gave me money to buy sweets as the tip for helping her.

Village life back then was very peaceful; the neighbors were always kind and friendly to each other. There were not as many people in those days, and almost everyone was a farmer. People never stole from another person in the same village. Sometimes, however, a person might steal something from other villages. The thief would sneak in at night and dig a hole in the ground to get inside the house. While the family slept, the thief would take things. If a thief were caught, all the people would run out of their houses and gang up on him, beating him severely. That kept crime down. People were very protective of their neighbors.

My parents lived in harmony, and so did we, their children. Before twilight, after performing our evening Muslim prayer, we gathered to learn Islamic religious teachings from my father. He was a *santri*, that is, one who strictly follows the teachings of Islam. We had to be serious and were supposed to be attentive. We had to be able to read and memorize short scriptures of the Koran. Sometimes, we also had to memorize the translation of those scriptures in the high form of the Javanese langauge. My mother and we children were very proud of my father. He was very clever in explaining all sorts of religious matters and was quite skillful in writing Arabic. Two or three thick books had been successfully written down by him in mixed languages, Javanese and Arabic, in Arabic alphabets. All of us could write and read Arabic very well. I can read those books written by my father. I teach my children to be able to read them, too. They are about religious rules and teachings.

My parents were very good to their children. They never treated us differently although we were not from the same blood. Our familial relations were very good, and that close feeling continues with my children now. We help each other very much. This is the Javanese way. What makes my father and me different from the average villager is just our formal education. My sisters never went to any formal school. My brother only went to school to finish his first year; after that he went to the "Pesantren" Islamic boarding school. So, I turned out to be the only child in my family that could finish elementary school. I also enjoyed reciting the Koran.

From this village only two boys graduated from elementary school. Back then [in the 1930s], the school was run by the Dutch and was named "The Number Two School" because it was different from the one for Dutch and Javanese blue-blooded children. My school was secondary to the latter. I was among the clever students at school, but I was still very afraid of the teacher. He seldom smiled and punished us severely if we played truant or did not do our assignments. He was a Javanese too, but he was a very fluent Dutch speaker. His handwriting was very good and neat. We were supposed to write well and neatly, too.[3] If our handwriting was poor and he could not read it, he would certainly punish us. But all of us liked him. He behaved mannerly to all of us and always wore neat clothes. His clothing was traditional Javanese. We did not pay anything for our education then. The teacher even provided us with necessary stationery.[4]

When I was about to continue my study at the high school, the Japanese came [in 1942]. They were, at first, very good to us. I was asked to enroll at the high school. Instead of Dutch, we now had to speak Malay at school.[5] We were also taught the Japanese language. I was, at that time, very good in Japanese. But, now, I can hardly remember anything of that language. It was, perhaps, because I learned it by force or more likely because, after a time, I grew to hate the Japanese very much.

Several months after their arrival, the Japanese became more despotic and mean. Rice and other farm products were taken from us by force. We did not know where they took the food we had grown.[6] Fortunately, we still had cassava. That was all that we could eat, but later they took cassava, too. What was left was dried cassava, and we ate this poor food. Food and supplies of cloth that they promised for us never appeared. In the second year of their occupation here they did not leave us anything to eat or wear. Yet, they always forced us to grow rice for them to take away. Later, they also ordered us to grow castor oil plants which, they told us, would be used for flying their airplanes. Of course, we did not know what they really wanted to do with this crop.

My experiences told me that the Japanese were even worse than the Dutch. I'm not saying the Dutch were good. They often treated us like we were animals. Yet, we were supposed to praise them. Let's say when meeting some Dutchmen on the road, we had to stop and squat, and more important, we were not supposed to look at their faces. We had to make a very low bow. [Laughs] If we happened to look at their faces, they would hit and kick us, and we would be abused. That was definitely annoying, to be treated like that in our own country.

But the Japanese, although we were allowed to speak to them, were even meaner and more harsh. They would jab their knives into our stomachs or hit our heads with their samurai swords for the smallest mistakes we made. Yes, everywhere and wherever they went they brought that samurai. As a teenage boy, I would have liked to have had one of those samurai, but who dared ask them for one?

The other bitter experiences we had in addition to the lack of food were the disappearance of cloth from market places and the resulting increase of skin diseases. During the Dutch occupation era, before the arrival of the Japanese, I had possessed several good clothes and trousers. They were all taken by the Japanese. Fortunately I was able to hide one sarong,[7] by quickly stuffing it into a piece of bamboo, before the Japanese soldier could see it. I wore it only when the Japanese were not here in the village. Usually they came here twice a week, regularly on the same days, and I kept this well in mind. It is still clear in my memory how they searched our houses when they came. They acted like they had to take at least one thing from our houses on every visit. Finally, they took away our domestic animals, too.

I had kept my only good sarong in a safe place, and I, like other children before the war, only wore sarongs made of a mixture of rubber and cloth. It produced noise when we walked, you know, because it was rubber. Still, it was better to have such a sarong. Under the Japanese occupation, most people had to wear jute. And this gunny-sack material was very attractive to insects. I used to wonder, at that time, why there were such massive numbers of bugs. After finishing our work in the rice fields each day, we had to spend more time searching for bugs in our poor dress. Probably because of all those bugs most of us suffered from skin diseases. Some people even suffered from open ulcers on their legs, which were hard to heal. There was no medicine or salve. The only thing we could do was to expose the open sores to the heat of the sun and then cover them with a mixture of certain leaves. But that did not cure the diseases.

It was worse because our clothes were always dirty and rarely washed. Only a very small number of people owned more than one piece of clothing then because when the Japanese found we had extra clothes, they would take them from us. It was true that some people managed to save nicer cotton sarongs, like I did. I was in my teenage years then, so I felt a strong need to look neat, a kind of display of my self-respect. As soon as the Japanese went away, and we could get more clothes, those damned bugs and skin diseases also went away.

As a young person, I had always wanted very much to do something for my people, say, by fighting against the colonialists. I considered both the Dutch and the Japanese our enemies. I remember quite vividly, from my childhood, that two men from this village had taken part in the anticolonial revolt. They were known as the bravest boys in our village. They joined the Hizbullah corp in the town.[8] We were very proud of them. I was too small to join them, so I stayed at home helping my father and mother cultivate our land. During the Japanese occupation, my mother had not been able to carry out her small business as a tobacco seller because her merchandise was stolen by a Japanese soldier. This meant the loss of her capital.

It was not until we proclaimed our independence [in 1945] and the Dutch returned here to reclaim their control that I took part in the revolution. I was then eighteen years old and was appointed the village secretary. I was very young, but I was motivated to work hard. As the secretary of the village, for my salary I was given a piece of land to cultivate. And as one of the village authorities who were obedient to the newly born Republic, I was determined to help our soldiers fight against the Dutch.

Anyway, the problem was there were two village heads here: One was chosen by the people, while the other was appointed by the Dutch. The one chosen by the people was very obedient to the Republic. The assistance I could give to the soldiers involved collecting food from the neighborhood to be delivered to the soldiers and giving them information about the Dutch. I also took their weapons to a safe place when they had no time to bring the weapons with them because they were in a hurry escaping into the bushes when the Dutch came in the daytime. They attacked the Dutch at night. My house was at that time the first place for the warriors to stay when they were here. They gathered and discussed everything about their plans here. The people and I collected food and prepared a safer place, where they could hide for several days at a time.

When the Dutch came to patrol the area, this house became their first suspicious object. But by that time we had sent the warriors to hide in other places. I liked helping our republican soldiers. I felt obliged to help them. The Dutch patrol seldom came here, at most once in two weeks. Usually a Dutch patrol group consisted of a Dutch commander and ten to twenty Indonesian loyalist soldiers. These soldiers were often very despotic.

Once I was ordered by those soldiers to meet their commander on the road because this Dutch commander did not take part in the actual search of my house. I was told to squat while approaching. I did this as ordered, but as I neared the Dutch commander I looked at his face. For this impertinent act, the soldiers kicked me in the buttocks. I fell, but from that angle I could see his face even more clearly. For us native people, the safest way to deal with the Dutch was to behave as foolishly as we could. Therefore, although I could understand what they were asking about I would just say, "No, sir, I do not know anything," in my most respectful form of high Javanese. They were glad if we talked to them in high Javanese when having a conversation with them, as a sign of honor for them. The farthest consequence for this cheating was, especially when they became annoyed, that we would be kicked or scorned. If we behaved as if we were educated, however, we would be brought to their headquarters for interrogation, and this could last for a week.

This village was almost never used as a battlefield. But, as long as I remember, I will not forget the time when once they met here and had to shoot at each other. Penetrating into the bushes, our fighters shot the Dutch patrol; meanwhile, the Dutch did the same thing, retreating and firing their guns. The victims were four republicans and two Dutch soldiers. After they moved away, we villagers buried the victims, of course not at the same place. The bodies of our heroes were buried within the area of our cemetery, while the Dutch bodies were buried outside. Those who were wounded in the fight had been carried to their posts while they were retreating so there was no winner or surrender. Both sides just wanted to return to their posts. Perhaps they thought their enemies were more powerful.

I suffered a very bitter experience during the second occupation of the Dutch, after the proclamation of independence. Somebody slandered me, accusing me of being a Dutch spy. Our soldiers thrashed me down. They punched me for two weeks. Fortunately, I was not seriously wounded. One soldier who punched me was my own relative. I remained steadfast in proclaiming my innocence to them, and I got the idea that the person who slandered me was the real Dutch spy. Later I proved my loyalty to the revolution, by catching him when he was working for the Dutch. We sent him to our headquarters. In fact, I took pity on him since he was my schoolmate. But I had to prove I was right.

Unfortunately, after everything worked out all right, my relative who had punched me died. I wish I could have met him to prove my innocence. That is one of the great regrets I have from the years of the revolution.

The village dual leadership, that is, under the two different village heads, did not end until the Dutch recognized the sovereignty of the Indonesian Republic. In 1953, our government held a people's election to choose a new village head. I successfully won the election over the other candidates. I was happy that I could continue my ideal in developing this village. I remained as village head for twenty-three years, even though I got married and stayed busy raising my family. At one point, I got to shake hands with President Sukarno when he visited this area in 1963. I admired him very much because he freed us from the colonialists. He was very clever. He was an intellectual, but he was also very close to his people.

During my official period as a village head, the most frightening experience I had was in 1965 when the communists rebelled. I was told that I was among those leaders who were supposed to be killed by them. I had married the daughter of a neighboring village head, and my four children at that time were still under ten. Every night I had to patrol around the village observing in disguise from one compound to the other. My wife was trained as a member of the voluntary women's corps to wipe out the communists. I was very proud of her. I always urged my people to keep our unity, our calmness. They helped me very much in keeping the village security. Almost all villagers were prepared to face any possible riots made by the communists. Younger people organized themselves in the Anshor youth movement and the older ones in a multipurpose corps to destroy the Communist party. Because there was no Communist party member in our village, the movement operated in other villages. They joined younger people and villagers of other areas in destroying the Communist party members who had threatened our lives.

It was true that the situation was very strained. We believed that they could show up at any time in front of our doors, ready to kill all of us. Their power here was not strong enough though. And this village was safe. As it turned out, there was never any physical contact between the communists and us. But at the time we did not know what would happen. Every night the children and women had to flee and find a more protected place to sleep. All adult men took part in the patrol or in destroying communists. Since a very long time ago, all villagers here have been faithful Muslims and very opposed to the communists who are against God. At that pressing economic period we helped each other. The inflation was horrible; prices went up almost every day.

I followed the trials of the Communist party leaders through the radio. And from the radio I understood that the Communist party wanted to change this country into a communist one. They deserved hard punishments because they were very cruel. They had killed several of our best generals. So, it was proper, I think, if people got up and took revenge on them. The most popular figure in destroying the communists in this part of the country was Colonel Sarwo Edhi Wibowo. His troop, the RPKAD (The Army's All Commando Regiment), moved very fast. People supported those brave soldiers.

When General Suharto put down the communists and was chosen to be our new president I was glad. I did not know everything that happened in Jakarta, during all this fighting. What I knew was limited to what the radio broadcasted. The most important decision Mr. Suharto made was the dissolution of the Indonesian Communist party. Since 1965, Indonesia has never seen their red flags with hammer and sickle on them. We have never seen their frightening black uniforms. We feel safe. This village has never held any idea of hatred toward that village because we are different in ideologies. Muslims have been freer since 1966, in holding prayers and studying our religion without any fear created by communists. In this sense, Indonesia has been luckier than many other nations, which never acted decisively to stamp out their communists.

Under President Suharto's New Order government, there have been several beneficial changes in this village. Governmental aid is given every year. Villagers began actively erecting bridges, dams, schools, and mosques. Prices are more or less stable, although in recent years it is getting more and more difficult for us to live on our rice fields alone. Some people can afford to buy motorcycles and television sets. Some others, especially those who are civil servants, can build concrete houses. I am very happy to see people getting more prosperous and living in peace.

What makes me feel happy now is that during my leadership

period I could help people, especially the economically weak. For example, I helped people who could not afford to pay their taxes. Every year I had to spend my personal money on them. It was a must for me to help them. In fact, I sometimes thought of buying my sons motorbikes with that money. But I didn't do that. I preferred helping poor people, even though I was not rich myself. The most important advance in our nation today is that I can send my children to schools, and they can get better jobs than mine. If they fail in their study, then they have to become farmers like their father.

After retiring from my position as a village head in 1975, at last I could give full attention to my family. I returned to my rice field and my dry land. I grow rice; it is a must. How can we eat rice if we don't grow it? Lately, though, mice have been destroying our harvests. For almost seven years our farming products have been going up to the sky. It has been very saddening. But I keep growing rice, without getting any, so I can never get any money from selling rice. Still, it is a kind of tradition or heritage. You can grow coffee or clove on dry land, but a rice field is for growing rice.

One of my sons advised me to dry my rice field and grow chili or other crops that could be of benefit, rather than growing rice just to be eaten by mice. But I said "no" because I believe those mice are a form of God's test. Perhaps we committed so many sins that God gives us a proper test. Can we afford it or not? I believe that I can have my harvest if I keep trying. Yes, maybe when God has forgiven all our sins.

Therefore, I ask people to make our mosque better. We work together in improving the mosque. We also improve the study of our religion because children today especially need more knowledge of Islam. We have to educate them seriously. I know young people behave so abruptly. They want to get everything fast so they become careless. They have to be taught religion and be closely taken care of. Otherwise, they will become destroyers of society.

Today, everything has changed. When I was a child, the situation was different from the present. Influences from outside the family are very strong on young people today. If parents and teachers are not careful and watchful, children only waste their time and money at school. For example, the cinema in the small town near here is a bad influence. I have seen a pornographic banner outside the build-

2. Man plowing rice field with oxen. *Photo: Hazairin Eko Prasetyo*

ing, and the spectators are underaged children. Who is responsible for this? Children are just copying what they see. Following good examples is harder than following bad ones. We can see this in young peoples' hair styles. They imitate what they see in films, television, and newspapers.

If their parents reprimand them, today's youths become angry. This kind of response never happened to children of my generation. I was not courageous enough to say "no" to my parents. Children of today do not know our Javanese customs and tradition. Most of them cannot even speak high Javanese correctly. It is difficult. I think it's the time for such changes to happen. But, once again, parents must be able to control their children. Otherwise, they won't be heard.

This is not so important for me personally because now all my children are grown and living independently. I am still willing to help them as far as I can afford to do so, but from now on I want to do whatever I can for my own sake and society—especially through religion. I want to spend the rest of my life doing daily activities. That is all. I will be happy to see my children's and my grandchildren's happiness.

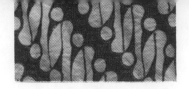

A Princess at the Sultan's Palace
of Surakarta

Members of the royal court at Surakarta lived a life isolated from the common people. But even royalty has been affected by the momentous events occuring since 1940. This woman began life in traditional Javanese courtly style, but then she was pushed into marriage with a Sundanese Islamic scholar from west Java. After moving to the Dutch colonial capital to be with her husband while he pursued his career as a public official, she discovered that he had different attitudes from those in which she was raised. She survived and prospered and made her own contributions to Indonesian history. In 1988, at age eighty-six, she was interviewed in Javanese by S. M. Darmastuti (female age thirty-three).

I was born on Thursday, August 14, 1902, or Kamis Paing 9 Jumadilawal of the Javanese calendar. My father was the son of Mangkunegoro V, the prince of the Mangkunegaran Palace of Surakarta. He was born on November 12, 1885, the seventh child and the third son of twenty-eight children. My mother, who was not of noble birth, was my father's first unofficial wife.

A short time before I was born, my mother, who was still young, was taken to my father's younger sister, named Suparti, who lived with her mother in the women's quarters of the palace. It was there that I was born. This was something quite out of the ordinary. Only a child of a reigning Mangkunegoro was allowed to be born in the palace, whereas I was only a grandchild. That was the first time a grandchild had ever been born in the palace.

After my birth my mother was unable to produce milk to nurse me so they had to search for a wet nurse. This was not so easy, and they tried several women in succession, until the fourth one was chosen. Not long after this my mother left the palace to return to her parents' home. I was taken care of and brought up by my aunt Suparti. I did not know my mother at all. I did have a mental image of a rather large woman, with light skin and thick hair, but I later discovered that this imagined mother was in fact a new wife of my father. Her name was Waginem, and she was good to me.

Everything I know about my childhood was told to me by my aunt Suparti. I regarded her as my own mother. But it seemed that she did not like Waginem, which bothered me. They were the ones I was closest to. The idea of not having a real mother present made me restless and unhappy. I would often wander about in the garden and on the paths of the palace garden, wondering about my mother. My head was full of unanswered questions. When I was tired and sat down for a while under a shady tree, I would often cry to myself. I felt very lonely and longed for my mother. I so much wanted Suparti to be my mother. She took care of me, watched over me, taught me everything I knew. She was always there when I needed her.

The Javanese word for "father" is Romo, but I could not pronounce the "r". So I called my father Momo. From that time on, my father was known at the palace as Momo, and he was often called Momo Bagus, which means Handsome Momo. One day my aunt told me that my father was going to leave the palace. This made me sad, for even though he lived in a room near us, in the palace men's quarters, I hardly ever saw him. Now I thought I would be without both father and mother. He wanted to get away from the palace, to go out into the world to see and do things. He took a position as a Dutch civil service secretary in another part of Java.

After my father left, I was still taken care of by aunt Suparti, whom I loved very much. She treated me as her own child, and I regarded her as my own mother. She taught me manners and discipline. She taught me how a resident of the palace was expected to behave: how to show deference to my elders, how to dress and wear my hair, and so on. To me, she was mother. She introduced me to all her brothers and sisters. They were twenty-eight children from fifteen unofficial wives of my grandfather Mangkunegoro. His first wife, who died at a very early age, had not presented him with a child.

It was the custom at the palace for the unofficial wives to be given a new name as soon as they had become legal wives. Mangkunegoro V divided his wives into groups with the same first name. Each group consisted of three persons. Of the fifteen wives I remember only nine of them, and I knew only thirteen uncles and seven aunts. I was not sure which uncles and aunts were brother and sister, and I did not even know which wife was their mother. This was no problem in the Mangkunegoro family because they were all one big family of brothers and sisters.

My grandfather loved animals. In his private garden he kept a great many, even tigers, alligators, monkeys, and many different kinds of birds. A number of deer walked about freely in the garden as well as wild pheasants. I often played in that garden.

One fine day aunt Suparti came with the news that my father was returning. He would become a translator for the Dutch colonial resident at Solo. He decided to live with his elder brother outside the palace. From that moment on, I went to my uncle's house where my father was staying so that he could teach me to speak Dutch. How cruel my father became in this teaching! He was often angry with me, especially when I could not distinguish between the Dutch dipthongs. If I made a mistake, then he would take a pitcher of water and pour it over my head. Once he was so angry that he lost his temper and broke the earthenware pitcher over my head. [Laughs] That was an unforgettable event in my life. After he had poured the water on me, I would cry, and then he would settle down and dry my face lovingly.

When father thought I had learned enough Dutch from him, he sent me to a Dutch kindergarten. There I learned to sing, accompanied on the piano by a Dutch teacher. About the same time, father moved from his brother's house to his own house near the palace. It was a large house, but old and in disrepair. The gardens were full of underbrush, and snakes could often be seen.

I went there twice a week to study different subjects with my father. One day he introduced me to his latest wife, who was childless. She was very kind to me. Not long afterward he brought another wife to live in the house, and she presented my father with a son. Unfortunately the baby only lived ten days. I was so sad because I had been longing for a playmate. Because I was all alone, I played with the youngest brother of my father. He was only six years older than me. He spoiled me, carrying me about and playing horseback. He and I also had to learn to read the Koran. A cousin of mine took part in these Islamic studies with us. She was very good at reading the Koran, reciting the versus with beautiful intonation.

My father arranged that I should spend every weekend at his home. I preferred to be with aunt Suparti. She was the one who had taken care of me since my birth. To persuade me to come, father would always give me new toys. I developed a great fondness for one of my father's new wives. The other one was irritated by me. At one point I became very ill. Aunt Suparti did many things to care for me, but I had such a high temperature that I was unconscious. One morning, as I was just coming out of this unconsciousness, I woke to find a lady kissing me gently and then quietly withdrawing. She disappeared before my eyes were wide open. Later I was told that she was my real mother. When I heard this I sobbed in aunt Suparti's lap. I tried so hard to remember the face of the woman who had kissed me. I wanted to know her gestures, to gaze a long time at her eyes, and see her face so full of love and care. Suparti told me that, without my ever having been aware of it, my mother had often come to the palace, just to look at me. She was remarried now, to an assistant at another palace.

When I was nearly eleven, my grandmother was dying. My father and his brothers and sisters carried her to a special place. No one was allowed to die within the palace except the Mangkunegoro, his official wife, and their children. A few days later she passed away. Later that same year my father decided to travel to Holland. I stared at aunt Suparti wide-eyed when she told me. Holland, that sounded so far away! Then my beloved aunt told me that she was going to get married. My father was going away, and Suparti was getting married—could any news have been worse than that? I could not imagine being left behind by the two people I loved so much. The wedding took place in 1913. I had to say goodbye to my beloved aunt because she had to go to another town to live with her husband.

After that I lived at my father's house with his two wives. He released them, so that they would not have to await his return from Holland but could marry anyone they wished. He took another wife, who accompanied him to Holland. As the son of the Mang-kunegoro my father was entitled to a monthly payment of three hundred gulden. Of this amount one-third was sent to him in Holland, one-third was set aside for payment of debts, and the rest was used for our living expenses with servants. I returned to live at the palace and was well provided for, yet I was so full of sadness at being parted from those I loved. I did not understand why, but it seemed that I could not please anyone in my heart. I was alone again.

Finally, after a few years, my father returned from Holland. At last I was happy. No longer did I have the feeling of being all alone, of having no one at all. He gave me such attention after he came back. Later, after my grandfather's death, my father became the Mangkunegoro, and I was the special child. We lived in the palace happily.

When I was age twenty-one my father arranged for me to marry a scholar from west Java. He was sixteen years older than me and had taken his doctor's degree at the University of Leiden in 1913. The first years of our marriage were years of adjustment. We often had misunderstandings. It could not have been otherwise; we came from different regions and different cultures. In addition, my husband was very well educated. What frequently caused conflict between us was *time*. My husband was, like the Dutch, as regular as clockwork, whereas the habits I had brought with me from the palace were entirely different. To me time had entirely different meaning: time was extensive, time was something to be felt and enjoyed, time was flexible. To give just one example, in Solo we never went to bed until past midnight, whereas my husband was always in bed at 10 p.m.

However, my husband was basically a very kind, patient, and thoughtful person. I learned to value his qualities highly. We moved to Batavia [the Dutch capital, which was renamed Jakarta by the nationalists], and unfortunately our first house was in bad condition. Before entering the house we had to cross a rickety bamboo bridge, and the roof of the house leaked badly. The move from the palace to this old house was a great change for me and required patience and endurance on my part. Fortunately we lived there for only six months. We got a much nicer house by paying a great amount of so-called "key money" as a bribe.

My husband was deputy adviser for native affairs for the Dutch resident. One day he told me we were invited to attend the farewell party for the Dutch governor general. I was apprehensive. This would be my first meeting, as a wife, with the world of high-ranking foreign officials. I felt very nervous as we stood in line with guests who were all strangers to me, awaiting my turn to shake hands with the governor general. I was impressed when I entered the Dutch palace. I saw a great many Westerners and only a few Indonesians. It was fascinating also to see the women in their glittering gowns.

In 1924 my husband was appointed professor in the Malay, Sundanese, and Javanese languages. He also began a thorough study of Islamic law and taught a course on that subject at the law school in Batavia. I was now becoming accustomed to associating with people connected with my husband's work. I also took part in so many women's activities in my own circle. Among other things, I became chair of an organization of Indonesian women. Although we were from three different ethnic groups—Javanese, Sundanese, and West Sumatran—we worked together very well. Ever since 1925, I had had a desire to realize the spirit that later became called "unity in diversity," now Indonesia's national motto.

My husband continued to become more prominent in the Dutch colonial government. In 1935 he was appointed a member of the Council of the Indies and adviser to the governor general for a five-year term. During this time he remained extremely busy. I tried to help him as much as I could, although my own time was largely occupied with our six children. In 1941 he was appointed acting director of the Department of Education and Religion. He had great ideas about reforms to be made, and we were on continuous contact with specialists in science and education.

Then war broke out in Europe, and Holland was overrun by the Germans. The political situation was changing, and I felt uneasy. The threat of war in Asia, with Japan as the aggressor, hung over our heads and frightened us. A number of my Dutch friends left Batavia and moved inland to Bandung. Then my husband had to go to Bandung, leaving us behind. After he left, things got worse, and I was very sad and very frightened. The situation was becoming more and more unsettled. In March 1942 the Japanese entered Batavia.

The years that followed were hard times. There were shortages of everything. It became more and more difficult to get enough food, clothing, and other necessities. The shops were practically empty, and people very seldom sold things in the market. I was extremely anxious about the situation. My husband did not come home. I was so afraid, especially when Japanese soldiers came to visit us, asking where my husband was. I always tried to avoid answering their questions. Even the school children were forced to labor for the Japanese, while not having nutritious food to eat. People suffered terribly.

After the surrender of the Japanese in 1945, we were relieved but the situation was very uncertain. The British landed with their Indian and Ghurka soldiers, who it was said were to maintain security. According to what I heard from people, they were trouble-makers. There were a lot of armed Indian soldiers in our neighborhood. I was afraid, especially when they knocked at the door at night, claiming to be looking for weapons that we might have hidden in our house. As had occurred with the Japanese, the Indian soldiers would come into our house saying they were looking for weapons, but in reality they only wanted to approach our daughter. Finally it was all over, and the situation returned to normal.

The independence of the Republic of Indonesia had been proclaimed, and the new government desparately needed skilled officials. My husband got involved, and he became chairman of the Indonesian delegation to Holland. That was my first trip abroad. My husband attended the inauguration of Princess Juliana as queen. Later he was a member of the Round Table Conference, where the final negotiations for the recognition of Indonesian independence were approved. He became Indonesia's secretary of the Department of Education, Culture and Science and later he was appointed professor of Islamic Studies at the University of Indonesia. In 1957 he became general director of the Language and Literature Foundation.

These functions resulted in a great number of activities that made me much busier, but they became too much for my husband. His health began to fail, and I was very anxious about him. It was God's will that he died quietly on November 12, 1960, at the age of seventy-three. I was terribly sad to lose him, and I felt that my life was nothing without him. I was so lonely.

Eventually I got over that loneliness. Life must go on. Now I am quite old. On my birthday recently my children and grandchildren held a big party. Many people were invited, and they performed a play. It was the biggest party we ever had.

During these last days of my life, I often think of life. As I look back, I come to the conclusion that everything that happens to us whether we think it good or bad—is in reality a great experience that enriches and adds meaning to our lives. I have had to form a family, educate my children, assist my husband in all his activities, and adjust to great changes. I have known life under three different governments, experiencing the joys and sorrows of each time. It is not we who determine our fate and the role we play in life, but it depends on us to play the best roles we can.

In this twilight of my life, I can look back with tranquility. I thank God that every experience I have had gave me wisdom and its own blessing and happiness. I am very happy in waiting for the end of my life, surrounded by my loving descendants.

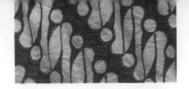

A Soldier in the Revolution

Though this man has been a farmer and a village leader, he most identifies himself with his role as a soldier. The first topic he began talking about, when asked about his life, was his role in the revolution. He is pleased with his children, but he hardly mentioned his family until that topic was brought up at the end of the interview. Born in 1928, he was educated in a Dutch school, worked with the Japanese during World War II, and then with the anticolonial resistance forces. While he feels somewhat uneasy about the killings in which he was involved, he feels that his efforts and those of his fellow soldiers have contributed much toward improving modern Indonesia. Today, he lives unpretentiously in his village near Yogyakarta, at peace with himself.

This interview took place at a quiet restaurant in Yogyakarta, where over many glasses of hot tea the man spoke with seeming candor to Hazairin Eko Prasetyo (male, age twenty-nine) and Walter L. Williams.

I was eighteen in 1946, when I joined the revolution by enlisting myself in the Hizbullah Muslim Volunteer Corps. That name is taken from the Arabic, which means "God's troops." It was then very famous among Muslims because we fought for the liberation of our country from foreign colonialists. Islam opposes domination of Muslims by unbelievers. Our troops were very brave. Three men from my village became revolutionary fighters. Besides me, the other two were rich and educated in a pesantren, the special Islamic religious school. I was just a layman and inferior to them. I honored them and doubted whether they would receive me as a soldier. Compared to them, I was far from their level of refinement. I suffered from skin rashes and was poorly dressed. I was doubtful about my abilities, but I overcame those doubts because of my strong courage and determination to fight against the Dutch.

I was accepted into the commander-in-chief's guards regiment and managed to become friends with most leading figures in the troop. I became secretary for the regiment because I could read and write well. Earlier, I had finished elementary school, under the Dutch administration. I can hardly remember what I experienced during the Dutch colonial era, before they were defeated by the Japanese. What I did do was devote myself to my studies. The Dutch school was very difficult and hard to finish. They had a five-year elementary school program, which had to be completed in two different schools. The first three years were in a school not far from our village. After getting that diploma, if we wanted to continue the program, we had to walk six kilometers farther to attend the fourth and fifth years. After taking the fifth-year diploma, one was considered a graduate of elementary school.

I finished elementary school and got my second diploma in 1938, long before the Japanese came. I still keep my diplomas on the wall, although they are now full of holes. By having the elementary school diploma, I could qualify for various clerical jobs. It was definitely worth the effort. Only two other people from this village, besides me, could afford to go to school then.

There were many fewer people at that time, not as many as now. Most people only went from their houses to the fields to work, seldom leaving their villages. They did not go to school. Only I could get the fifth-year diploma. So, most people knew very little, except for their immediate surroundings. Back then, the young people were very afraid of elderly people. They were afraid because they knew so little. Now things have changed, as more children have become educated. Today, young people are becoming more active in society.

When Japanese occupied our country, I was a young man. At age fourteen, I was drafted by them to become a laborer. We worked hard, building railroad tracks. But my position was good because I dared to speak to them. And I could write and read. They chose me as a notetaker in one of their big warehouses. As a result of this job, I got good clothes and enough food to eat. I was closely supervised by a Japanese official, so I could not help my neighbors when they were tired of working and needed a rest. Even though the Japanese treated me well, after a time I decided to escape because they were becoming more and more cruel. The laborers suffered very much. I joined some men from my district, and we succeeded in escaping from the Japanese work camp even though it was well-guarded. They did not catch us, and I eventually got back to my village.

It was a terrible time back then, and after the Japanese left the Dutch tried to come back in. That is when the revolution began, and I got involved in it. The rebels had two separate headquarters in my town, but most people only knew about one. My office was in the secret headquarters, some distance away, where the important generals stayed. We had to march to the mosque guarding General Sudirman every Friday afternoon for him to do his prayers on the Muslim holy day. He was a good Muslim and leader. We also escorted other generals who were going to the mosque when we were in Yogyakarta. That was the only duty to which we were assigned, when we were not involved in a military operation. We were very proud of our generals. They had given up everything to fight the Dutch.

One time during the revolution, when I was on holiday at home, some neighboring villagers reported to me that they met two strangers walking toward my village. These strangers were Indonesians, but we suspected that they might be Dutch spies. I decided that, as a soldier, I had to do what must be done. If they found out that I was working for the revolution, they would shoot me dead. I must do the same to them. The simple reason was that we needed to protect our safety: kill or be killed, that was our doctrine when meeting our enemies. The spirit of fighting for our country was deeply rooted in my heart [proudly beating his chest]. Being in the army made me proud and satisfied. I killed the enemy for only one reason: to struggle for our country and religion.

Those two suspects were of different ethnic groups, one was Javanese and the other Ambonese. The second man had a gun wrapped under a sarong that was hanging over his shoulder. I stopped them and pointed my gun at the armed guy, saying, "Come on, sir, hands up. Come on, hurry up. Hands up." And they did so. People came around and tied them fast. We brought them to my headquarters, but the Ambonese one tried to escape. I called him to come back, but he would not stop. So I had no choice but to shoot him. The bullet went through his head, and he died at once.

I did not want to deal with the other suspect because I knew him. He lived in a neighboring village. But I also knew that he was a Dutch spy. So, I let the villagers do what they wanted to him. They hit and kicked him, you know, a lot of angry people. After this went on for awhile, at last he died. The villagers were satisfied and buried them in our graveyard. Yes, people hated spies even more than soldiers. What was surprising to us was the Dutch reaction.

After the following day, we had no doubt at all that these suspects were spies. The Dutch would not have retaliated for the killing of civilians. What the Dutch did to my village was awful. I can only say that it must have been what God willed. From the fields, I could see and hear a horrible uproar taking place in my compound. The Dutch came and burned twelve houses down. It was like a mountain hit by fire. My father was at home. I do not think they knew he was my father, but they killed him anyway. There is a vivid saying, "Whoever makes experiences, gets the result."[1] Nobody saw the murder because people fled. We soldiers had to run away because we were less in number than the Dutch. We could not afford to resist the raid. I only saw my father's body later, when it was ready for burial. We used his sarong for his shroud. [long pause] We did that because we were in a state of emergency.

When my father died and my house was burnt by the Dutch, I felt very broken. But my mother had immediately become aware of the danger. She hid herself in the kitchen. After the Dutch left, by herself, she managed to extinguish the fire. I was glad that she was safe and our house was only slightly damaged, but I was very sad about my father. My older brother always blamed me for causing father's death. He told me over and over again that if I had never killed the Dutch spy, our father would still have been alive. "Do not be cruel, brother," he said, "otherwise, you get the results." I answered, "You and I have different ideas about some things. You, as a compound and civil leader, have the duty of keeping people in order. That's all. I am a soldier. In wartime like this, I have to kill my enemies, or they will kill me. It is my way of fighting for our country and religion."

It was the rule of warfare at that time. He who attacked first would become the winner. Later, in 1948, I was a government soldier helping to suppress a communist revolt in Madiun. In the Madiun affair, we attacked the communists first, and they lost the battle. Our army won a great victory. But I cried then because when I stopped fighting long enough to take my compulsory prayers, my regiment ran after the rebels, and I did not know where to find them. So, everything was left when we won the fight or we lost it. That is why a soldier must be brave.

Still, what my brother said continued to haunt me, and I felt very guilty for my father's death. After 1948, I decided to quit the army. If I did not quit, I am sure I would have a high rank now. I know one man, my fieldmate in the regiment, who later became a major even though he could not read and write. Furthermore, he could not speak in front of his mates as I could.

Although I am not a high-ranking military man now, I still receive my veteran pension. The government pays my pension every month, which is sufficient for my personal needs, especially when I must buy medicine for curing some disease. Thankfully, the government does not forget about revolutionary fighters like me. I do not know what would have happened to our country if there had not been so many brave fighters. It is good that the veterans, who have built this country, are being honored.

I am sure that everything will be all right. When I am in town, I feel very satisfied. I have the feeling that all the progress our people are now making is, in part, due to my share. I take part in it. I participated in providing the foundation on which the towns are now prospering, even though I am not a leader. But I am not at the back either. Deep in my heart, I always feel that I have contributed something to them. I am proud because I have done something for my beloved country and religion.

People of today are getting fatter and fatter. They do not experience any struggle. They know nothing of the revolution. Look, I still keep in my mind what General Sudirman always told us. "This country is a heritage. It doesn't belong to the Dutch or to the Japanese or to the Chinese. It is not a loan. Come on [beats his chest], let's chase the Dutch and all their agents." The fighters were very proud of him. We were prepared to sacrifice our lives for our country and nation. And, I think, it is right that our country is a heritage. Our forefathers had made it for us to live. President Sukarno and General Sudirman had emblazoned my soul and mind with nationalistic and patriotic fervor. They gave all their lives for the country. We are safe now, and everything is much easier.

The next military event to threaten our country was the communist rebellion of 1965, which was the continuation of the previous one in Madiun. But the 1965 rebellion was national. All villages in our country were involved. In Jakarta, the communists proclaimed their victory. They killed our generals, like Ahmad Yani and the others. They were very sure that they won the rebellion. They announced their regime, but it only lasted for five or six hours. Because they were cruel to both military and civilian people, we began a countermovement. They assassinated any people who were different from them. So, in return, people began catching them and transporting them to some imprisonment places. I did not know for sure. Many of them were killed.

I also took part in this movement to sweep the communists away. I went to some neighboring villages where communists were active and, joining people from other villages, caught the leaders. We persuaded them to surrender peacefully. Otherwise, we would have killed them because they were considered dangerous for the unity of our nation and religion.

In the recent decades, I became a village official for the government. As a caretaker of the society, I have to be well-mannered to all people. If I press them or say hard words to them, they will be contemptuous of me. I have had various experiences in getting people to cooperate. Because I am experienced, I know that I have to be skillful. For example, once a week people here have to do their public work for society, like cleaning the mosque and improving the condition of the roads. If some people do not come, I just keep quiet. I must not reprimand them. I must not say something hard to them because, who knows, they might be sick or have something important to do. I have to be careful.

What I can do is politely try to persuade someone who is not doing a fair share of work, to make them understand the need for every person's cooperation. I tell them, "This village is not the village-head's. This village belongs to all of us. Since a very long time ago the people of the village have been doing social work. What we need is your presence. You have to be cooperative. The most important thing is that you come. I do not care whether you work or just fool around. I will certainly be glad if you come. I will not give you any order because you will be insulted. It is easy. If you dare to do nothing or just heat your body in the sun, I will not care. You have to come, that's all."

This approach seems to produce something worth considering. A few years ago only ten to twenty people showed up. Now, it's getting better. If some men are absent, I ask them to show up, and they do so. I say, "If you do not show up, your neighbors will slight you. Or else you let your village run down. This village is your heritage from your ancestors. This will be forever like this. When I die, the next generation will come. When the next generation dies, the next following generation will take their place. It is going on this way forever."

If I tried to force them to do their social work, they would certainly be angry and would not listen to me any more. Almost all villagers here are experienced. They go to towns looking for better jobs besides farming, especially the young people.

What I think about young people of today is that they are getting better. They were hard to manage a few years ago, but they are easier now. As Islam is becoming more prominent in society nowadays, its influence is great. The Koran forbids Muslims from doing any bad things. But, frankly speaking, it seems that young people today are naughtier when compared to those of my youth. I think they have become different because of their different milieu. What I always tell younger people is that they should be educated and self-critical. They have to be aware of their limited strength.

I feel satisfied because I am old. What else can I do? I have no more power to do anything. My first wife died ten years ago, and now I just spend my time with my second wife at her house. I need not worry about my children anymore. All five of them have been working. And, it is unnecessary for me to fear about food and clothing. I get my veteran's pension, and my children can support their own needs. In any case, I always tell them to do good quality work. I recommend that they should obey their employers, for unless they do so, I, their father, will get a bad reputation. They should be honest; otherwise, I will be ashamed. I am satisfied because my children understand what they should do for me. They give me some money once a month. It is not much, but I am satisfied.

A Seamstress

To this seventy-six-year-old woman, the most important aspects of her life are her children and her business. For most Javanese women, motherhood and work outside the home are not mutually exclusive roles; both are required. For the average Javanese woman, at least until recently, there was no expectation that marriage would involve a husband supporting her. Woman's role means work. This woman sees success as having lots of children, having those children become well educated, and then having them married with several children of their own. Having many children is a strong traditional Javanese value, which continues even during the present era of population control programs.

This woman, focusing on her family and her business, stays away from politics. After the turmoil of the 1960s and the massacre of dissidents, many Indonesians have learned to avoid direct political statements. She is intensely loyal to Indonesia and grateful for the stability of the past two decades. As she approaches her final years, her religious faith—a combination of Muslim and Buddhist ideas—provides her with a serene satisfaction in life. A determination to help her children and society at large gives her a sense of purpose in life that could be a model for many.

The interviews with this woman were conducted in Javanese by S. M. Darmastuti, (female, age thirty-three), they talked in the back room of the woman's busy seamstress shop. The interview was interrupted several times, as workers asked the woman for directions and advice on how to handle a problem. Despite the woman's advanced age, she is still actively involved in running her business.

When I look back on my life, I think the most important things to me are my children. I have four daughters and three sons. I think I am not very successful in encouraging them to finish their education because only one got a graduate degree and two never even went to a university. My oldest daughter went to a high school that trained teachers for young children. When she finished her study, she taught kindergarten for two years. Then she stopped because she got married. Unfortunately, her husband died a year later. Now she has married again, but I don't think she will go back to school. My fifth son just barely finished high school because he is not too bright. Thank God, though, he has been a success in his business. He works hard as owner of a grocery shop, and he lives happily with his loyal wife. Because they have not been able to have children, they adopted a son.

I am proud that four of my children graduated from college. My second son is the most successful in a material sense; he is director of a sugar company and also owner of five big ships. He has only two daughters, and both of them are already students at the university. His life is easy, but . . . [pause] I don't think he is as generous as my other children. My third son, in contrast, devotes himself to helping the next generation. He is a high school teacher. He has six children. His life seems happy, although I know life is hard for him financially because teachers' salaries are so low. I help him out, by letting him use one of my houses without charge. I pay the electricity charge, the water tax, and the land tax.

My fourth daughter married a university lecturer after she finished college. He also owns a tailor shop to supplement his meager university salary.[1] They have three children. I think she is the happiest among all my children. Her husband does not let her take a job, even though she has her college degree. He is the most understanding man I have ever seen. My sixth daughter married a medical doctor, and she is now an ordinary housewife with two children. My youngest daughter is the only child who finished her graduate degree. She is now a lecturer, and her husband has his own business. She has only one son. I hope she intends to have more children soon.

The other thing that is important in my life, besides my children, is my business. When I got married fifty-five years ago [in 1933], my father gave me ten rupiahs to start my own business. My father-in-law did the same thing for my husband. With that money we rented a little shop and began selling cigarettes, sugar, tea, and rice. I lived happily with my husband, and our business grew bigger and bigger. Everything went well until 1942, when I was pregnant with my fifth son. Then the war began, and the Japanese came to our town.

I hated the Japanese very much. They took things for no reason. For example, my husband collected ties and safety matches; he began his collection when his Dutch friends gave him ties and matches from other nations. He also bought more from Chinese traders. It was a harmless little hobby, but it gave him much enjoyment. And do you know that the Japanese, when they saw this collection, stole it all! My husband was so disappointed that I felt a great pity for him. The Japanese troops who came to Indonesia were wild. There were a few, especially those in the high officer ranks, who were polite and sympathetic. I know this because they frequently came to our shop to buy cigarettes.

Still, I was so glad when the Japanese left. But then the Dutch came here again, and the revolution began. This time we had to fight against the Dutch troops. Most of the Dutch army were young people, and they were much more polite than the Japanese. The wildest troops employed by the Dutch were the Green Berets. They were Molucans, from the islands east of here, and they joined the Dutch army to kill Javanese. Two kilometers from our shop was a market that was always full of people selling and buying. When the Green Berets first came and occupied this town, they showed their force by slaughtering people in the market—not only adults but also many children.

Today a monument in the middle of that marketplace commemorates that sad event. My husband was one person who helped the Dutch soldiers bury the bodies. You know, he did not want to eat anything for three days after seeing that horrible sight. My husband said that actually the Dutch soldiers did not want the Green Berets to do the cruel things to the people. But when those bad things happened, then the Dutch were just silent and did nothing to bring the murderers to justice. It was not fair, and the people of this town were angry with the Dutch as well as the Green Berets. We wanted to drive the Dutch from Indonesia.

I totally agreed with that idea. I wanted to be a citizen of an independent country. But still, I was afraid of war. That was why I did not let my husband join the guerillas. I did not want to lose him in battle. My children were still young. I think everybody can fight oppression in their own way, not always by open warfare. I decided to help the guerillas by supplying them with food—that was how I fought.

One of my nephews joined the guerillas, and he came to our house with his friends three times a week, usually at night, to get food for their camp. They pretended to be vendors who were bringing their merchandise home to sell to the rural peasants. Well, I am glad to say that God allowed them to live through that fighting and even up to the present. One of those guerilla friends of my nephew is now a general in the army. He still remembers me. I am proud that a general sends me holiday letters twice a year. My nephew did not want to stay in the army after the revolution ended. Instead, he got a job in the government customs house, where he worked until he retired. His life today is very successful; he has seven children, and five of them have already graduated from the university and gotten married.

Unlike the young people today, I did not have much of an education. I regret that I was only able to finish my fourth year of elementary school. My mother had died when I was eight years old, and my father quickly remarried. My stepmother did not want me to continue my schooling so I just stayed at home helping her rear my new stepbrother and helping my father work in his cigarette business. I was not free from this hard life until I got married. Later, after my father died, my stepmother regularly came to my house for me to care for her in her old age. Her son had married a woman who never took good care of my stepmother.

Despite my personal feelings, I could not turn her away. Even though I am a Muslim, I believe in *karma*. I believe that God will reincarnate us again for our redemption, if in our lifetime we still have many sins that cannot yet be redeemed. I dare not do bad things to others because then God will know it and he will do the same bad things to me through human actions. While it has not happened to me, I have witnessed such things many times in my life. Even though I did not have much opportunity to learn to be clever at school, I learned life's lessons from seeing the sufferings of others. I hope such bad experiences will never happen to me and to my descendants as have happened to my stepmother who was turned away by her own son.

I have been very fortunate lately. Besides the house where I live, I also own seven houses, which I gave to my five children who are living here in town. The other two houses are for rent. People say I am successful in my business. But they never knew how hard my life was after my husband died and I was pregnant with my youngest daughter. Two of my children were students at the university, three more still had to be put through school, and the youngest was still in my stomach. My business was ruined. I had to sell my house to pay the bills. I tried to run my business while raising the children by myself, but I failed again and again.

One day my fifth son, the one whom I thought was the most stupid, came home with his friend who asked me if I would help him sell emblems for a political party. I did it in pity for him, but to my surprise people bought them gladly. That was the first time I realized there was an opportunity for a new kind of business, one that people were never before aware of. I told my son's friend to make more emblems, and soon people were coming regularly to buy them. Not only that, but they started requesting uniforms for their political parties as well.[2] My children really pitched in and helped me greatly in this business. They kept the shop open every day after they got out of school. At night, after finishing their homework, they helped me sew clothes and print the shirts with the pictures of the parties on them.

I love all my children. I still run my business today, as old as I am, because I love them and want to give them all I have. I never think of asking them to help support me, the way my cruel stepmother did to me. Instead I want to help them create a prosperous life for themselves and their children. I want them to be successful entrepreneurs so that they do not need to ask the government to pay for them. Instead, I want them to help the government by paying taxes. Only three of my children are government officers, and the rest are in business. I am very proud of them, even though not all of them are rich.

I know nothing about political life and always remained neutral in dealing with the various parties that came here for their uniforms. From the Dutch era until today, I have just focused on my business. During the colonial era I did not feel life was hard. My business was good. But I preferred to be occupied by the Dutch rather than by the Japanese. Anyhow, I like best to be free from anyone's occupation. Independence was our idealism in the 1940s, and every good citizen of Indonesia knew it.

The time when everything got out of hand was in the 1960s. Oh, I still remember how people would have to stand in long lines when they wanted to buy rice, oil, and sugar. That was the time when communism was still alive here. When I watch the television news programs, I can see that similar situations are still happening in other parts of the world where communism exists. I do not know why people will fight for communism, and I asked my sons and daughters about it. Most of them told me that communism will grow bigger in a poor country.

Fortunately, Indonesia has started to move beyond that. I am proud of our late president Sukarno. He is a real hero for Indonesia. But, the bad thing about him was that . . . I don't like the way he treated women. He cohabited with many women, without taking care of his reputation as a president. Maybe you think it was just human nature, but still I don't like it. My late grandfather was a strong supporter of Sukarno. Grandfather was a village leader, and Sultan Mangkunegoro VII spoke of him as a strong and wise man. Grandfather told me, long before the revolution, that Indonesians would have their independence if there would emerge a man who can make people hear him and who also could hear what the people want. You know, Sukarno means "super ear." That Javanese word means someone who has a super ear to hear what the people say and want. Well, we wanted independence. And Sukarno proclaimed independence.

My grandfather also told me that, later, Indonesia will have a leader who can make people full of "harta" or wealth. Now we have President Suharto, and his name means someone who has super wealth. I think President Suharto is very successful. He has given Indonesia an era of stability, with no more riots, rebellions, and difficulties in getting food. He has given us a feeling of safety.

Well, I am not a fortune teller, and my grandfather was not a fortune teller, but once he told me that the nation's third leader, who will bring Indonesia into a really good era, is one who has a super love. Well, well, well . . . Now we have General Tri Sutrisno [a high officer in the army] Will he be our third president? We just have to wait and see. You know, Tri means "third," and Sutrisno means someone who can love people deeply. That is precisely what my grandfather meant.

I always vote in the presidential election every five years. But I have no intention of being an active member in a political party. I don't like politics. I am just an uneducated old woman. I am happy enough with the success of my business, and that is all I need. I pay my taxes diligently and honestly. That is my way of showing my obedience to my dear Indonesia. I encourage my children to be entrepreneurs, rather than government bureaucrats just waiting for their salaries like so many government officials do. What I did is solely because I love this country. I want to give Indonesia something, rather than ask for something.

I am not boasting, but each year I donate money to the orphanage and to the Muslim hospital. I worked at my business not only for helping my children and grandchildren but also for contributing to society. I always remember what the prophet Mohammed said: "Find your wealth as if you will live for a thousand years more, but find your creed and faith in God as if you will die tomorrow." I always repeated this saying to my children. But my second son, the richest, seems not to obey what I told him. He finds his wealth very seriously, but he never thinks about his faith to God. Instead, he goes to a *dukun* [shaman]. He believes in all those superstitions, and he doesn't even do his prayers to God as a good Muslim should. Oh, I get very sad when I think about him. I think dukun conjuring is forbidden by Islam and also, I believe, by Christianity.

Actually I am not an extreme Muslim. I let my children choose their own religions. One daughter is a Catholic, and one son is a Protestant. They are obedient devotees to their faiths, and I respect them more than those people who say that they are Muslims but never pray or do anything for their beliefs.

Nowadays I live quite simply. My grandchildren come and stay with me on the weekends. My oldest daughter helps me run my seamstress shop. Thank God I am fortunate to have two loyal live-in servants and four assistants to work in the shop. I pay them a generous salary, and they are very understanding of my situation. They treat me quite respectfully and never leave me alone—even during holidays. They arrange their days off in a certain way so that I can always have at least one of them here to accompany me every day and every night. My children trust them, too.

Life is much easier if we accept whatever happens to us by believing that God's will comes our way and that it is best for us in the long run. Even in our hardest times, if we still believe that whatever happens to us is best for us, then we will be given our real strength by God. By doing this, life is easier. It is important for us to know this because it will help tame our extreme individual ambition. Every minute our lives are getting shorter, so every minute we have to think and do good things. When God asks us to be with him, we can then accept it easily. Life is not like waiting in line. We do not know who will be the first to be called. But every person will be called at last. Many people are afraid of that reality. We have to face this bravely, without forgetting what the prophet Mohammed said about working and faith.

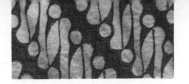

A Policeman

This man, like many of his generation, was active in the revolution. Yet his narrative focuses mostly on his work as a policeman in the years following independence. He was particularly active in helping to suppress some rebellions that ransacked Indonesia during the chaotic early years of the nation's independence. Because the rebel groups were partly motivated by economic pressures, it is difficult to determine to what degree these groups were encouraging real political revolt or merely stealing food as outlaw bands.

Born in 1922, this inside observer of Dutch colonialism became particularly aware of the relationship between poverty and crime. While feeling the need for political and social stability, he is also sympathetic to the plight of the poor who might have to steal to survive. Feeling that he did his job with the greatest possible sense of justice, he held a secure sense of accomplishment in his old age. Typical of Javanese people, the extreme respect for the elderly is a comfort for him as he prepares to face the end of his life. The man is self-assured in a quiet unassuming way. He has always recognized the power of spiritual forces, not so much from a Muslim perspective but from the ancestor-spirit focus of ancient Javanese animist religion. He indicates his satisfaction in knowing that he has done his best and seems content for the next generation to be in charge.

This interview took place at the man's home in a small village near Yogyakarta. The interview was conducted in Javanese by Priyanto (male, age thirty-nine), translating for Walter L. Williams.

I was a policeman. It is a profession I loved and still love. It was my ambition since I was a small boy. Dedication was the ideal in my days. When I think about the past, I recall my times in the police forces. I feel that I have done good things for others. I am very proud of my profession! There is a difference between the work of a soldier and the work of a policeman. A soldier should kill his enemy, but a policeman should not kill. Police work is based on humanism. I could not kill or even hurt my enemies, although they have committed crimes.

I began to get acquainted with police when I was only a small child. My father was an *ambtenaar,* a high government official, during the Dutch colonial time. He was chief of a district in the southern part of central Java. Today the police are under the military forces. But in the Dutch administration, the police activities were supervised by the central Dutch administration in the Department of Internal Affairs. My father was always involved in disputes with the Dutch, but still he had to work together with them. They had a strong influence upon my father's daily activities.

As a small child I was captivated by the arrogant performance of the police. Gradually I was told that they were assigned to enforce colonial law. Only a small number of people could take up this profession, mostly the ambtenaar's relatives. When I revealed to my father my ambition to become a policeman, he said calmly, "Son, I am happy to hear of your great interest in humanity. Being a policeman will provide you with a kind of psychological satisfaction. You have to know, though, that it is not a pleasant profession. Your enemies are your friends, your people, and maybe even your family. How would you do that? You are expected to protect the people from the criminal acts of offenders, no matter who they are. It is your duty to prevent as well as detect crimes."

I can understand my father's wise words because he saw his policemen did not do the right things. As colonial policemen, they were bound to obey the Dutch rule. They even controlled and supervised my father's activities. I used to see them whipping farmers who refused to plant sugar. For a certain period each year the Dutch required that the land be planted with sugarcane, under the government's supervision; as soon as the sugar was mature they were to sell it to the local sugar mill. But the price set by the Dutch was such a low rate that people hardly had enough money to buy food. With so much land devoted to sugarcane, there was not enough time or space to cultivate food crops. Because there was not much rice, people began to commit crimes. I can see today that the problem of rural development is very complex. The peasants never think about demanding equality, rights, or more opportunities to improve their lives; they simply want enough rice to eat, as there are now more mouths to feed.

I was twenty years old when the Japanese came to rule this country. At first we welcomed them as liberators from the Dutch colonialism. However, the warmth of welcome was soon stamped out by the brutalities of their war machine. I was smart enough to understand the political chaos in Indonesia. When the Japanese imperial forces occupied Indonesia, the Indonesian Nationalist Movement faced a new situation. The most prominent leaders of the movement, under the leadership of Sukarno and Hatta, cooperated with the Japanese forces. To prepare for independence, our youths received military training under the Japanese commanders. I was among the youths who received the military training in east Java. I thought I should do something for my nation. Meanwhile, my ambition to become a policeman was fading.

After the Japanese Empire lost the Second World War and surrendered to the Allies, the Indonesian Proclamation was announced by the committee for the preparation of Indonesia's independence. At this time we began to live in the independent era. The era of colonialism was over, but the new nation faced serious problems of structure, organization, and administration. In a speech Sukarno said, "To proclaim independence is easy. To make a constitution is not very difficult. But to establish the organs of the offices of authority for administration of state is not an easy task." He was such a great person, and he made this nation enjoy freedom. People have to admit that he was one of the most prominent leaders and the founding father of this country. However, he was only a common human being, and by the end of his administration he had done some things wrong. I think we expected too much from him.

During the four years of the revolution I joined the student military forces. I was stationed in the northern part of central Java. As far as I remember the British came first to accept the Japanese surrender and acted as a caretaker until the Dutch could arrive. In 1947 when the Dutch troops and armored tanks rolled into the territory of the new republic, they caused a dreadful situation. The Dutch military forces invaded Java and other islands. Fighting broke out in every part of the country. What was different from the prewar times, however, was that the Japanese, for all the bad things they did, at least had given us the training and the confidence that the whites could be beaten. We who were trained by them now trained others. If we did not have guns, we made sharp pointed sticks. We were no longer afraid of the white man.

When the war was over I was happy to return to my family, but I found out that during the fighting my father, charged by the Dutch with protecting the Indonesian guerillas, was executed. His tragic death was a great blow to me. When I heard the news, I thought the world was shaking. I believe that the deaths of our parents are tragedies in our lives. It is impossible to replace their positions in someone's life. Much to my regret, I was unable to make his spirit happy. As a son, I should have been there when he died to "dig his grave deeply and hold his coffin highly." It is the duty of the children to give respect and glorify the parents' name.

I got out of the student military forces a year after the revolution was over. Meanwhile my ambition to become a policeman still remained in my heart. When the new republic encouraged youths to join the police forces, I took the opportunity for the transition, and I volunteered for the state police. For the first six months I tried to adjust to my new profession. I was learning by doing, and my experiences in the war helped me do the job. I now realize my military experiences were very useful.

During the early period of the new republic, there was not much for the police forces to do. Most people gave their serious attention to building the nation. The crucial moment emerged, however, when a contradiction developed among the politicians and extremists. By that time the situation was becoming worse and uncontrolled; it led to turbulent mobs. Robberies, murders, and crimes continually distressed the society. I was assigned to fight the Merapi Merbabu Complex terrorists, who were based in the slope of the Merapi mountain between Yogyakarta and Solo. They robbed and terrorized the farmers with threats and violence.

One night, when I was stationed at a police post north of Yogyakarta, I heard the sound of gunfire. I was certain that the terrorists had begun to rob the people's belongings. I was terrified by the shouts for help that I could hear coming from people who lived down from my post. We were only fifteen people, and I was appointed to command them. I told my members to get ready, as the sound of gunfire was getting closer. I was informed that they numbered about fifty. I held my *keris* dagger for a while to my forehead, in hopes that I might receive spiritual power.[1] It's my ancestor's keris, and my father gave it to me before I joined the war; I still have it with me. Without wasting time, I instructed ten of my members to run to the village and told them to use their firearms in case of trouble. First, I realized that I needed to reduce the number of the terrorists and then attack suddenly.

Few terrorists had firearms. Mostly they used swords, knives, and spears. As we got closer to the area, I made a shot, hoping that I could capture some of them. Fighting broke out. I was in a difficult position because I could not differentiate between farmers and terrorists. However, our arrival had encouraged the farmers to join us in the fight. Just before the sun rose, the fight was over. We captured ten terrorists. I sent the captives, plus two of my members who were wounded, to the central office. I asked my commander to send me more reinforcements. In addition, I also mentioned my difficulties in knowing the difference between farmers and terrorists. They were all dressed alike, and it was impossible for us to find them in the daytime.

When the chief of the village came to see me, he expressed his gratitude on behalf of the farmers and said he would be pleased to do something. He asked me if we were prepared to repel an attack. He said that the people of the village were worried that the terrorists would come back to take revenge. He seemed to understand my difficult position, saying, "I think you have to win the next fight, otherwise this village will be burnt."

The chief recommended that I should visit the village cemetery to ask for spiritual help at the grave of the village's founder. He said, "As a stranger you should pay your respects to the owner of the village who 'sleeps' there. He knows that you do not do any harm to us. Perhaps you will gain a spiritual power from him." Well, I realized that I was a stranger in this part. I should have visited that grave upon my arrival. Followed by my two members, I went to the cemetery early in the morning. Under a big banyan tree I found a graveyard; the owner of the village slept in the middle. According to the chief, he was the first man to live here. We sat around his tomb and began to pray. As told by the chief, I asked the spirit's permission to stay in his domain. I also begged his blessings should any danger come to us.

This Thursday evening was also the *kliwon*, the sacred day according to the Javanese calendar. It's believed that at that sacred day all the bad spirits are roaming about the world. People, hoping they can keep themselves from falling under the spirits' influences, are expected to stay awake until late at night. I was about to fall asleep when the sound of an explosion broke the night. I told all my members to get ready. Our post was surrounded by terrorists.

Suddenly the terrorists rushed into view, attacking one of my members. The big fight began. They came from different directions, and the number of the terrorists increased. Meanwhile I had already lost two of my members from the first fight. We fought in defence of our post, but we could no longer hold it. It was useless to fight them; we were so outnumbered we did not have a chance to win. To save our lives, we had to jump into the valley.

I was the last person who left the post, and they blocked the exit. I could not escape. There was another way to reach the valley, by climbing over a very high wall. Before I could make up my mind three terrorists successfully broke through the back door. I had only two bullets left in my revolver. I tried to shoot them to reach the back door. Before I reached the wall, more people were rushing to surround me. Only a miracle could save my life.

Without my awareness, something happened at that moment. As if I were moved by a power outside of myself, I suddenly jumped completely over the high wall. I rolled down in the valley. I did not know what happened to me after that.

The next day, when I opened my eyes, I was being taken care of in a house of a sympathetic farmer. My legs were both broken, and I was severely wounded. Yet I was grateful because the spirit had saved my life! As soon as I recovered, I was transferred to the central office.

Two years later I was transferred to a police district in Sumatra. There were no important activities there, beyond the daily police routine. While there, I married the daughter of the village chief. Two years passed, and my wife never got pregnant. I began to worry that there would be no child in my family. The following year I was transferred to east Java, but my wife preferred to stay with her parents so we split up. I was living alone for a year until I married a Javanese girl. Now, I have three children, and they are all grown and living with their own families. During the Lebaran Holy Day, at the end of the Islamic fasting month, they come to visit me and my wife. They bring their families, too. To me, this occasion is the most important moment in our lives. I have been asked several times to stay with them, but I don't want to disturb their happiness.

During my time in east Java my policework mainly concerned cases of people cutting teak wood illegally. When the dry season came there was always big trouble in that impoverished area. The peasants lost their livelihood. It was too dry to plant the crops without water so they would steal wood from the govenment-owned forests to get money. I always remember when my father once told me about the problem of being a policeman. That time I had to meet the poor peasants who cut the wood. They would plead with me, "I have to feed my family, and I lost my job. Can't you help me?" I know for a fact that poverty means crime. It was against my will to send them to jail because there was no one to look after their families. This type of policework was emotionally difficult for me.

After a few years in east Java I was promoted to instructor in the police-training academy. The government realized that the nation needed to build stronger state police forces to promote stability. I liked that job as an instructor. At three o'clock in the morning I started to have exercises with the students. The day was filled with physical training. After a time I tried to introduce my opinions about improving the training system. My suggestions were accepted, and then I was asked to complete the syllabus for the police training course. That gave me a good sense of accomplishment.

Several years passed when an old friend of mine came to see me. He held an important position in the police forces. As a good friend he said, "It's about time you enjoy yourself. You deserve a better position. Don't you want to move to Jakarta for a promotion? There are some important positions available. Perhaps you would like it, and I will certainly help you." I know he told me the truth. Yet I didn't want to accept his generous offer. So many people, thinking only of their personal advantages, try to get a better position; they don't want to think about their duties, only their own good. I could have risen higher, but I suppose being an instructor was also one of my ambitions. I don't want to personally know the rulers of this country or hold a high post. I get my satisfaction from knowing that I have done something for this country. I still want to do more for Indonesia.

We older people, however, must now realize that it's time for us to step aside for a new generation, a generation that will continue our mission. Let's not try so hard to hang onto power, but instead focus on preparing a better generation to follow. One time the members of my village asked me to become the *lurah*, the chief of the village. But I told them, "There isn't any limit for anybody to dedicate his life to service of their country, but time will give him the limit. His time means his age. I am sure that it is time for the older generation to give the opportunities to the young generation. Their sacrifices, I am certain, have not been in vain."

Now I am seventy years old, retired and living with my wife. My pension isn't very much, but I can live on it. All my children live with their families. I am proud of my profession. As a policeman, you can't be rich, but you will be happy. Your people, and even your enemies, are your friends! I know today the reputation of the police is declining because of financial reasons—the pay is not enough to live on. Some police have abused their authority to gain personal advantages. Still, as a retired policeman I get much respect from people, and I feel that I deserve it. I chose to live in this quiet village because I am now getting older and I am going to get closer to God. Someday, somehow, I am prepared to meet him.

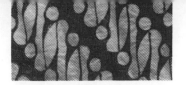

A Writer

In contrast to many other men, this man expresses little interest in political developments. Most important to him are his writing and his ability to do what he wishes in life. Unlike most Javanese of elite background, he states that he does not care about social status; instead he praises the simple village peasant. Sometimes he has gotten himself in trouble by impulsively following his desires, but in the final analysis he is happy with his life and content about his contributions to Javanese literature.

Although he modestly claims that he is "old and forgotten," this man is a well-respected Javanese writer. He was sought out for this interview in the central Java town of Magelang by Ratna Indriani (female, age twenty-nine), a scholar of Javanese literature. She conducted this interview in Javanese, with questions offered in English and in Indonesian from Walter L. Williams. This man is indeed living in modest circumstances, but he says that being independent and making his own choices in life are more important to him than any material comforts.

I was born June 1, 1919, in a little town in central Java. My father, a middle-level *priyayi*,[1] worked as a street overseer in the Department of Public Works for Central Java province. My mother was a daughter of a Muslim leader in Blora. I am an only child so I was spoiled as a boy because my parents were well off. In morality and education, my father was strict, and my mother was very restrained. Fortunately I received gentleness and loving care from the wife of my father's friend. After her husband died, she joined our family as a companion. She knew many classical folk tales and fairy tales. With her rich imagination, she told me stories at night.

I still remember my favorite story. It is about a Dutch girl who is devoured by a gigantic giant called Buto Ijo, the Green Giant. Yet, in this story the girl remains alive inside his body. She asks about every part of the giant's physique. The story is interesting for me because this is how I learned about the anatomy of a human being. Nowadays I still retell that story to my grandchildren. My interest in story telling drove me into writing both short and long stories.

I did not stay long in my birthplace because my father was appointed to work in other cities of central Java. My real childhood began in the city of Semarang, where I entered the social environment of the middle class by studying in a Dutch primary school. I was given a Dutch name, Nicolaas or Nico. It was only for a year though because my father suddenly decided to stop working for the Public Works. He wanted to enjoy his days in his birthplace, a little village in east Java, where he was offered an opportunity to become a railway surveyor. At that time the Dutch government was building sugar factories and private railway lines for the lorries.

My environment changed from the urban context of Semarang to the small village milieu in Gelung. There, my friends were children of the sugar planters, sugar factory clerks, cart drivers, and farmers. I stood higher in class status than the other children; I was highly respected because I was the son of a member of the bureaucratic elite. I became conspicuous among those who belonged to the lower classes. They called me *Gus* or *Den Baqus*, which means handsome, good quality, or respectable.

My father did not like my intimacy with lower-class people. He expected me to become a *priyagung*, respectable gentleman, who had to be well educated. For this reason, he sent me to a country town for private school in which most students were Chinese. He did this to avoid my intimacy with the lower-class people and to fill my spare time before I really entered a Dutch school in Ngawi.

In 1926, I entered the Hollansch Inlandsche School in Ngawi. The lessons were given in Dutch or Javanese. In this school we were trained to read many books from the time we were in the fourth grade. The students were ordered to borrow Dutch books in the library and required to finish reading a book in a week. Later, this habit had an important effect on my life and helped me to be a good writer. You cannot write well if you do not read a lot. I finished my elementary school in 1933; then I continued my study

in a Dutch junior high school in Madiun. For transportation from
Paron to Madiun, I used the train.

I became a regular passenger on this train. I met a beautiful
Dutch girl who also was a regular passenger. We often shared the
cabin, and we had an intimate relationship. My love affair almost
got my father into serious trouble. In fact, the girl's father had
reported my conduct to my father's boss so that my father was
severely punished. It was just not accepted for a Javanese male to be
in love with a Dutch female. My father, realizing that he was only
an inlander of lower position, decided to accept defeat. From then
on, he ordered me to stay in a boarding house in Madiun. It was my
first lesson about love.

In 1936, I finished my junior high school. I asked my father's
permission to continue my study in Solo, but he and my uncle
insisted that I should continue my study in a public high school
either in Yogyakarta or Semarang. At the end, I was so persistent
that I was allowed to enter school in Solo. Again, I was a regular
passenger on the train, and history repeated itself. I fell in love with
a girl from Sragen who shared my cabin every day. I often went
home late, and I often stopped at Sragen. My father was so angry
that he refused to pay my school fee. I dropped out.

After that point, I became a do-nothing. I gambled, became a
reyog player,[2] and engaged in other disgraceful activities. In my
father's eyes, I was a failure.

There was a Dutch man who sympathized with my situation. He
trusted me and asked me to join him in his effort to build a private
school in Paron. I agreed, and we became partners; but actually I
did the work. While still a teenager, I became headmaster of the
school. Everything was going fine, until several months later. Then
something important happened: I fell in love again. This time it was
with a teacher who worked in my school. I wanted to marry her,
but my mother disagreed with my choice. Saying I was too young
to be married, she did not allow me to continue my relationship
with the girl. I was angry and broken-hearted. I gave up my job and
left Paron for good. I wanted to try to forget my love. In fact, my
love for her was unforgettable. A few years ago I saw her once
again, and I still felt a thrill in my heart. This warm feeling of love
has inspired several of my stories.

As soon as I had left Paron, the first city I visited was Semarang;

I have fond memories of that city. In Semarang I worked as a daily clerk in the Department of Irrigation. I worked there for three months, but I was not satisfied with my job. After that I moved from one place to another, changing jobs as often as I liked. I worked as a shopkeeper and a salesman, among other things. Then I assisted my uncle in his land surveying. I showed such a good performance in this job tht I was promoted and appointed a land surveyor in Kendal. At that time, I was still very young by today's measurement. In 1939 at the age of twenty I married a Kendal girl. She is my first wife. She still lives with me. She gave me nine children, and eight of them are still alive. We live with my third daughter and her family.

By 1940, I changed my job again and joined the Dutch army. I worked for two years in Cilacap, but I must confess that I am a restless person who gets bored easily. In 1942, I decided to return to Paron. When the Japanese began to invade Indonesia, I returned to Paron and sold gasoline to support my family there. A year later, I moved to Jember, east Java, and became a clerk in the Railway Department. It is not yet the end of my story of changing jobs.

By 1945, I was in Kaliwungu, a little town to the west of Semarang, where I worked in a paper factory. Again I felt bored to death. I left and joined a theatrical troupe in Semarang. That looked like it was going to be fun, but three days later the British and the Dutch bombed Semarang. I wanted to get out of there, so I returned to Kendal. There I worked as a developer in the Public Works Office until the day of the independence proclamation. Two months after that I joined the army again, and this time I worked somewhat longer—three years. In 1949 I returned to Kendal as a land surveyor until 1951, and from then to 1955 I moved around changing my jobs once again.

The year 1955 was an important date in my family life. In that year, I could not resist falling in love again with another woman in Paron. I married her, and she moved in with my family. She gave me a son within the same year. Although one of our daughters died when she was in her teens, we have a happy family life. Both my wives are good women, they are on good terms with each other, and now I feel happy and contented living here. It is really just a simple way of living.

The year 1955 was also important for me because I began to

work seriously as an editor for *Java Baya* magazine in Surabaya. At that time, I really enjoyed my work so I stayed at this job for ten years. For me, that was really amazing. While working there, I also doubled as an editor for *Crita Cekak* magazine and *Gotong Royonq*, both published in the city of Surabaya.

Then, in 1965, after a decade of stability, I felt my restlessness growing again. In that year, my natural drive to enjoy a free life was again realized. Since that time I have been focusing on my writing. I became a professional writer. My realization that writing could produce money happened when my first short story was published in *Panji Pustaka* on February 15, 1944. My reading habit is another factor that enriched my imagination. When I worked as a teacher, the thing I enjoyed most was telling stories to the children.

I have never really studied how to write or taken journalism courses to help me understand the techniques of writing. I write because it is the best possible work that I could both do and enjoy. In fact, it is difficult for me to describe writing as my job. Actually it is my hobby, though I later depended on it financially more than I figured, especially now in my old age. I do not care whether people consider it my hobby or my source of income. Becoming rich is not my concern. As a result, here I am now, an old and forgotten writer, who actually has to confess that he cannot depend on his writing to adequately finance a proper life.

I have written more than three hundred pieces of work, so many that I sometimes forget and reuse a title that I had already published. Yet, not one of our own children inherited my talent in writing. They mostly considered writing as my job, just like when I was working as an editor. They did not object to my working on my old typewriter, but neither did they especially encourage me. They just showed indifference. They did not pay attention to my manuscripts, and many original documents were lost. My second wife showed interest in my work by reading my manuscripts and commenting on them now and then, here and there.

I have no pretension to be a famous author, to be known by people. My passion in writing is quite personal. I want to find happiness by expressing myself through my characters. I think my own identification with my favorite characters usually enters the writing. I want my readers to worship a hero or heroine. Maybe I want to become a hero—I don't really know. I often look to the past for these heroic figures. I have written many historical romances. I love history, and every time I write about historical romances I open my history book and study. I can say the descent of the Mataram kings without looking at the book![3] I have memorized it. Studying Java's past always excites me and expands my imagination.

In terms of writing style, I do not like symbolism. Simple people like me are too unsophisticated to use symbolism. I prefer straightforwardness in writing because I like realism in my style. That is probably why I do not write many poems. For me poetry is difficult because it needs more imagination, more feelings, and a better grasp of aesthetics.

In my writing, I am in command of active Javanese, Indonesian, and Dutch, besides passive English. I often write essays in the Indonesian language, but most of my writing is in Javanese. I realize that writing in Javanese will never make me rich. I do not care what other people think. They may consider me foolish, but I enjoy being a free human being.

Through my motto *sanajan gepeng ilir tak lakoni*—meaning "although very difficult, I'll commit myself to it"—I dedicate my faith to the continued development of Javanese literature. For me, writing is like my wife, and the Javanese language is a medium to express my love. I feel a great responsibility that I should enliven my own literature. Javanese is the best way through which I can express my feelings perfectly. In this spirit, I never felt betrayed by my fellow writers who turned to Indonesian as their medium of expression.

Many people have predicted that the Javanese language and literature will become submerged under the power of the Indonesian language. I disagree with that idea, even though the government is pushing people to speak and write in the new Indonesian language. As long as the Javanese people still speak Javanese, Javanese literature will be alive. I am optimistic. Maybe there will be a decay in quality because younger generations do not often use the language and they sometimes have problems in writing. It is important for modern Javanese writers to be attentive to the demands of the society. I think the government's involvement in the development of Javanese language and literature is absolutely necessary; this maintains a mutual relationship between the readers and the writers.

The process of my writing is unmethodological; it is simple and common. In my opinion, content is more important than outside appearance. I usually prepare the title after I think about the topic. Then I begin to write, often by hand rather than using a typewriter. I use any kind of paper; sometimes I even prefer second-hand paper to a clean new sheet. In one sense, I feel more free writing on dirty paper. Because my inspiration can come anywhere, sometimes I do not employ my typewriter at all. When I feel ready to write that means I have finished the story in my mind. I rarely make an outline because the story forms itself in my imagination and develops during the process of writing. The same thing also happens when I write long stories or novels.

On average I can finish a short story in two or three hours, but long stories, of course, take longer. When my drive to write comes, I can write several stories at one sitting. Because I might submit several stories to the same magazine at once, I sometimes use pseudonyms such as Prabhasari, Laharjingga, Harja Lawu, Sri Ningsih, and Habra Markata. Sometimes the names have a special meaning. Habra Makarta, for example, means that we should praise honesty and accept the consequences of one's [karmic] acts. Laharjingga means something warm and shiny, which reflects my hope that my writing will give warmth and light to ignorant people.

My stories often express the hardness of life and show the problems faced by the lower-class people. This focus comes out of my own view of life. My childhood was colored by many and various experiences that have become the source of my inspiration to write. I was the son of a priyayi, but I consider myself fortunate to have been brought up in the village. In this way, I received an intimate relationship with nature and the village life. The common peasants are the people I love. They are just plain and ignorant people, usually honest, simple, and submissive. The peasants have become my positive object because they are not fake immitations, like many people of the higher classes. They are genuine. I do not like to take city life as my object because it is artificial and corrupted. Attention has been poured down on city people; it is the duty of artists like me to pay attention to unimportant people. That is my life's work, and that is what I enjoy doing.

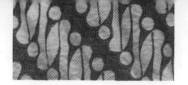

A Pedicab Driver

In the context of past generations of Javanese village life, a person who did not inherit any land was almost certainly doomed to a life of poverty. An orphan, or anyone without relatives, was a tragic figure. This explains why Javanese put so much emphasis on having children and keeping their family together. Even today, there is no security for the lower-class elderly unless they have a child to take care of them. This poor man is a case in point.

The only thing that he and his wife can do is to hope to scrape by from week to week, until their children can help support them. He is not concerned with the passage of historical time, and when asked to tell his life story he focuses on the struggle for daily survival. He never mentions the revolution, the disturbances of the 1960s, or any other political event. The great change in his life was due not to any political change but to his movement from the farm to the city.

This man is now a *becak* driver, pedaling a three-wheeled pedicab for passengers along the streets of Surakarta. Every urban area in central Java swarms with becak drivers, mostly rural men who cannot find jobs in their villages. This man was interviewed by Walter L. Williams while sitting at a roadside food stall, next to his becak, waiting for a customer. He spoke about his life over a meal paid for by the interviewer. Kedah (male, age twenty-seven) translated from the Javanese.

Whenever he has the chance this man longs to return to his village north of the city. This narrative tells much about the reasons for rural to urban migration and the structure of urban poverty. Because this man and his wife cannot afford to pay the school fees, their children will remain uneducated, and the family will most likely remain impoverished in the next generation. The Indonesian government's transmigration program was addressed to meet the needs of

3. Pedicab driver taking two women with their goods for sale to market, on a becak. *Photo: Martha Pardede*

the lower class, but this man explains why that program does not work for the truly poor.

There seems to be no way out for people like him. Perhaps he is right to simply resign himself to his "fate." Still, he wishes that he could somehow get land in the village so that he could be a farmer and continue his traditional life. His experience admits to no sense of progress in life. For him, life under the Dutch, Japanese, or Indonesian governments is equally difficult. In all the political systems he has known, life is hard.

I was born about fifty-five years ago, in a village near Klatan. I have been driving a *becak* [pedicab] for eighteen years. Before that, I was a farmer in my village. But my family did not own any land so I had to rent land from others. I gathered wood to sell, worked on building houses for people, plowed, or did whatever kind of work I could get helping people. When I was a child, everyday I had to gather grass from the fields and roadsides to feed my parents' cows and goats. They would borrow an animal from its owner and promise to feed and take care of it. Then when the animal reproduced my parents would sell the offspring and split the profits with the owner. I did not have any time to go to school, and even today I cannot read. It was more important to work hard to get enough money for food.

I married when I was in my twenties. My parents picked out a woman for me to marry. I did not know her before then. That was the way it was back then, just following your parents' desires. Before a person gets married, his life is not complete. I got married to have descendants, to continue my life after I die. We need to teach our children to be good in their attitude, and their behavior, so that they can improve the reputation of their parents, when the parents are old and later dead.

Formerly, people said that the more children you have, the more fortune in your life. That is no longer true. My wife and I had six children. It used to be an advantage to have a big family because they could work when they got old enough. We still need children to take care of us when we get old, but only two or three. Nowadays it costs so much to raise a big family, and besides a lot of times the children cannot find work. We wanted our children to continue in school, but they stopped because of the fees required from secondary school students. It is not expensive for parents who have good jobs, but it is too much money for a simple becak driver.

It is very difficult to get enough work to live on, when you do not have your own land in the village. The government offers its transmigration program to get people to leave Java and go to the less populated islands. I know a young man, an orphan without any family. His parents died when he was twelve, and since then he has been driving a becak like me. He is desparately poor, and he would be very happy if he could join the government's transmigration program. He wants to work hard to be a farmer, if he could just get a chance to have his own land. He tried to join the transmigration, but when he went there the official told him to go to this place and then another place and get this form and that form. It confused him.

The government has a television program explaining how to do transmigration, but when do poor people have a chance to watch television? If they could afford a television, they would not be interested in migrating. They also print up articles in the newspaper, but he does not even have money to buy newspapers; besides, he cannot read very well so he doesn't really understand. Recently, the government says people who want to transmigrate should be married. How can a very poor man like that get married. What kind of woman today would want to marry a man in his situation?

Still, I did not encourage him. I don't know if transmigration is a good thing. Some people near here who did it came back without money. The government assigns you land: it might not be good land, but you still have to work it. This very hard work, cutting down trees and clearing the land to prepare it for farming, might not be worth much after you get the land cleared. Much of that soil in the other islands is not fertile like Java's soil. There is no use having a lot of land if you cannot farm it.

Here in Java, people can easily get everything, and a marketplace is usually nearby. My wife can do her selling in the market. In the islands where the transmigration sends people the transportation is not good, and it is hard to get crops to market. Everything there is difficult, harder than imaginable. You are isolated, far from neighbors, without electricity or good roads. The only sound at night is from the crickets. Besides that, to go so far away to another island you have to leave your relatives and your village. Eating, or not eating, it is still better to stay together.

I prefer farming work, but so much farm labor is being done by machines that there are fewer jobs in the rural areas. Especially if there is a bad harvest, there is no other choice but to leave. With all this in mind, and realizing I had to do something, I had no alternative but to get work in the city. I tried to get many different kinds of jobs but could not. The only thing left for me was to become a becak driver, pedaling people around town on this pedicab tricycle. Even though I was forced to do this, I am happy at least that it is honest labor. I am most proud that I never resorted to stealing to get money. Pedaling this bicycle is the only way I can get money to support my family, so I must be happy with that. My wife sells chickens, but that by itself is not enough for our children to live on.

I really cannot say anything good about being a becak driver. I have to endure the work because it is my duty to give food to my family and try to send my children to school. But if I get an opportunity to do another kind of work I will take it. I cannot afford to buy my own becak, and I have to rent it from a bicycle company. There is so much competition, with so many men who cannot get jobs, trying to get some money by offering becaks. The driver has little ability to turn down an offer from a passenger, no matter how low, because there is always another driver nearby who will do it for less. Somedays I cannot get even one passenger. Yet, I still have to pay the fee to rent the becak. I do not regret it if I cannot get passengers because I know that is just my fate and I cannot help it. Sometimes I take passengers even if they do not have money to pay me, just because I pity them walking in the hot sun. But I do that only if they genuinely do not have any money because it is hard work for me.

I would advise young men not to become becak drivers if they can avoid it. They are still young and can get experience in a better type of work. Being a becak driver is too physically demanding, and it does not bring in enough money. I would rather take another job, even if it paid less money, just so long as the pay was dependable each week. The worst thing about being a becak driver, however, is that it depends entirely on my good health. If I am sick and not strong enough to pedal the people up and down the hills around town, I cannot get any income. Then I have to depend on my wife and children to bring in enough money. The older children try to get work to bring in some money to help. I am counting on them to support us after I get too old to drive a becak.

I live with a friend of mine in the city, and I leave home early each morning and return after dark. I can only afford cheap food from the roadside food stalls. Fortunately, my friend does not charge me to stay at his house, but if there is anything broken around the house I volunteer to fix it for him. If I have enough money I buy the repair supplies myself.

I try to take a bus to go home for a day to visit my family, usually once every two weeks. That is my one enjoyment, to be reunited with my family in my village. If I could get my own land, I would return to farming. In the city, there are many entertainments and more opportunity to sell things in shops or along the streets. But as far as I am concerned it is just a place to look for money. In the city, everything you need, you must buy. You cannot work together with your friends in the city; you must compete against them. People become hardened, and they are not concerned about the other person's life. It is all individual.

If you do not have experience or education, it is not good to go to the city because you have to do the hard labor. But many young people prefer to move to the city, and that is good for them because their future opportunity for fortune will come from following their own desires. If a person goes to the city and does well, it is his or her fate. Likewise, they could stay in the village, and if it is their fate, they will be able to live well there. I must accept my fate: I am only able to be a becak driver.

Still, I hope that fate will eventually allow me to return to live in my village. In the village it is not so expensive to live, and we can grow our own food. If you need something, you can ask your neighbor to help you or to share their food. Then later you can do something to help them in return. Village people are more dependable to help each other. There is not so much stress in the village, and it is not so noisy a place to live. It is a happier and more peaceful life.

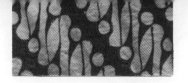

A Cake Seller

In contemporary Indonesia, as in many developing countries economists and government planners have mainly focused on the creation
of jobs for men. The resulting policies often ignore work for women.
The underlying assumption of many Western development programs is that Third World women are simply housewives. This
woman's narrative, along with those of the other women in this
collection, show that assumption to be false. Among the Javanese
masses, women have always made important economic contributions
to the survival of the family by working outside the home. The most
significant economic role for most village women was and is selling
food in the market. Peasant women expect that they will earn a living
from their own labor, rather than just being supported by their
husband. The three constants for nonelite Javanese women are marriage, motherhood, and work.

This woman was interviewed in her small bamboo-thatch house,
at the end of a long day. She was obviously weary as she patiently
answered questions put by Robertus Widjojo (male, age thirty-three)
and Walter L. Williams. She sees no hope that her future will differ
from her past. For the underclass, there is little expectation of real
economic progress.

I don't know exactly how old I am. As far as I know, I am in my
fifties. My parents were poor farm workers, working on our neighbors' lands. I did not go to school because I was the oldest child and
had to help my parents earn the living and take care of my four
brothers and two sisters. This happened to the other oldest children
of poor farm families.

I got married in 1954, when I was about eighteen years old. A year later, I gave birth to my first child. My oldest daughter is an elementary school graduate. She lives in Klaten with her husband and her three children. In 1962 I gave birth to my second child. He is also an elementary graduate. After he had passed his elementary school, he took a carpentry course that the government ran in the town. Now he works for a contractor in Klaten. He got married three months ago. My youngest son is fifteen years old, and he still lives at home with us.

My husband is a few years older than I am. He is from this village. He got some land from his parents, but it is not enough to support ourselves. Therefore, my husband also does many odd jobs, any kind of job that pays him cash. He works hard, yet what he earns is not enough to support the family. So I also have to work. I decided to cook rice and corn cakes to sell. Formerly, many women of this village used to sell cakes, but now only about four women are still in this business.

I leave my house at 4:30 a.m. and walk ten kilometers to Klaten. There are no buses in this road. I get to the town at 6:00 a.m. I go from house to house and sell my cakes. I take the same route every day. Each woman of this village who does the same business has her own area and customers, and we agree not to go into the other's area. At 1:00 p.m. I walk to the market and buy two kilograms of cassava, one kilogram of brown sugar, two kilograms of corn, three kilograms of sticky rice, and two coconuts. I carry that home on my back and arrive there two hours later. Then I go to the river to take a bath and wash the clothes. After that I cook for my family. After cooking, I peel the cassavas and prepare everything for the following day's business. I work in the kitchen until 8:00 p.m. and then I go to bed.

At 2:00 a.m. I get up and continue my work until 4:00 a.m. I have to work in the kitchen twice because I have to cook the sticky rice shortly before leaving or it will get too soft. I also have to cook the corn twice, in the evening and early in the morning. After I finish everything, I go to the river and take a bath. Then I leave my house and walk to the town carrying another bamboo basket full of cakes on my back. I have done the same routine every day for twenty-eight years.

When I go home, after a day's work I bring about Rp. 5,500 [U.S. $3.30] with me. During the last week of the month, when

4. Woman preparing rice cakes at home. *Photo: Hazairin Eko Prasetyo*

people are running out of money, business does not run well; then I let my customers take my cakes and pay for them later. This means I bring home less. My business does not run as well as it did ten years ago. Today there are hundreds of kinds of factory-made cakes, in beautiful colors and attractive packages. With so many unemployed people, and with big businesses moving in, everything is very competitive today. I am lucky I can stand this for twenty-eight years.

Time goes by. The woman's hair grows grey. She looks older than her husband. Everything in society has changed, but the woman's work.

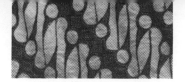

A *Chinese Businessman*

Chinese people, migrating out of their homeland for centuries, have moved into many areas of Southeast Asia. With strong family values and a commitment to preserving Chinese language and culture, they have been a remarkably persistent ethnic group in their new homes. In Indonesia, Chinese were brought in by the Dutch first as contract laborers and later as lower-level administrators in the Dutch East Indies Company. Characteristic of overseas Chinese families is their emphasis on socializing their children to save money. This makes sense for an immigrant landless group that is trying to make a niche for itself in a new nation. In contrast to the Javanese, who were seldom given much of a chance to save money under Dutch colonial exploitation, the Chinese in Indonesia developed a reputation for working hard and not spending much money. A common statement in Indonesia is that Javanese people value land, a leisurely life-style, and social status, while Chinese people value money, devotion to career, and education. It is said that when Javanese people get extra money, they buy land; when Chinese get money, they start a business.

After the Dutch left Indonesia, the Chinese often had enough cash savings to start businesses. As a result, though ethnic Chinese constitute only 10 percent of Indonesia's population, they own probably 90 percent of the nation's businesses. Chinese families tend to stress education; thus, the professionally high position is passed down to the next generation. This economic dominance has led to some resentments and ethnic tensions toward Chinese by the normally tolerant Javanese. This frugal entrepreneurial ethic in Indonesian Chinese families can be seen in this man's life story. His father's emphasis on saving money, in hopes of returning to China and living off the savings, is probably more typical of overseas Chinese than of China's people in general. When this man returned to China during his childhood, he noticed the difference between his values and those of the mainland Chinese. He expresses how glad he was to escape China.

This man is now, at age sixty-five, a leading businessman in Surakarta. He and his wife still spend long hours at their beauty salon and beautician school, yet they live quite comfortably in a large house with several servants. He was interviewed by English teacher F. X. Andrianto (male, age thirty-three), who is himself an Indonesian Chinese.

I was born in a small town of central Java in 1923. I was the eldest son in a family that was active in the Chinese community. My father was a teacher in a Chinese elementary school that was funded and managed by Indonesian Chinese businessmen. My father's salary as a teacher was two hundred guldens, almost three hundred Chinese dollars, which was considered very high at that time when the average elementary school teacher's salary in China was only twenty Chinese dollars. In comparison, my father's salary was really very high. We did not live in any luxury, however, because my father saved almost all his money. He hoped that one day we could return to China and lead a good life with our savings.

But then, after ten years of saving money, the depression came. Business was very bad in Java, and the school could not afford to pay my father anymore. That was 1934, and I had just finished my elementary school, when my father decided that we should go to China. There were five of us: my father, my mother, my grandmother, my younger sister, and me. We went by ship from the port city of Surabaya, and after ten days we arrived in Foochow, the capital of Hokkian province. It was quite a big city, and more than that it was my father's hometown. Yet, I felt as if I had come to a strange place. The children did not dress as neatly as people in Java, and they spoke a language different from what I spoke at home. I had sometimes heard my father speak in his native Foochow dialect, but it was something new for a child like me who always spoke good Mandarin at home.

With the help of his friend my father got a job as a teacher in a good elementary school, and later he became headmaster. It was quite a good job in a poor country like China. My father was very proud of his situation, especially because of all the money he had saved in Java. But this comfortable situation did not last very long. In 1937, when I graduated from junior high school, the war with Japan began. Hearing that the Japanese invaders were very cruel and believing that China would soon be defeated, my father wanted us to go back to Java. But my mother refused to uproot the family once again. My father was the one most in danger, so he went alone to Java with the hope of bringing us along later.

As the Japanese invaded Foochow, the Chinese government evacuated almost two thousand of us students to a small town in the interior, where they hoped the Japanese army would not expand. That is why I went to a senior high school away from my family. After one year of schooling there, suddenly the Chinese government decided to send us to an even more isolated mountain area to receive military training. Actually we learned not only how to shoot guns but also how to cultivate the land, make fertilizer from feces, and develop other necessary skills. We did this training for four months. After that I had to teach the urban refugees how to survive in the countryside and how to fight against the Japanese. Even though I was still in high school, I had the rank of sergeant.

After graduating in 1941 and passing the entrance exam to the university, I was fortunate enough to enter the Department of Animal Husbandry and Veterinary Science at Chung Cheng National University. I was one among only two hundred university students in all of China. That was really something special for me. Moreover, I heard from my former classmates that most of those who could not enter a university were sent to fight in the war.

I graduated from the university in May 1945, when the war with Japan was still going on. China's economy was in massive confusion, and it was very difficult for me to find a job. During all this time, I had not had any contact with my family. Sometimes I ran into some of my classmates, who were now soldiers. Others of them had died in the war. I wondered why the government did not draft me, but later on I understood that the government did not want to send its scholars to the front, in fear of losing its few skilled citizens.

In August 1945 the Japanese surrendered. Four months later I finally got my first job, as a teacher in a teacher's training high school. I worked in that job for one year. At last I was able to make contact with my family. They were still in Foochow and had sold almost all our belongings in order to get food. I began to send them money. Later on they also managed to make contact with my father, and he too began to send them money. He was going to bring them to Indonesia, but the revolution had broken out there, and my mother did not want to leave China now that the Japanese were gone.

I was looking for a job that would be more suitable for my training as a veterinarian. After one year I was lucky to be hired at a government dairy farm. Even though the salary was low I was very proud to have this job while many others in China were unemployed. I was still young and highly educated, so I expected to have a very good future working for the government. After all the years of fighting Japan, I looked forward to a bright future for China and for myself.

Then, another war began. Life is so unpredictable. This time it was a civil war between the nationalists and the communists. The nationalists under the leadership of Chiang forced a lot of young farmers to fight against the communists. I myself saw many farmers in the villages captured by Chiang's soldiers during the night, and in the morning they were forced to march through the city streets to the military barracks. These young uneducated farmers were supposed to be the backbone of the anticommunist movement, but it turned out to be Chiang's biggest mistake. The rude treatment of the nationalist soldiers toward the farmers was used by the communist propagandists to win the sympathy of the people. This propaganda was very successful. Very soon almost all the Chinese people, including my family and me, were in sympathy with the communists.

In 1949 the corrupt nationalists were defeated, and the communists came to power under Mao. The people, especially us young people, were happy and very optimistic to have a new virtuous government. But after a year the situation grew from bad to worse. People began to realize that the new government treated them even more cruelly than the nationalists had done. They began to live under a long nightmare. Young Communist party members began to demand money from people, and people were afraid to do or say anything against the government. A small mistake in a conversation, implying something critical, would lead to a severe punishment. This happened to one of my best friends in my company.

He was among the best employees in the dairy farm. It had even previously been said that he would be one of our bosses in a short time. I did not know what his offense was, but in the morning when I came to work other friends told me that he was arrested by the police and was sent to do forced labor far away in the mountains. That place was used by the communist government to "reeducate" the citizens who were considered to be against party doctrine. I understood that my friend, if he came back alive, would not be the same person again. What a pity. He was an outstanding engineer who had never said anything relating to politics that I had known of, and yet he had to suffer that punishment.

That night, after coming home from work, I began to realize that the same thing could also happen to me. I might not say anything against the government, but probably a neighbor who was jealous of me would make a false accusation, and as a result I could be severely punished. It was really a nightmare for me.

That night I decided to leave China. Actually I had nowhere to go, but after much thought I decided to try to join my father who was then working in Jakarta. I went back to Foochow and told my family about my decision. My mother was very sad, and my younger brother who was born in China told me that I had betrayed my country. But I had already made up my mind to go to Indonesia. After some preparation I left China. It was not very difficult to leave China at that time because the new government was not yet in total order. I just asked for a visiting permit to go to Hong Kong for a few days vacation. Once I got into Hong Kong I went straight to the new Indonesian consulate, showed them my birth certificate, and told them that all my family was in Jakarta. They permitted me to enter Indonesia. I arrived in Jakarta on August 12, 1950, as a free man.

I soon found my father's address in Jakarta and was reunited with him after all those years. I found out that he had taken a new wife. He worked as a manager in a building construction company, and he got me a job working there. My salary was just enough to live in a small boarding house, have decent meals, and buy a new shirt once in a while. Yet I was so happy to live in Indonesia because I could see my father and more than that I was a free man.

After a year I realized that I had no talent in the construction industry. I decided to apply for a teaching position in a private Chinese school. I taught in that school for five years. In 1956 I moved to Solo and got married. I had saved some money and was determined to start my own business, even though it was not a climate favorable to starting a business. The economic and political situation in Indonesia was not stable at that time. Government cabinets were replaced every two months or sometimes even within a month. Nevertheless, my wife was good at sewing dresses, so we decided that she would make the dresses, and I would sell them and manage the store. Though our capital was not big and the economic situation was so uncertain, we still managed to rent a little shop and make some profit. My wife made the garments at home, and I sold them in our shop. Also, I arranged with my wife's relatives to display the dresses in their shops on the main street.

Meanwhile, the Indonesian economy was going from bad to worse. The Indonesian leaders were so occupied with politics that they neglected almost completely the economic development of the country. This had a very bad impact on our business. People were not interested any more in buying new dresses. They had to spend their salary just to get food. And even worse, the unemployed Javanese, especially the youths, began to come to the Chinese people's shops to ask for money. They would use violence if the Chinese businessman refused. This happened in our shop. At first they came once a month, but later they came more frequently. Between 1965 and 1967 different groups of young men would come into our shop asking for money almost every week. It was really a difficult time for business. As a result, we decided to close our shop and live on our savings.

After Suharto got control of the government, the political and economic situation started getting better. After we closed the dress shop my wife had gone to beautician school, so rather than sell garments again we decided to open a beauty salon instead. In 1978, when we opened our salon, it was the only well-equipped and up-to-date one in the city. Very soon we had plenty of customers. I decided to start a beautician school, and it is now the biggest one in this area. We are considered to be among the top beauty salons in the city. I am proud of my business. Besides the salon and school, we now own two large houses. All our daughters are married. I am now satisfied with myself, even though I did not end up working in my field of training as a veternarian. That is what I mean about life being so unpredictable. Don't try to look too far ahead because you can never tell what will happen in the meantime. The only important thing is to be flexible enough to make your own independent decision and then act on it, no matter what others might say.

That's what I had to do in deciding to leave China. Now, I would never consider going back there, even if I were still young. As far as I am concerned, both the nationalist and the communist governments there are corrupt. Trying to do a business there would be awful. I'm not saying that doing business in Indonesia is always easy. Besides the unemployed young men who still often come to our school and salon to ask for money, there is the problem of bribing officials to get anything done. Still, with all this, I think that doing business in Indonesia is much easier than doing it somewhere else, let alone in China. I am happy to be an Indonesian citizen and to live here in Solo. Looking back on my life, I always think that my decision to leave China was the best decision I ever made in my life.

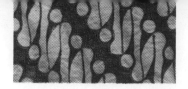

A Feminist Psychologist

Even though Indonesia is a remarkably diverse nation, with many cultures in the various islands, each particular geographic area is characterized by one dominant ethnic group. In contrast to the multi-ethnic situation in the national capital city of Jakarta, and with the exception of the Chinese who live in the urban areas, central Java is ethnically dominated by Javanese. Still, some individuals from other cultures live in Java. Foreigners, mainly Dutch, English, Australians, and Americans, live in various cities as teachers, missionaries, and business and development officials. Indonesians from other islands come to Java to attend universities, to work in government offices, and to do business. Some Javanese who lived in other islands, usually as government officials, marry local persons and bring them back to Java.

This is the case with this woman, whose mother moved from the Minangkabau area in the neighboring island of Sumatra. Even though this woman was born in Java, she absorbed many of her attitudes on gender roles from her mother. The Minangkabau is a woman-centered society, where kinship, land ownership, and households are controlled by related groups of females. Women have high status and are not dominated by men in the same way that they are in most patriarchal societies. Because a man upon marriage traditionally moves in with his wife's family, there is little chance that he can mistreat her or be violent toward her, with all her relatives nearby. Because women perform important work activities that contribute significantly toward the survival of the family, because women control distribution of the resources that they produce, and because property is passed down from mother to daughter, women's economic position does not just depend on her husband.

This woman is an exceptional person in Java, not just because of her ethnic background. A highly educated woman, she lived for a year in France and for eight years in the United States, where she has been greatly influenced by American feminism. At age fifty, she is the youngest person included in this book; therefore, she represents a generation different from many of the women and men included here. More important, there is a cultural difference. This woman illustrates some ways that international trends are coming into Indonesia, especially from those who are going abroad for their advanced education and corporate training. She typifies a new generation of well-educated multinational people, a type becoming more common as worldwide travel increases.

This woman was interviewed in Indonesian by Claire Siverson (female, age twenty-five), an American sociologist who was studying Javanese language and society at Gadjah Mada University in 1987–1988.

Growing up I was influenced greatly by my mother in terms of developing my ideas on the injustice toward women in society. At home she had a great deal of say in the family, and a great deal of respect was accorded to her. My mother came from the Minangkabau culture, where the status of women is very high due to the matrilineal nature of the culture. There, women have a lot of power over our lives compared to women from other parts of the archipelago—not in everything but in many things. The lines of decendancy come from the mother, not the father. In terms of property, the daughter is the one who inherits it all. Women are born with a higher status than men in society. They are respected more as women.

I was born in Surakarta in Central Java and was raised there, until I graduated from the university. But I am Minang through and through, even though I've never lived in the Minangkabau area of Sumatra. I've gone there to do research twice, and it was incredible to see women talking among themselves there, speaking out and respected by society. It was wonderful.

Although I share the view of feminists that we need feminism as a kind of dedication of our lives to the improvement of the quality of life for women, since I am a Muslim I got married according to Islam. But I realized that I wanted the protection of the state, which recognizes a civil marriage more than a religious one, so we had it legalized in a civil ceremony. The state can protect you in cases where the husband wants to have four wives at once, as allowable under Islam. It's also harder to get a divorce if your marriage is only recognized by Islam.

After my marriage I had a real sense of despair. My husband comes from a patrilineal background. We would often argue. Once we moved to America, for his education, I was really depressed about the terrible situation for women. That's where I really became a feminist because I was really unhappy there. I felt like I was in a hopeless situation. I had to do all the domestic work by myself. Finally I rebelled and said I didn't want to deal with it any more. My husband agreed to help me around the house and with shopping.

That never would have happened if we hadn't gone to America. He never helped me in Indonesia. He would never make his own tea or join me in taking care of the children's needs. If they were already bathed and dressed then he would hold them and play with them. But as far as bathing them or changing their diapers was concerned, not once did he help. After we got to America he had to help because if he didn't I would go on strike!

For nine years I lived in the West—eight years in the United States and one in France. My husband was working on his Ph.D. at the time, and so I followed him without having any real occupational or educational purpose of my own. My job was to take care of my husband and our children. I was pretty unhappy in that respect, especially since I had already obtained my master's degree in psychology from an Indonesian university and wasn't putting it to use.

My experience in America had a tremendous impact on me in terms of understanding women's oppression. It's no wonder the feminist movement sprung up from the States. When I was there I felt that American women were really suffering because compared to Indonesia, there are hardly any paid household workers, so there are fewer women to exploit. There are so many pressures on women who are raising families there because they are so often expected to perform two roles: as an unpaid worker in the home and as a paid worker outside the home.

Here in Indonesia I am much freer. I don't have to do any chores at home. I have my private practice in psychology, I participate in seminars, for five years I have been writing a newspaper column for a national paper, and I give lectures at a university. All that hard, routine, uninteresting work to keep up the house is done by the three *pembantu*, the paid, live-in housekeepers who work for us. Having paid domestic workers is the norm for Indonesian professional families.

In the traditional American family situation, all the housework is done by the wife. Thus, American women's lives are full of daily pressures. It's completely understandable why women would revolt.

I sometimes feel as though, given my views on men and women in society, I am living in a vacuum. You know, it is commonly believed that men are emotionally stronger and more rational than women. But as a psychologist I am often approached by men so emotionally confused they are contemplating suicide. So I believe that idea of men never being out of control or weak is nonsense.

I believe the most important issue facing Indonesian women today is that, without knowing it, women today are still handcuffed. They still aren't conscious. They just go along with whatever their husbands say or do. They resign themselves to being passive and following from behind in the man's shadow. I can't understand why they accept that. Their place in society is so low.

Indonesia is entrenched in tradition. The older generation has strongly clung to the traditional ways. Maybe this is because they haven't been exposed enough to outside influences. Now we have more progressive education. More and more Indonesian women are going abroad, and they're hearing about feminism and attending speeches on women; new viewpoints are flooding Indonesia.

Things are changing because we have more effective communication with what's going on abroad, and so our culture is quickly affected by and also affects other cultures. Then suddenly women become aware, "Hey, look at this situation I'm in! Look at the situation we're *all* in!" Before you know it, they are turning around, though, and exploiting other women—the housekeepers—in the name of "liberation." But I see that this doesn't happen as much in America—it's harder for women there to exploit anyone. It's too expensive, right?

It's interesting to me that Indonesian women who go abroad come back and, I'm sorry to say, are spoiled. In the passive roles they play they have housekeepers, not just the upper classes but even the lower-middle-class women, too, because the housekeepers are paid such low wages. The Indonesian women's movement here isn't big enough or dynamic [enough] or visible enough. We lack an aggressive women's movement because the women resign themselves to remain on the pedestals set up for them by their husbands. And they seem to ENJOY that life! I don't get it!

There is a government -sponsored women's group for wives of civil servants called "Dharma Wanita" [Women's Duty]. It is a program meant to establish, formally, women's participation in Indonesian development. The women organize to do charitable work for the rural and urban poor, like donating the proceeds of home-cooked food sales or going into the villages to teach literacy or do basic health work.

It is a good idea, but the organizational hierarchy is set up in a very strange way. For example, if the husband's civil service job is a low-paying one and the wife is a professor, let's say at some private school, she must still participate in the Dharma Wanita activities which may be far less stimulating than those around her own work. It is compulsory for wives of the civil servants to join Dharma Wanita.

The wives of top male officials, who may have no education in the least, suddenly fill key positions in the Dharma Wanita structure simply due to their marital status as the wife of a big official. So the women participate in Dharma Wanita on the heels of their husbands, which is precarious for them because if their husbands are fired, retire, or quit then their wives must automatically drop out of the organization.

Here's another example of a common situation we must remedy: In Indonesia, if we have three children, like two girls and one boy, and the family only has enough money to pay for one child's education, without a question they always educate the boy. I think that's wrong. To me, if there is only an opportunity for one of the children to get an education, the determining factor should not be gender, but rather who has the greatest intellectual potential. If it turns out to be the girl, then give her the chance to study.

Another example involves violence against women. It is not nearly as bad as in America, but it does happen. Let me tell you about a recent court case for which I was called in as a psychological consultant. A wife burned her husband to death. I interviewed the woman and found out that during their twelve-year marriage the husband and wife both worked but the husband made his wife turn over all her earnings to keep the household running. The husband only contributed a tiny portion of his earnings to the household, just Rp. 5,000 to 10,000 out of his Rp. 100,000 per month paycheck. That's less than the Rp. 40,000 a month the students pay for their rented rooms at a university. The wife contributed all of her Rp. 60,000 paycheck, which just wasn't fair. The man used the rest of his money on having a good time—going to nightclubs and spending it on other women. Whenever the wife asked him where he went, he never told her. He would come home and beat his wife, whether with his bare hands or with some kind of blunt instrument. He even tried to strangle her. This happened again and again. He beat his children, too. He started seeing one woman in particular, and his wife found letters from her and her picture. That's how she found out about his affairs.

This is after twelve years of marriage during which time the wife tried to get a divorce from him twice, but neither time would the husband comply. One morning the wife received a letter with a military letterhead. It was written anonymously by a woman who said that she and the husband had been involved for five years and were planning to get married. That poor wife! She was despondent.

When her husband came home very late that night, she remained silent about it all and tried to sleep but couldn't. So she got some kerosene and doused her husband. She says she only wanted to burn him a little. The husband suddenly awoke, all wet, and the wife was so afraid that he would hit her again that she threw a lit match on him and he burned to death.

The judge thinks that this was a premeditated murder. I defended her. I said their life was not harmonious: the wife was under a tremendous amount of undue stress, and the husband was incredibly egocentric and aggressive. At last the wife got furious and realized that she had been lied to about everything he did. It is completely understandable that the woman killed him.

The case is still in court. I really sympathize with her, but the court seems very hostile to her as if to say, "Who does this women think she is for taking matters into her own hands!" Such a thing rarely happens in Indonesia. In cases where the husband kills the wife, he often gets away unpunished.

The judge sees this case as a sign of the growing women's

movement in Indonesia because the wife actually did something to oppose her husband's treatment of her. I don't think they'll give her the death penalty because the court feels that she did this in a fit of anger and she wasn't completely conscious of what she was doing. They are saying she was "temporarily insane." I think a fair sentence for her should be only a very light one. Because she was abused for years and years by this man!

Drastic changes are needed in Indonesia, but to go through with such a thing is difficult. Women need to be given lots of information—if they can hear other women speak out and read about how to make changes, women's consciousness can be raised to the extent that in their position in society they are not walked all over by men. They must be treated as equals. If we look chiefly at Java, it is clear that women have really low status in society.

To improve the status of Indonesian women in society everything needs to be changed, including both cultural attitudes and structural attitudes. Not only the women need to change. Men need to make real changes in their attitudes. Men here have it great. Why would they want to give up anything for women? They're completely spoiled!

If I were to convey a message to Western feminists, struggling to improve the quality of women's lives, I would say: Keep struggling! That I believe we must do wholeheartedly.

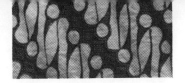

A Businesswoman

Javanese women have traditionally taken an active role in work outside the home, in terms of their buying and selling food products in the marketplace. This work often means that wives bring more money into the family than do husbands. This narrative describes how a woman handles this economic superiority, when the dominant Islamic ideology says that the husband should be the head of the family. This woman owns a successful business, but she is not at peace with herself. In the past she felt she devoted so much attention to her business that she was ignoring her husband. Now that she is spending more time at home, she still worries that she contributes so much more to her children's survival than her husband does through his civil service salary. She is anxious about the uncertainties of business in an increasingly competitive capitalist system. And she reflects the concerns of entrepreneurs: complaints about taxes, bureaucracy, and government policy. Yet she is also defensive about being in business. She hopes her children will get government positions or academic posts, even though she knows these pay much less money.

Her attitudes reflect a Javanese mentality that is somewhat disdainful of business, even though she herself is successful. Much more economically well off than most Indonesians, she seems less satisfied with her life than the small-scale market woman (interviewed at the beginning of the book) who is grateful for being able to afford a radio and a concrete floor in her house. That difference may be due in part to age and also to the more comfortable life-style in which this businesswoman grew up. This narrative shows that, even when women contribute more financial support to the family, if they do not question an ideology that sees the husband as dominant, then they will suffer internal conflict. This woman revealed her personal troubles to Hazairin Eko Prasetyo (male, age twenty-nine), while watching over her shop selling onions and potatoes in the new city marketplace.

When I was young, I was not the only beautiful girl in my village, but I had the chance to choose in my own way who would become my husband. Choice violated the rules of Javanese marriage at that time when girls were supposed to obey what their parents said, especially regarding their marriage partners. My father was different from his royal-blooded contemporaries. He was especially good to me. He gave me freedom and opportunities to go to school and later, to work. That attitude, I think, made me feel I should get a husband of dignity and good future. The first guy I fell in love with was the one I married; he is still my husband.

He was a police officer, a man of fortune, future, and name. Most important, he is very proud of himself—the kind of man I prefer and like very much. He is now retired, but the qualities he has as a man, husband, and officer are still with him. Yet, somehow life changes things, and everything between him and me has also changed, at least in my eyes and feeling. I do not know if all the changes are due to our growing older, or to the fact that we continually experience what is going on in our society and family and perceive it differently.

We were married when we were very young, shortly after the Dutch recognized our country's independence and self-government. At first my parents seemed to dislike his profession. But when we had time to converse and they found out that my husband also took part in the revolution before entering the police department, they started to change their attitude. My parents' dislike of police officers is understandable because, like others who are suspicious of what the police do, I see many dishonest and disobedient policemen in their roles and functions. Most elderly Javanese people do not like policemen, judges, bank workers, and merchants.

Policemen are considered bad because, instead of becoming "shelters" for the people, they frighten people by always finding faults with civilians. Judges are considered too money oriented because many of them decide cases on the basis of which party gives the biggest bribe; they only add more trouble to the troubled. Bank workers—employees and employers—earn their living from rent, and this money-rent is filthy. Merchants get the profit by cheating their buyers. They say the price they pay for something is, say, one hundred rupiahs when its real price is fifty rupiahs, only because they want to profit fifty rupiahs. So neither my parents nor I liked these professions.

However, I became everything we did not like. I married a policeman because he was then the only man that suited my requirements. And, now I am a market woman, a merchant, because this is the only field of work, after several experiments, that is most suitable for me. I am not bound to time and place to work. I can go anywhere, anytime to buy or sell farm products like onions and potatoes. I do not buy or sell fruit because this commodity is easy to damage. For the past twenty-five years I have bought potatoes and onions in some other big cities, transported them in trucks, and sold them in this city, or vice versa.

The difference of price between those places and the bonus I get from the brokers becomes my profit, of course, after subtracting the transportation costs. I tell my customers frankly the price I pay and the other costs I have to bear. But I do not tell them that I get a bonus from my brokers because I am sure they get their profits in the same manner I do. I give a price discount to them if they buy my commodities in big lots. I do not think this is unfair dealing because I do not cheat them by, for example, telling a false price to them to get profits. I never do that.

About my husband I never overhear any wrongs he does in his capacity as a policeman. I always ask him whether he gets annoyed by the criminals he deals with. He is a careful officer. He never gives me money he cannot account for. Sometimes I secretly follow him doing his work. And I find he is a real good policeman because, to my knowledge, he never threatens people. I do all this because I have to maintain my parents' good attitudes toward him. I tell them that my husband is really good as a police officer by explaining what I find and know about his work. I honor him both as my husband and as a police officer. Everything done produces its own result.

My husband retired from the police department twelve years ago. After retiring, his behavior totally changed due to financial reasons. He knows my business keeps getting bigger and better. His

5. Women selling goods in the marketplace. *Photo: Hazairin Eko Prasetyo*

income before retirement was not as much as one-tenth of mine, and the ratio became worse after he retired and my business swiftly expanded. In fact, I never mind whether he gives me money or not because I realize that he needs to spend some money on his hobby—playing tennis. Besides, I can easily finance all our family needs. I pay all our children's necessities both at home and at school. I am happy to see my children having no problem with what they need. But I am truly sad to see my husband becoming more remote from his family.

Ten years ago, I traveled a lot from one city to another for my business. I could be at home once a week, and even once a month during the harvest time, and very often I found my husband was not at home. He traveled a lot too, playing tennis with his contemporary veterans from one big city to another. So we seldom met. Thank God that my childen are good children. They are all active Muslims. I know they need me at home, but they understand that all I do is for the sake of their future lives. I do not know if my husband also does the same thing. All I know is that he just plays tennis day after day—and this makes me sadder.

My children know what their father does so they are becoming closer to me and more distant from him. Perhaps the worsening relations between my husband and me, between my husband and the children, was caused by gossip five years ago. People said that he took another woman, much younger than I am, for his second wife. And people told me that he did not return home not because he played tennis in a distant city but simply because he visited his second wife. At first, I did not believe it. But as more people told me the same story and some said they had witnessed it themselves, I asked my husband about the marriage. He said NO. I believe him. But I do not know what my children felt and thought about it.

We have to think about our children. To prove that the gossip was not true we decided to decrease our travels. I began to handle more of my business over the telephone, and I suggested to my husband that he sould be home and together with the family as often as he could. After we did this, the gossip faded away. But the role of my husband as the father of our children decreased sharply. I do not know the reason: whether he is poorer than me and appears less strong than ever. I always tell the children to be good and obedient to him because in my mind there is no denying the vital role of a father as the head of the family. I never imagine betraying him in this role, although in terms of family economy I am superior to him.

When my children ask me what school they should choose, I tell them to consult my husband, their father and the head of my family. And when I want to plan something for my business, I ask for his approval although he never deliberately involves himself in it. He always lets me do what is best for my business, but I always listen to his careful suggestions. If I know my children are reluctant and doubtful to do what he suggests, I say, "Obey your father, or you won't get my support."

I try hard to control the family affairs in their right place—that is, my husband leading the family and me supporting him. However, as I told you before, everything changes, and we, he and I, react to the changes in different ways. He is retired and stays at home more than I do. I mean, he stays at home all day except on Sundays when he plays tennis and we have no objections to his outings. I go to the market everyday and stay there until evenings. So, I meet my children at night and in the morning; or, if necessary, they can go to the market to see me, but this rarely happens. My husband never goes to the market. But he always tells the children, especially during their school holidays, to go the market to help me. But, you know, young people are ashamed of being in the market selling onions and potatoes, aren't they? Especially boys because the market is considered women's work.

We have four children, all boys. The eldest son married his schoolmate shortly after his graduation from high school. And now he has given me two entertaining grandchildren, one boy and one girl. He had no intention of studying in the university because, as he told me, he had "no good brains." So, what else could I do except suggest that he should work with me in the market. I told him to accompany his uncle, my younger brother and representative in business, to go from one place to the other dealing with the buying of potatoes and onions. They were also responsible for the transportation.

My brother graduated from the faculty of law at a famous state university in this country, but, as it turned out, he preferred helping me with the business rather than working in law. At first I always gave him and my son directions by telephone, but later I gave them freedom to go where they wanted and to buy or to sell the commodities as long as the deals were profitable. They could decide whether to buy and sell the commodities in a certain place; however, the decision of buying and selling in this city was in my hands. When my brother died three years ago, it was the time for my eldest son to become my full representative. He is careful and quick in dealing with brokers, but sometimes he phones me twice a day just to ensure that his decision is justifiable. He travels a lot, but I always remind him not to forget his duty as a father and husband.

Because he has his own family to support, I give him a suitable house to live in and a certain amount of regular income to spend. I bought him a motorcycle a few years ago and an automobile to travel from one city to another. But this very case is, as I realized later, the source of my husband's inferiority. My children know who buys them motorcycles, cars, television sets, houses, everything. I am sad to realize that it is not my husband who finances them. But, isn't it good to have progress? The saddest truth is that my children only think of who gives them everything rather than who is responsible for the whole affairs of the family.

They do not want to accept the fact that whatever I do is under the knowledge and guidance of my husband, their father. What they show me, as I understand it, is that their mother is everything. It is not true. My husband is a somebody. My husband is everything to me but not to my children. They do not want to listen to him any more, but I force them to do so. I even asked my husband to take part in the business, even to take my place. But he always says that it is too late for such a person like him to deal with the business now. It is the time and turn for the children. He wants only to be the father of our children as long as they need him. I cry when I hear this. However, I cannot and must not let my eldest son run the business alone. It is not really a good time nowadays for a freshman like him to go on a business venture when everything is becoming harder and more competitive. The business of today is not as good as it was ten or twenty years ago. Therefore, experienced persons are badly needed.

Nowadays more people are going into the same kind of business, and they bring with them more money and facilities. They can import onions and potatoes if they think it is more profitable. Or they can damage the price of these commodities by bringing cheaper ones from other islands. And I am beyond all this sort of play. All I can do to prevent my business from being broken into pieces is to rely on good relationships with the contemporary market people, those old people who still value continuity and friendship over immediate financial profits. Most of them are old Javanese who think that the loss of friends and relatives is not comparable to the loss of money. And we have our own customers who are also of the same opinion. So, it is unnecessary for people like me to compete with the new wealthier merchants. Let them do what they want to do; we have a certain way to keep our business going.

One of several keys to keeping our customers is to keep the high quality of our merchandise. We buy only the best potatoes and onions to sell to supermarkets and individual buyers. The latter hold wedding parties or celebrate certain holy days; most important, they should be given the best potatoes and onions. They trust us, and so they become our customers. However, sometimes we have to buy the merchandise a little more expensively because of short supply. The brokers do not want to ruin our relationship and friendship. They just sell their potatoes and onions to buyers they believe they can trust. We believe that these new merchants are not in the business for the long term; they will turn to another more profitable field if possible and leave us. So, trading with familiar people who promise a better profit in terms of both finance and personal relationships is preferable.

The other difficulties for business are from the government. A lot of new regulations are difficult to understand and difficult to carry out. We have to have a trading license, which is not easy to possess. We must visit several offices and fulfill several requirements before the license can be given. It takes almost three months to finish all these procedures. Besides the daily market retribution, we also pay yearly contributions for the security cost. There are various taxes we must pay annually: income tax, earth and building tax, and selling tax.

My objection to the taxation is that the tax forms we have to fill out are beyond our knowledge. We do not know how to fill out the forms correctly, and so we do not know how much money we must pay every year. This knowledge is important for traders like me because it certainly helps us settle our budget. It is not easy for my second son who is now studying business management in a university to fill out the forms either. So, I give the forms to the tax officer to fill out, and I do not know whether the amount I pay is proper.

Another problem with business today is the opportunity for small retail traders. This market was rebuilt three years ago. Before the restoration, I had three kiosks [stores], but now I only have one. Hundreds of small retail traders have to leave their kiosks because they could not afford to pay the increased rent after the restoration. Most of them returned home and opened small kiosks inside their houses. But many of them can no longer run their business because their capital is consumed at home. Here they can, at least, separate the capital from their domestic budget. Some of them could only afford to rent second floor kiosks, cheaper but less strategic. How many customers are willing to walk up to those kiosks when people can obtain the same thing on the ground floor?

It is true that after the restoration the market looks nicer and cleaner. The kiosks are bigger than before. But this is the government's biggest mistake: all it seems to think about is how much money it can get from taxes. The government does not pay much attention to improving economic opportunities for small traders.

People who move into the restored kiosks are richer merchants who are enlarging their business by buying new kiosks. And, as usual, they are Chinese. Therefore, we sometimes think that whenever there is a market restoration, it is not for small traders.

What I want to do from now on is to train my children to run my business if they do not succeed in their studies or they cannot get government positions. I am very willing to support their study in whatever fields they take, as long as they are sure that they will be successful. I have bought them each a house, which is now being rented and generating income to finance their study. I pray night and day that my children will, at some time, be able to place their father in his right place.

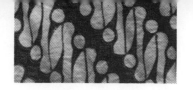

PART II

Holding onto the Past

The Artistic and Spiritual Traditions

A Dance Teacher in the Sultan's Palace of Yogyakarta

Among the most distinctive aspects of Javanese culture are its artistic traditions. Java is justifiably famous, worldwide, for its classical dances. These slow and methodical movements, accompanied by gamelan orchestras with their mesmerizing melodies, are taught at the sultan's courts. Traditionally, the sultans of Yogyakarta and Surakarta were the main patrons of the arts. The classical dances were performed mainly for the courts. Historically, there has been some rivalry between the two courts, and this man's comments about the relative refinement of Yogyakarta dancing over Surakarta dancing reflect this rivalry.

This dance teacher participates in the old style of life in Yogyakarta, a deliberately leisurely pace that recognizes more important things in life than material wealth and modernization. Although he was born in 1928 and has lived through the dramatic changes of the last half-century, this man has been relatively insulated from these changes. He concerns himself with retaining the cultural heritage of his people. He recognizes the reality of change, but he sees its impact in things like the necessity of staging abbreviated dances for tourists rushing in and out of Java. He regrets these changes, but, given his traditional value in not becoming upset over anything, he adapts to realities. This man is not unrealistic; rather, he prefers to keep his distance from the realities of a new order and its more frantic approach to life.

He was interviewed at the sultan's court, lounging in his sarong under a cool veranda while sipping tea brought to him by a palace servant. The interview was conducted in Javanese by Priyanto (male, age thirty-nine), translating for Walter L. Williams.

Perhaps I was born to be a dancer. My mother was a dancer during the reign of Sultan Hamengkubuwono VIII [1880–1939], and I trained to dance the classical Javanese style when I was a very young boy. There was no formal dancing school during the Dutch time. I learned to dance in the prince's house, and the prince himself was the instructor.

When I had to go to the school for the noble family, I did not feel at home. I was in the same class with the sultan's sons; I felt very awkward because they were royalty and I was not. In addition, my ability to speak Dutch was not very good; therefore, I left the school. I had to realize that I was not a prince. My chance to attain a formal education was very limited. I quit school even before I was circumcised. At that time boys were circumcised at about the time they were ready to get married. There were no doctors, and the job was done by a person who specialized in circumcizing boys. I was circumcised at the same time with some princes. We were nine boys all together.

Only a few people are interested in Javanese classical dance because it is difficult to learn and it takes time. You have to start very early, when you are very young. When you begin to learn dances too old your movement becomes awkward and stiff. The basic dances of Yogyakarta style and Surakarta style differ. Yogyakarta style is more difficult; it is smooth, elegant, and very refined. Surakarta style is more dynamic and perhaps much easier to learn. Yogyakarta style, in the old time, was performed only in the palace. In contrast, Surakarta style was also performed outside the palace, for commercial purposes.

I have been teaching dance here for more than thirty years. I teach students only in the afternoon from five to seven, but when there is a general rehearsal I conduct my class later at night. I have to pay homage to the royal household once every ten days from nine to twelve in the morning. In addition, I have to train the prince's children to dance in the *Kasatriyan*, the ceremony marking the passage of a sultan's son from childhood to adulthood when the boy is about twelve years old. My other duties involve working in the palace department that oversees the maintenance of the palace heritage—care for the royal artifacts, coordination of cultural activities, and tourism. The high official in charge of this department is Prince Hadiwinoto, the second son of Sultan Hamengkubuwono

IX [1912–1988]. The prince is a university graduate with a degree in anthropology.

I receive only a little sum of money as salary, but I receive a supplement as a dance teacher. I don't expect too much. I have no wife or children, so I can manage—just enough to live. A small apartment is given to me, where I stay in the house for nobles in the palace. But most of all I am happy that I can do something for somebody else.

I think everybody knows that nowadays the sultan actually resides in Jakarta. For a time Sultan Hamengkubuwono IX was the vice president of Indonesia. After the republic took over governmental administration, the royal families gave up the power to control their kingdoms. Today there are no more kingdoms, even though Yogyakarta continues to hold the status of "Special Territory." But even Yogya's sultan does not have the power to rule like he did before the revolution. He is more or less a figurehead. While the sultan is involved with the national government in Jakarta, the authority to maintain the palace is with his brother, Prince Puruboyo, who married some eight years ago, when he was seventy years old. The "lucky girl" was only twenty-seven when the prince married her. Her parents were very proud, and it was a real tribute to them; besides they received some money to start a small business. The prince has two sons from his first wife, but with the second one he doesn't have any child yet. Perhaps they will have children in the future, I don't know.

Prince Pujokusumo is my cousin, and I am surrounded by those royalty whom I have known my entire life. I am living in the same house where my mother lived when she was a dancer here. My mother died when I was only twelve years old. I blame her death on my father, who treated her badly. The lives of the noble families are very complicated. One thousand days after my mother's death, as is the custom here, my father married again. He married his cousin and had three children with her. If you marry, you should treat your wife respectfully, at a distance. Only in the Western culture are husbands and wives intimate with each other. In Javanese, the saying is that a wife is "only a friend when we are in the kitchen."

I have two brothers and one sister. They are all married and have children. My sister is married to a batik merchant, and she is living with her family in East Java; my two brothers are living in Jakarta. I would rather stay here in Yogyakarta. Yogya is a nice place to live; it isn't too busy. I don't like busy life. People must make a living to provide for their needs, but they also have to enjoy their lives. I think many Westerners are so caught up in making money to buy material goods that they forget to do this. Don't work too hard. Do things as you can, don't press yourself too much, and you will live longer.

That is the attitude we follow at the palace. People who want to get a position at the palace do it, not because they want to make money, but because they have other special reasons. Lots of people, mostly farmers, want such positions. When there is not much work to do in the fields, after the harvest or in a drought, instead of sitting around worrying about rain they would rather be able to enjoy participating in the many social activities of the court. In the old days, when the sultan had a lot of land, he would often reward those with a position at his court by giving them a piece of land. More important for most people, however, is that they apply for a position at the palace to gain high social status. This provides a kind of psychological satisfaction. They receive only a very small amount of money, but they are very proud and happy to be part of the palace. You will see that life is not always measured by wealth. The Javanese philosophy says: "Be rich without treasure and win without warriors." It means that we are expected to be wealthy in the sense of our mental attitude; then we will be honored by love and fulfillment. People always want to achieve happiness, but they think wealth is the way to get it. You can more likely become happy by not being demanding. With the right mental attitude, you can achieve victory without fighting.

In my own life, though I have very little money, I feel that I have achieved this. I do not have to worry about the future, and I know that when I am old I will be cared for adequately. Other people worry about having children to take care of them, but children can die or even turn against a parent. I am assured that I will be well attended to at the sultan's court. I enjoy my daily activities, and I do not feel under pressure. I enjoy my dance teaching the most of any of my activities. Besides the prince's children, I have twenty-five students from the Academy of Dance and almost that many who come from the villages.

I prefer to teach them the classical dance styles. Some of the newly created dances or modern Javanese dances are good and very

6. Javanese classical dance, at the Sultan's Palace in Yogyakarta. *Photo: Walter L. Williams*

attractive, but in my opinion they are not real dancing. These new dances are more like performing exercises or sport: there are no specific rules, and its basic movement varies. It is a kind of mixed dance, I would say, with elements of Sundanese, Balinese, or Sumatra movement all jumbled together. Most people admire them only in the first show, and then they get bored very soon. The classical dance has its own rules and several meanings. When you are watching the classical dances you have to see its background and the meaning. Then you will understand.

Nowadays I am often called on to organize a dance event for tourists, in which I have to change the rules and shorten the time of the performance. I hate to do that, but there is nothing else I can do. Most tourists want to see only the main part because they don't have enough time. Each night we have different performances, but the tourists' favorite is the Ramayana Ballet. The sultan has decided that we are going to promote our culture so that more people will visit Yogya. The cultural show is the main attraction here. But we also must not forget the importance of the dancers' social security. In this case, we have to consider that these performances are like special requests, and thus we have to ask for payments for the dancers. Perhaps you might think that I am too commercial; but what else could we do? They must make a living to support themselves also.

Life has changed today. We are no longer living in the traditional times. The life in the palace has changed drastically since the sultan moved to Jakarta. The princes don't have enough money to support the financial needs of the palace. That is why we are now encouraging tourism—to bring in enough money to continue our culture. You see, some princes have even had to sell their antique family treasures and houses. They begin to live in different ways. However, we don't lose everything! Thank goodness we still have our traditional way of living, as a part of our daily activity at the palace.

Javanese people, especially Yogyakarta people, are trying to rebuild their sense of glory from the past. Have you see the palace warriors under Prince Hadiwinoto's command? Oh, what a stirring sight. Protecting our culture depends entirely on the people. The only thing we can do is to create "self-awareness." We have to bear in mind that the development of the Javanese culture is our responsibility. I am sixty years old, but I intend to do all I can to keep our traditions and values alive.

By paying attention to the traditions, I think people today can get important messages for how best to live their lives. For example, my favorite character in the wayang puppet shows is Semar. Wayang stories reflect our basic philosophy. In his job Semar is just a lowly servant; but at the same time he is also the mainifestation of Batara Ismoyo, a god who protects the good spirit and truth. He is a servant on the one hand, and on the other hand he is a god. In applying this to society, I think Semar is the symbol of democracy. His masters cannot do anything without him. The message of the Semar stories is that leaders can do nothing without the help of the common people. I grew up under the Sultan's rule, and now I live in the Indonesian Republic. I cannot truly decide if democracy is a better system than monarchy. Both forms of government have advantages as well as disadvantages. I only want to say that, whatever system exists, the people's voice *must* be heard.

You have to know the Javanese saying *Djo Dumeh*, which means you have to care for others. If you are able to achieve something better than other people, then you have to think of the others. Those who don't do this eventually find themselves alone and without support when they need it. You see, life is a wheel, and you are on that same wheel with everyone else. So, when you are on top, it is to your benefit to help others who are currently on the bottom. Because the wheel never stops moving: It moves up and down, and round and round.

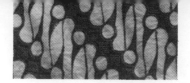

A Singer

Throughout the world Java is famous for its dance and wayang puppet theater. The basis of both art forms is gamelan, the Javanese classical music noted for its haunting and complex melodies and rhythms. The gamelan orchestra is made up of a number of male musicians who play metal gongs, drums, and other percussion instruments, as well as some stringed pieces. Prominent in the orchestra is the singer, who is always female. One, two, or three women sing high-pitched slow lyrics that convey a mood of serenity and peace. In contrast to the men's music, which comes from their manufactured instruments (objects of culture), the woman's contribution comes from the body (objects of nature).

Although greatly honored for her singing talents, the female singer has something of a reputation as a woman of loose morals. Singers traditionally come from families of low status; becoming a singer offers impoverished females a means of rapid upward mobility. However, the role has its price because these young women usually become concubines or prostitutes for either the musicians or the patrons of the orchestra. This woman's life story confirms this, showing the advantages and disadvantages of the singer's life from her own perspective. As with many popular singers who become stars, the young person often has no emotional basis to handle either the instant fame or the later descent into obscurity. In the end such individuals often regret their self-centeredness, as this woman does.

She expresses a deep sense of tragedy about her life—her mistakes and missed opportunities. In a society that attaches such importance to family togetherness, to children, and to a sense of attachment to a particular group, this woman blames herself for the poverty, loneliness, and lack of support she finds in her old age. She never questions social norms that treat a divorced woman as a threat; her only response is to try to get married. At last she succeeds, but it is an unhappy marriage; after her husband dies she is left alone again. Unable to have children, she seems never to have considered adoption. In fact, she never expresses much desire to help others. As a result, she has tragically lost the family togetherness, the one positive thing she remembers about her childhood.

After trying without success to integrate herself into her native village, in an impoverished near-desert area southeast of Yogyakarta, this woman came back to the city where she lives alone in a tiny room in a lower-class urban neighborhood. She has no savings or any resources in case she gets sick. With no public health care system or retirement programs for the aged, elderly people without relatives to care for them face a fragile existence. Recognition of all these uncertainties contribute to her depression. She was interviewed in Javanese by Priyanto (male, age thirty-nine) and Walter L. Williams.

I am of a humble and uneducated origin. Both my parents were unable to read or write, and I myself have never attended any formal school. There was not even a school in my area during my youth. I spent most of my childhood helping my parents collect firewood and teak leaves in the forest because there was not much work in the fields. The land was too dry and infertile; besides, there was no water. We had to walk several kilometers just to fetch water to drink. The only crop that could grow year round in the dry soil was cassava, so that was about the only food source we could raise.

When I was a little girl the most wonderful event I had seen was the *wayang* shadow-puppet performances, with their musical entertainment. As a child I was captivated, especially with the lady singer, the *pesinden*, who performed with the gamelan orchestra. I was sure that the voices of all lady singers were magical and their faces were charming. Indeed, I was charmed to see their elegant performance and admire their attractive appearance. All the time I kept thinking that someday I would become a famous lady singer in my village. Most people said that I possessed a beautiful face and a good voice, suitable for a singer. They often heard me singing in the forest, such songs that I learned by listening to the singers.

When I was fifteen years old, one of our neighbors who worked in the city came home for a short visit. She told us about her various experiences working as a servant for a city family. She also mentioned that my singing talent could be easily developed if I moved to the city. I was very pleased when she offered me a place to work. When I revealed it to my parents, my father said, "You are a girl, whatever you reach and wherever you go, you will stay in the kitchen. Don't force yourself to work too much. Go slow to make sure that you'll get the right things. Life is a struggle, but we have to accept it accordingly. Do not be too demanding." He did not really want me to leave, but he was always so smooth and indirect about the way he expressed himself. He asked me, "Do you think you will find a better life there? Remember that our main achievement is being together as a family. It is nice to stay together to share the joys and bitterness of life."

Despite my father's misgivings I left my parents and followed the woman to find a job in the city. I promised that as soon as I could find what I wanted I'd return home. In the city everything was different. There were many more chances to see musical performances. My new master, who hired me to work as a servant, was very glad to hear my plan to become a singer. He sent me to an elderly singer. Under her guidance I began to learn the Javanese transcript and singing technique. It didn't take too long for me to get acquainted with the instruments, as well as the musicians. They sometimes helped me improve my skill and comprehend various verses. The other thing I liked most: the men in the orchestra often teased me. I think all women liked to be teased or praised.

My life certainly changed. From a humble and simple girl I became a coquettish celebrity. The elderly singer was so jealous of my popularity and successful performance that she did not want to train me any more. At this point an elderly musician offered me his house free of charge. He told me that I would not have to have a job other than my singing, and he told me that he would help me improve my skill. Without suspicion I accepted his generous offer, and I stayed in his house which was not very far from his own home. Now I am sixty years old, and I know all about the world, but then I was too foolish to know the trick. I realize that a woman's defense is within the confines of her clothes. This man has ruined my life; I was only seventeen years old when I was made his concubine. I considered that my experience was usual, that it could happen to any woman. It has been decreed in the Koran that men can have more than one woman and marriage should not be based on love. I was always told, "Woman has to accept as you are provided and to accept anything without making protest."

In general, woman's life depends on her husband; or I might say she has to share the husband's joys, but she cannot get away from the husband's disgrace. What else could I do? However, it was not so bad. Above anything else, I still felt that I was a lucky person because I did not lose my freedom.

Meanwhile, my skill had improved a lot. I often received many invitations to give singing performances for various occasions. People admired my performances; they teased and praised me. I was becoming famous and was very proud and conceited. When there wasn't any activity, however, I began to feel that I was only the musician's ornament. I realized that as soon as he got bored he would throw me out. I began to realize that I needed to look after myself.

After that, I used to go alone without his company. One day, a Babah, a wealthy Chinese tobacco trader, invited me to sing for his celebration. I was a great success and received good payment, but beyond that I received additional payment from him. This was the beginning of my relationship with him. He promised to marry me. But before our plan could take place, the Japanese soldiers reached the city, and they began to rule the territory.

I remembered the verses mentioned in the prophecy of Joyoboyo [an ancient Javanese king]. It predicted that a dwarf people from the East will come to Java to chase the white buffalo to their stables, and they will rule this territory for about as long as it takes for corn to ripen. The tiny Japanese chased out the big white Dutch "buffaloes," but they ruled Java for longer than the ripening of one corn crop. During the Japanese time life changed drastically. There were no art or music activities, and the people were forced to work hard without payment. The Japanese took everything. Almost every day I caught sight of people in the street who died because of hunger. This country was penetrated by a big famine. Because I was alone much of the time, I was afraid and scared that the Japanese soldiers might approach me.

Meanwhile my elderly "husband" could no longer afford to give me his house. He returned to his wife and family. I took all my belongings and went under Babah's custody. Babah was very fond of me, and he asked me to help him maintain his business. I began to learn how to run a business. I remember when he said that the Javanese people are not very good at trading. He said. "It is very hard to trust what a Javanese says. You never really know whether they are pleased or sad, whether they agree or disagree with anything, because they try so hard to mask their emotions. Moreover, they don't want to say things straightforward. It is very hard to judge their expectations. They prefer to reach for status than to work hard for the sake of their own good. Their main goal is social status." I have to admit he was right about this. Look at Javanese people's concern for their names. They call themselves by the honorable title "Prawiro" as soon as they get a position as a bureaucrat or soldier, but everyone who labors or works is derided.

I lived happily with Babah, but still I felt lonesome. Life without entertainment is flat and monotonous. I persuaded him to agree to sponsor a gamelan unit for our daily entertainment, and I invited several musicians to practice at our home. Among them there was a young good-looking musician who played the drum. Well, I was captivated by his appearance. In our society it is disgraceful for a girl to pursue a man for his looks. Actually I wanted to get a real marriage and build a family. As I grew older I became worried about my future.

Finally, the dwarf people went away, and Indonesia was free. I wanted to be free also. Without Babah's permission I escaped from his house and moved in with the handsome young musician in the northern part of the city. I spent my money to support both of us. We stayed together for several years. One day he said that he wanted to have children and that I had not been able to have any. He told me, "What is the use of marriage if we don't have children. There is no one who will look after us when we get older; besides there is nobody who will continue our name." I tried to get pregnant but could not. I visited several *dukun* [shamans] to get advice. I realized that I would never be able to have children. Later this man left me behind and married a village girl. I met him two years ago when I went to the city; he told me that he is now expecting his first grandchild.

After he left I was a divorcée until a dalang puppeteer with five children proposed to me. In fact, I did not have any courage to get married again, but being a divorcée had created big problems for me. People used to gossip a lot about me. They accused me of being a woman who liked to chase young men or entice away somebody's husband. My profession as a singer has a reputation of being cheap. Well, perhaps God punished me for my being conceited and ungrateful. Yes, I think I was all that. But my heaviest sin was that I forgot to pay attention to my parents! I had been so concerned about my own career and my personal relationships that I did not care for my mother and father in their old age. And then before I knew it, they were dead. Now I realize that our parents, as a matter of fact, are the physical manifestation of God. They are visible God. If we turn our backs on them, then we are turning against God.

My life with the puppeteer was not very happy; however, I had come to see that this unhappy home life was my fate and punishment for being ungrateful and conceited. Then one night, when we were having our show, he died suddenly of a heart attack. I was alone again. Several years later I made up my mind to return to my village. I was longing for the past, for the happier times I had had in my youth. But by this time, almost everyone in the village I had known in my childhood was gone. Most people looked at me as a stranger.

Nowadays I do not have any family, and I live alone. Formerly I was rich and famous; today I have to make rice cakes to sell in the market just to get enough money to live. I am trying to train young girls who wish to be gamelan singers. I know that our old Javanese ways are declining, but I still hope that our generation can be responsible enough to teach the young ones. Otherwise we will lose our traditions. Besides, I have to do something beneficial to counter the mistakes I made in the past. That past will never come back again. It was a beautiful life, yet it was painful.

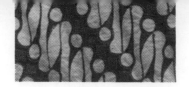

A Dalang Shadow-Puppet Teacher

Java's famous wayang shadow-puppet theater is under the control of the dalang, the master puppeteer. The dalang not only operates the puppets, but he also enacts the dialogues and monologues of every character. He narrates the whole story by constructing the script as he goes along. Wayang tells the classical mythology of Javanese culture. The performances go on for hours, usually all night long; the dalang, sitting in one position, takes no more of a break than to sip hot tea that is placed near him. Dalangs are admired for their mastery of the complex cosmology of the wayang stories, their voice control, and their skills in telling the stories in a dramatic and sometimes humorous way. Their ability to perform for many hours is considered a spiritual gift.

A dalang is practically a religious figure, so devoted are his listeners to his words. Recognizing the propaganda value of wayang, the Indonesian government subsidizes performances at Independence Day celebrations and other holidays. The government also pays musicians, dancers, and dalangs to appear on government radio and television stations. Sultan Hamengkubuwono IX (1912–1988) was particularly important in encouraging the arts. He granted large plots of land to universities and arts training institutes. He allowed free rehearsal space for classical dance, music, and wayang groups in the palace, which has become one of Java's major tourist attractions. Some artists receive personal subsidies. Among artists these policies have promoted a feeling of loyalty to the government, and they have made Yogyakarta an internationally recognized center for the arts. This is immediately apparent to a visitor strolling the streets of the city: batik art shops are everywhere, and the many resident clothing designers often sponsor well-attended fashion shows. Wayang is only one art form centered in Yogyakarta, but it is perhaps the most prestigious.

This dalang evidences a boastful manner, reflecting his high status. He rather proudly recounts his disinterest in making money and his lack of success in business. He was interviewed at his studio for teaching wayang, near the palace. The interview was conducted in Indonesian, with translation by Hernie (male, age twenty-seven) and questions by Walter L. Williams.

I began my profession as a dalang before I was born. I say that because I am a possessed dalang. My grandfather and my father were dalangs. I only continue the culture that was passed down to me. I never went to a dalang school but obtained my skill, in playing the shadow puppets, from my elders. I was motivated by the environment that is in my family, as a possessed dalang. Since my childhood I have associated with dalangs that attracted me to wayang.

Before I became a dalang, I was a merchant. But the job was not appropriate to me, and I went bankrupt. After that, I decided that my talents were in preserving the arts and traditions of my people. I began working in the culture department at the sultan's palace. In this position I deal with not only wayang but also other Javanese arts. I have also written some books on Javanese culture.

There are so many conditions to become a dalang, and they are rather hard to do. For me, the conditions are not so hard because, as I said, I am a possessed dalang. For other people they are hard because they do not have strong instincts in wayang; they do not have the spiritual possession. Before they become dalang, they must watch shadow playing so much. Gradually, they learn. The knowledge they gain becomes their basis for admittance to a dalang school. Before a few years ago, there was no dalang school. With all the changes occurring around us, some people began to fear that wayang and our other arts would decline. Aware of such a situation, Sultan Hamengkubuwono IX founded a dalang school located in the area of the palace. The school is open for everyone, female as well as male, who wants to be a dalang.

A dalang changes his voice a lot when he plays wayang, to

differentiate among the characters in a wayang story. For example, if the dalang is using the puppet of Semar, he must use the voice given to determine Semar. The same is done for the others. To do all these different voices requires hard training and much time. And the voice change should be done carefully. It takes students a long time to learn this. My students at the dalang school I lead are from various palaces, and they also have various educational backgrounds and status. The bulk of them are from Java, but a few come from foreign countries, such as England and Australia. Because teachers still use Javanese as the language in the teaching-learning process, the students have to study Javanese before entering the school. Besides studying the shadow puppet performance itself, students also learn the songs to accompany the dalang while he is playing wayang, as well as classical Javanese dance and music.

Of course, for a person to be a dalang, he or she must have a magic condition. A real dalang will never be sleepy or have to take breaks while playing the night-long shadow-puppet performance. If those cases happen, the dalang is not professional. A dalang should look for magical abilities to resist feeling hungry, sleepy, and so on.

The dalang determines the story of the play. Sometimes, a dalang asks the committee that sponsors the show what story they like. Usually, they let the dalang choose whatever story he thinks is best for that particular gathering. But, generally, all dalangs are ready to play what people want. I actively played wayang when Indonesia was still under the Dutch. In those times, I only told the pure wayang story. Now that Indonesia is independent I always add messages to the spectators about our national development so that they might understand and help the government in development projects. I did not want to support the development by the Dutch because I don't like imperialism. I was not willing for the Dutch to colonize my country. But now, I suggest that all dalang should support the government in developing our country by explaining the need for cooperation with such programs through wayang. The puppet show not only tells our traditions but also gives lessons for the best way for people to live their lives.

An important and necessary role has been played by Sultan Hamengkubuwono IX. He is a great patriot, who strongly supported the revolution. He also gives a strong spirit for us to develop Javanese art. We can get many positive things from this activity, such as having many friends or learning self-control. In dancing or playing in the gamelan orchestra, we develop concentration and good cooperation. We can also learn a lot and can recognize feelings and behavior from the rhythm of their music.

I like almost all the wayang stories, but I like the stories that are most applicable to our present situation better than the others. Today is the development period of our country. So, the theme of the story I play is development; I mean that I relate the wayang story with a development situation. So many aspects of life can be related to the wayang story because the stories themselves picture the whole human life.

I am happy if there are many spectators and they look satisfied when I play the shadow puppets. That is why I always tell the wayang story that I think will lead to their greatest pleasure. I am sometimes unhappy if there is a misunderstanding between the dalang and the music players. The rhythm of their music must be exactly suitable for the dalang. Sometimes it might not be a good mix if I go to another place to play wayang alone, without my group. If an unfamiliar music group accompanies me in playing the wayang, it can make me very tired. If I played for one night in such a situation, I felt as if I had played for several nights.

I am not like other dalangs. I never make a set fee because I feel that my art is not for sale. For me it is necessary that people should get pleasure seeing me play wayang and give me some money to pay for my transportation. I believe the committee who invites me should decide the amount of the fee. As long as I have played wayang, however, those who invite me have given me more money than those dalangs who have a set fee. Generally, the dalang and the inviting committee bargain to determine the fee.[1]

Having enough to live on does not depend on how much money a person makes. It depends on his emotional control. Few people are satisifed with what they can make for their living. This means that the sufficiency of their economy does not depend on the money they make. In reality, less or much is sufficient for them. They think that the income is a blessing of God. But some others do not think so. They think they have to make as much money as they can to have as much wealth as possible. For me, the standard of economic sufficiency is that I can finance my family and pay for my children's school fees. I do not work hard to collect much wealth.

Generally, because a dalang professional cannot finance his family sufficiently, he should look for other jobs to add to his income.

There are so many dalangs, and their fates are different; therefore, the responses of the society to them are different too. Generally, however, people admire a dalang as a person who is above other people and has magic. The young generation, especially Javanese youth, is still interested in wayang. I say that because many young people watch a wayang show whenever it is done, especially if the wayang story is told in the Indonesian language. That's why I often suggest that dalang should conduct shadow playing in Indonesian in order that most Indonesian people can enjoy it. Wayang can still compete with modern recreations such as music, cinema, and the like because it is one of the major Indonesian arts. I do not think it is in danger of disappearing.

A Trance Dancer

The Indonesian government has wisely been encouraging all the arts, including different forms of dances. It supports not only the refined classical court dances but also the folk dances of the common village people. In part, this support is offered to create loyalty among the people; moreover, the government hopes an active artistic tradition will attract more tourism to Indonesia.

Indonesia has an amazing number of folk dances. Usually the performance is given by dancers of only one sex. Probably the majority of Javanese dances publically performed are men's dances. One male dance, the *jatilan*, involves the dancers going into trances, when they fall about uncontrollably. The end of the dance is a frenzied climax as dancer after dancer goes into trance and then collapses in exhaustion. Other men carry the dancers away to a private house, where they are nursed back to consciousness.

The uninhibited actions of the dancers are in sharp contrast to the usual deliberately reserved and controlled emotions of the Javanese. That is part of the spectacle of the performance for the audience. For the dancers themselves, the trance offers the young male dancers an opportunity to release their tensions in a way that does not harm others. It provides a socially approved means of emotional catharsis for them, without the violence associated with young men in many cultures.

This eighty-five-year-old former jatilan dancer was interviewed after two different jatilan performances in the same village west of Yogyakarta. The interviews were conducted by Walter L. Williams, with Kedah (male, age twenty-seven) translating into Javanese. The man sat on the floor mat as he ate his rice dish, drank hot tea, and smoked the Indonesian clove cigarettes so common among village men.

From as far back in time as anybody knows, jatilan dancing has been done by men of our village. *Jatilan* is a Javanese word, meaning "Horse Trance." This kind of folk dancing done by the common people in the villages of central Java is called "Kuda Lumping" in the Indonesian language. In the dance, the men are dressed like cavalrymen on horseback. They "ride" bamboo horses that are held between the legs and go into trances at the end. We don't know the origin of the story, but when I was young, an old man told me that a cavalry soldier from an ancient Javanese kingdom settled in this village centuries ago; that soldier brought the story of his days on horseback and his trance experience. Since then it has become part of our culture.

There should be at least six horse dancers, plus a white-masked dancer and a black-masked dancer. Sometimes there is a *barong*, a monster-like dragon spirit, but it is not necessary to have a barong in jatilan. There should be at least six musicians in the orchestra, playing two gongs, a drum, a cymbal, and three *angklung* [bamboo instruments]. They play the same melody over and over, varying the tempo from slow to fast and going continuously for hours. Replacement musicians come in and continue playing without missing a beat. A dance begins about ten o'clock in the morning and goes until about five or six in the evening.

No one knows why it became so established here; that was so long ago. Formerly, dancers and musicians came from other nearby villages, too, because the population was lower then, but in recent decades we have enough boys to recruit them solely from our village. Today jatilan is performed by only a small percentage of villages in Java, but mine is one that does it. People come from many villages outside Yogyakarta to watch our performances.

I began dancing when I was fifteen years old and continued until five years ago when I finally retired, at age eighty. I was head of the jatilan group here. I and my group have done jatilan in many different villages of central Java. Long ago, dancers began participating at about thirteen years of age, but more recently they usually begin dancing between fifteen and twenty. They dance for an indeterminate number of years, as long as they have the feeling. One dancer in our village is now forty-five years old, and he continues dancing every year even though the other dancers are a younger generation. The typical dancer is in his early twenties.

7. "Jatilan" Men's Horse Trance Dance performance, on Indonesian Independence Day, at a village in central Java. *Photo: Walter L. Williams*

The boys who dance are just typical boys; there is nothing special or different about them. Some young men of the village are not active in the group because they are shy about dancing in public, but all formally belong to the group. All feel the good results of jatilan, even if they do not dance themselves. Today there are about sixty young men in the group, and most are active. One man performs with both our group and another jatilan group in a different village.

Jatilan is usually performed about three to five times a year; the number varies depending on the demand. There has never been a year when there was not at least one jatilan performance. Someone might pay us to dance at a circumcision ceremony, or the parents of the bride or the groom might have us perform at a wedding. Our most recent jatilan celebrated the dedication of a new volleyball court in our village.

The government asks us to dance in the government ceremonies, and we always perform as part of the Indonesian Independence Day celebrations. Several years ago, the government sponsored a jatilan contest, and our group came in second in the competition. We like the fact that the government has become so active in promoting our traditional culture.

The attitudes of Islam toward jatilan are mixed. Formerly, someone who was a strict Muslim [santri] was not permitted by the Muslims to become a jatilan dancer. When I was young I was santri, and they tried to prevent me from dancing. But I joined jatilan anyway. Today people are divided; some santri say it is alright, while others do not approve. Some of our dancers are santri, and they feel it is not a problem to be a Muslim and a jatilan dancer at the same time. A few people believe that Islam does not permit jatilan because they think that going into a trance puts one under the influence of the devil.

The melody of the music puts you into the trance and probably there is also the influence of the devil. But that is alright. When I am in trance, I feel like I am in a dream, like I am riding on a real horse. It feels very nice to completely abandon the emotions and get carried away, following the rhythm of the music. Sometimes a trancer will put his head in a bucket of water and hold it there for a long time without breathing. Sometimes he will eat food or just wander around the dance area. There are always other men to keep him from hurting himself. At the end he gets completely carried away by the music and collapses into their arms. They carry him back to a house and slowly help him come out of the trance.

Not all the dancers go into trances during every dance. Some never have the feeling, but others do it every time they dance. When another person goes into a trance, if you desire to go into that state it can spread through the air to put you into a trance also. It is like an electric current. If I want to avoid going into a trance, I can control that; I only go into trance when I desire it and want to absorb this current from the others. If many people were watching it, they liked to watch a trance, and so I allowed myself to do it for them. Otherwise, if there were not many people, I did not go into a trance. If there was no audience, I would not feel it to be as valuable for me to try to do it.

Formerly, the trance was very soft, not violent, the way it sometimes gets today. Nowadays the person in trance will sometimes beg to be whipped and things like that. The person using the whip is not in trance, but sometimes the effect of whipping his friend is so sharp on him that it will throw him into a trance. I don't know where this originated; it just gradually became more violent. I do not think it is good to be so emotional. The leader of the group gives advice to the young men not to be violent when they go into trance, but the trancers just lose control. They do not obey the advice of the leader. Even though you never see a violent trancer hurt another person, they might get hurt themselves. I do not like it when they go into a violent trance. If a man does too many violent trances, the long-term effect on his body will not be good.

Trance is not done to get personal advantage. Afterward, I feel a bit of a headache, like I have been drinking alcohol. The next day trance dancers usually feel sick: exhausted with pains in the body. Afterward I felt very weak. Many dancers get body massages from their friends to help them recover. But there has been no long-term effect on the dancer's personality. It does not make you insane or anything like that. Later, they feel good about doing it, satisfied and appreciated by the onlookers. The young men especially enjoy dancing because it is very exciting with the music and the crowds. I felt proud when so many people showed up to watch us, and I danced seriously.

The members of the jatilan group do exercises and dance practice together every month. All the active members are very close, like brothers. When one goes into trance, the rest of us offer him support, like we are his father or brother. We help bring him gently out of the trance. Afterward, everyone shares a meal together. The jatilan group effort keeps the members together and supportive of each other. It ties the men of the village, both younger and older, together.

The money that the group makes from special performances is kept in a fund to pay for the jatilan equipment, supplies, dance costumes, and expenses. The profits are put into a bank account earning interest, or the group buys rice at harvest time when it is cheap. Then we store it in the homes of the members so it can be sold later when the price rises. With these profits, when someone in the village dies, the group donates money to the family to help them pay for funeral expenses. Also, any member of the group can borrow money from this fund if he needs it.

I enjoyed doing jatilan because it made me feel happy. It was my hobby. I think it is good to do it because it was handed down to us by our ancestors, and the people respect those who continue to do jatilan. If jatilan were not done in our village, it would be too quiet; there would not be these exciting events provided by the dances. It would be a loss of our culture. I don't know what would happen if it ever stopped. The members enjoy doing it, though, not because of the people's entertainment, but because we want to keep the culture. Art, to me is a tradition of the ancestors, and we have to keep it alive.

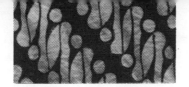

A *Dukun* Who Arranges Weddings

For the members of the sultan's courts, who do not economically depend on their spouse, marriage is not the basis of their survival. Some people may remain unmarried, while others may take casual "unofficial" spouses. In contrast, among Javanese villagers marriage assumes an economic importance rivaled by few other social institutions. Both men and women economically depend on their spouse and in old age on their children. Marriage is, therefore, an extremely important economic decision for a person and for that person's parents because the spouse will later be involved in caring for the parents. Given this view, choosing a spouse is considered the parents' prerogative. The couple traditionally do not even meet each other until their wedding ceremony.

The Javanese wedding ceremony itself is important, therefore, to create a bond between the new husband and wife. Magic is called upon to do this, in the person of a female *dukun*, or shaman, who has the magical powers to help insure a successful marriage. The ceremony must create a sense of shared unity among the two partners because traditionally no prior love relationship draws them together. Yet, despite the husband and wife not knowing each other before their marriage, Java's divorce rate is no higher than America's (in each country, about half the marriages continue for a lifetime).

How is it that marriages where the spouses do not even know each other last as long as freely chosen romantic marriages? In part, the impact of Islam, which stresses woman's duty to be faithful to her husband, is strong. More important, however, the marriage ceremony stresses the mutual obligations of the husband and wife to each other, to their parents, and to the wider community. A crucial factor in the stability of marriages in Java seems to be that, unlike in the contemporary West, a Javanese husband and wife do not feel the necessity of "being in love" all the time. In their view, such romantic ideals only lead to grief because they promote so much longing and such high expectations of blissful happiness that families are broken apart when couples fall out of love. Elders know that love is, as likely as not, a fleeting emotion. They feel that, even if two young people know each other intimately and think they are completely right for each other, they are so inexperienced in human relationships that they cannot possible know anything definite about the other person. Plus, each of them changes so much as they mature that it does not much matter what kind of person the spouse is at the time of the wedding. The important advantage of an arranged marriage, in the traditional Javanese view, is that the two young people are *not* in love; therefore, they are not disillusioned later when they fall out of love.

In Java today, many of the younger generation have been influenced by Western ideals of romantic love, especially as displayed in American and European movies. They seem more intent on choosing a life-mate by "falling in love." As individual salaries become more and more a part of Indonesia's cash economy, an increase in both marrying for love and in falling out of love and divorcing will likely become more common. Women and men in cash-paying jobs are not as economically dependent on each other as in agrarian families.

For traditional marriages, however, part of the reason for their success involves a certain emotional distance between husband and wife. Marriages are entered into, first and foremost, to produce children. The husband and wife must of course be close enough to cooperate in providing economic support for the family, but it is considered less important that they be emotionally close. A man continues to have his relatives and male age-mates as his most intimate friends, and a woman does likewise with her female friends and relatives. They do not expect their spouses to be their best friends; instead, they continue to meet most of their emotional needs in their same-sex friendships. Men spend most of their work time in all-male labor groups, and much of their leisure time is spent with male friends. Women do likewise, in their association with other women at the marketplace and in their neighborhoods.

In this context, close same-sex friendships are vital to the stability of the Javanese family. The family stays together for two important reasons: it is so economically important that the marriage succeed, and ironically not much is expected of the marriage on an emtional

level. Long-term same-sex intimate friendships provide the necessary balance for heterosexual marriage. The Javanese example shows
that such relationships are not contradictory, but complimentary.

The wedding ceremony itself symbolizes this gendered nature of
society by the seating arrangements. The bride remains on the same
side of the room where all the women are sitting. The groom is
likewise on the side where the men sit together. The two sexes face
each other across a central aisle that indicates the separate worlds of
women and men. Only the dukun, with her magical powers, crosses
the boundaries.

A few days after she had completed a wedding ceremony in her
village east of Surakarta, this dukun, born in 1928, was interviewed
in Indonesian by Martha Pardede (female, age thirty) and Walter L.
Williams.

A *dukun manten*, a sorceress as well as a beautician, helps a bride
prepare herself to receive the marriage life. The first duty of a
dukun manten is to make a bride as beautiful as possible. Not just in
her appearance, but a dukun manten has to try hard to make a bride
reflect an inner beauty. All dukun mantens have to prepare themselves mentally to be successful in doing that duty. We call this
preparation "our apprehensive time." One of our programs is fasting. I observe my fasting time before and as long as I do my work.
Some dukun manten do not fast; instead, they eat only rice and
water. The bride also does the same thing.

The second step is taking a bath. The bridegroom and the bride
have to do this part of the program together. Most of today's bride-
grooms do not want to do this with me and their bride; some of
them want to do it in a separate place or by themselves. First, I have
to prepare a room for this ceremony. I put an offering there. This
offering is dedicated to the spirits of the bride's ancestors, to ask
them for their blessing. The offering consists of bananas, a coconut,
coconut sugars, many kinds of cake, plus betel leaf and spices for
the female spirits and cigarettes for the male spirits. Then I burn
incense. After that I pray. It is a special prayer. It is only I who
know and understand it. Then, I prepare water and put some
flowers, pandanus leaves, and some leaves of coconut with the
yellow colored hull.

I take the bride in. She dresses only in simple cloth, a white material of cloth used in painting batik. I spray the water on her three times by using a cup made of coconut. This is followed by a prayer, too. After that, her parents and the other members of the family do the same thing. They must be the oldest members of the family and the number should be uneven, seven or nine. The largest number is nine. I do not know why the number must be uneven; I got this knowledge from my ancestors. It is what I learned from them. The intention of this ceremony is to clean and to purify the bride physically as well as mentally. When this ceremony is over, the offering should be given to the small children of the family.

The next ceremony we call the "fairy night." I take the bride into the brideroom to carry out this ceremony. As with the first ceremony, this room also is decorated with some fragrant flowers, and once more I put an offering here. Still, the offering in this ceremony must be better. It consists of yellow rice, some delicious cakes, and a chicken.

The second ceremony differs from the first: when this ceremony is over, this offering becomes my share. Here, I also burn incense. After I clean her skin once more by using traditional cosmetics to make her skin look soft and shiny, I'll start to make up the bride. Most of today's brides prefer the up-to-date cosmetics. I myself prefer the traditional ones, mixtures of many kinds of leaves and rice powder. But if they insist on the modern I always give in to them.

The bride sits on a pillow that is filled with many kinds of leaves. The intention is to keep the bride in good health, safety, and prosperity. It is hoped that she will get many children, who will bring her many opportunities. Her hair will be steamed to make it smell nice. Still, today's brides prefer to use modern hair spray, for they do not like the smell of that old concoction. Once more, I have to give in to them.

There are two kinds of Javanese bride's knot of hair—Solo style and Yogya style. They differ in the number of the accessories and the form of the silhouette painting of lily of the forehead (I also pray a long time before putting this on her head).

After all this, the bride puts on her clothes. Usually they are green. When she is finished dressing, I'll take her to her mother and the other women who wait outside. All along this ceremony, the bridegroom is not allowed to see her. It is why we call this the fairy night. I have to make her as beautiful as possible so the bridegroom will be surprised when he sees her in the wedding ceremony when the couple finally face each other.

The next stage is the ceremony done only with the bridegroom. He is still not allowed to see the bride. This ceremony is held in front of the village chief and the Muslim official. The bridegroom is asked about his reason and willingness to marry the bride. He signs the marriage certificate then, and the bride signs it in her room.

Next is the *temu* wedding ceremony. At this time, the bridegroom is brought by his family to face his future wife. He and his family come and bring with them a bowl filled with a small and very delicious bananas. Both the bride and groom are prepared with sacred sirih leaves. They throw that sirih at each other three times. The bridesmaid has to try her best to throw them earlier than the bridegroom. According to our belief, if she is successful in throwing them earlier, she will not be dominated by her husband. If she fails, however, she'll be defeated all her life by her husband.

Next, I put a bowl with an egg in it on the floor. The bridegroom, then, breaks the egg, and the bride washes his leg by spraying it with rose water three times. This ceremony has symbolical meanings. It means that the bridegroom will marry the girl and "break her egg"; that is, they will have a number of children. And the washing means the girl will devote her life to her husband and serve him.

I, then, take them to sit down on the elaborately adorned seat for a bridal couple. I have to burn incense here, too. The bridegroom sits on the right side and the bride on the left. The bridegroom will be given a basket filled with yellow rice. He then pours the rice, and the bride tries to catch it with her scarf. She has to try her best not to let the rice fall out. It has symbolic meaning: that is, the husband will work hard to earn their livelihood, to get money, and to look for financial opportunity; then he will turn over the fruits of his labor to his wife. The wife then has to work hard not to "spill" their resources, but to manage their finances carefully.

After showing their obligation to each other, the next part of the ceremony focuses on the couple's obligations to their parents. First, they kneel in front of their mothers and then in front of the fathers, to show how much they appreciate all the things their parents have

8. Traditional Javanese wedding ceremony, with the dukun directing the bride and groom. *Photo: Walter L. Williams*

done for them. The parents make a statement forgiving the children's past mistakes and formally blessing the marriage. Then a speechmaker presents an address on behalf of the parents of the bride, expressing hope that the young couple will become responsible members of society so that their parents can hold their heads high in respect. He also emphasizes the respect that the couple owes to all their ancestors, not to dishonor them. Next, a speechmaker representing the bridegroom's parents does the same thing. These speakers also give a lot of practical advice, telling them how to divide their work responsibilities at home so that it is fair to both husband and wife and how to be good parents for their future children. Of course, they have already heard a lot of that from me, but as part of the ceremony the repetition reinforces the ideas still more, for both them and other married people in the audience. After this, a representative of the community, usually a local government official, makes another speech. He gives more advice, emphasizing the importance of the couple contributing to the village as a whole.

The final part of the ceremony involves the couple eating a meal together. They are given sticky rice; it means that they will never be separated but will stick together always and live happily ever after. The couple feed each other three times, signifying the three meals of the day. Every part of the ceremony is symbolic of our traditional values. It is a beautiful event.

I enjoy my work as dukun not because I get a lot of money from it but because I get a special satisfaction. I mean I get spiritual satisfaction in doing it. Still, sometimes I feel disappointed, for none of my children follows in my footsteps to learn my ability and work as a dukun manten.

I have many experiences dealing with my job. As I said, every dukun has special prayers. I myself have special prayers, too, which can help me in knowing the readiness of the bride. One day I was called to help a bride. As usual I put some jasmines under her bed, and I also prayed. But, on that occasion, as soon as I put them there, they lost their fragrance. It seemed that they had vanished. Right then, I understood there was something wrong. Then, I asked her tenderly about her condition. At last she admitted that she was pregnant. Another time I had to observe my fasting time for three days before I started to work, for the bride's house was full of evil spirits. And my assistants could not work there.

I am very sad today because weddings now are not like they were in the past. Many young people look down on the traditional wedding ceremony. They should be proud to have such a beautiful and valuable cultural inheritance.

I had an experience with such a person, a bridegroom who just returned from abroad. When they were sitting on the bridal seat, he was smoking! As a consequence, the guests were shocked and blamed me. They thought that I did not remind him not to smoke there. Actually I had reminded him, but he said that he could not stand to be without his cigarette.

I have seen much impact of modernization in my sixty years on this earth. The modern impact is seen even in the Javenese wedding ceremony. As I explained, the traditional cosmetics have been replaced by manufactured cosmetics. And we have great changes in the beautician field. Many young girls go to school to learn to be beauticians; thus, many brides today are made up by younger persons, sometimes even younger than the bride.

That is not allowed in Javanese tradition. The beautician should be an older woman, who has lived a good and right life. Such a person brings with her valuable blessings for the bride. Another problem is that today's beauticians know nothing about the spiritual side of life, about the special prayers. They just work to make a bride look beautiful; they do not know how to prepare a bride mentally.

Some of today's brides just go to beauty parlors; consequently, they lose the glory and the greatness of the ceremony. I think it has some effects on the marriage itself. A wedding day is a special and important event in a person's life. The difficulty and the hardness of the ceremony are not without meaning. They remind the couple that marriage is not an easy business. It needs many great preparations, physical and mental.

I am sad in finding that most of the young generation look down on this traditional ceremony. Actually, we have to keep it, not only as our ancestor's inheritance, but also as a valuable gift and lesson to take care; it shows the meaning of marriage. I'm not surprised to see that many couples today break up their marriage easily. They know nothing about the value of their obligations. Increased divorce is one result of a wrong attitude toward the traditional values.

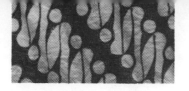

A Dukun Healer

Catholicism was first brought to Java by Dutch missionaries, and today it is a significant minority religion in Indonesia. Besides the majority of Javanese who identify themselves as Muslim, there are Catholics, Protestant Christians, Hindus, and Buddhists. Many people who follow these international religions, however, also consult the *dukun* for spiritual advice. A dukun is a Javanese folk shaman, who performs healings, sorcery, and other ceremonial acts. A survivor from Java's ancient pre-Hindu native "animist" religions, the dukun gets his or her power by using the cosmic energies of the universe. Dukuns differ from ordinary people in their ability to spiritually connect themselves with these mysterious energies.

This interview took place before, during, and after a night-long seance presided over by this dukun at his house in a village near the ancient Buddist sanctuary of Borobudur. The interview was conducted in Indonesian by Robertus Widjojo (male, age thirty-three) and Walter L. Williams. Eleven men participated in this seance, which was done for personal reasons to resolve problems or gain spiritual insight. Some of the men were Muslim, and some were Catholic; but they did not acknowledge any contradiciton between their professed religions and their participation in dukun ceremonies. Indeed, this dukun himself professes to be Catholic, and because he learned his particular healing practice from a Catholic priest he accepts it as part of his faith. There are many different types of dukun ceremonialism, and it is not clear how much of this particular practice comes from the nineteenth-century European "magnetism" technique for healing, which is the term this man uses to describe it, and to what extent it draws on Javanese customs. It probably combines both. As with the dukun who arranges weddings, this dukun's practice mixes ritual, healing, and meditation together. The notion that there is a kind of electrical (or "magnetic") energy in the universe prompts this dukun to try to plug his mind into that energy to gain psychic power. He assumes that if he can transfer that energy to others then that transference can cure physical or mental illness.

In this dukun's practice, much of the ceremony consists of him sitting in a chair meditating, while holding a stick with string attached to it. At the end of the string is a magnet, which the dukun continually twirls. There are various metal objects on the table beside his chair. Which object the magnet attracts gives the dukun a message, which he then interprets to benefit his follower. The men present at this seance believed that if they could manage to stay awake for the entire night, then their wishes would be granted.

My father worked as a mechanic in a sugar factory. He also ran a motor repair service at home. Actually what he earned was more than enough to support himself, but he had two wives and he chose to spend more money to please his second wife. He did not care about my mother and me. I did not get parental love from either my father or my mother. My childhood was full of bitterness.

As a boy, I was wild. I liked to fight and have exciting adventures. I went wherever I liked. I even used to sleep in the cemeteries. Other people were afraid to do that, saying that cemeteries are full of ghosts, but I always slept soundly, and nothing happened to me. Javanese people put some offerings in cemeteries, at crossroads, near wells and other places on certain days. The offerings consisted of rice, cooked vegetables, some kinds of cakes, some flowers, and some coins. I liked to take the cakes and coins. I was very naughty.

From the time I was small, however, I liked to read books on mysticism and religions. I wanted to know about different beliefs and religions before I made a choice. After years of study, I finally decided to become a Catholic. I had taught Catholicism in my village for years before I was baptized. It sounds strange, doesn't it? [Laughing] A Catholic teacher who lived in the neighboring village asked me to teach his class. Even though I was only fifteen, I felt that teaching about a religion was a good way to learn it. I knew more about Catholicism than anyone else in our village.

I was a good reader, even though I only finished my education through elementary school. I could not go to secondary school because I did not belong to the noble class. Besides, I did not have the money. My father certainly would not have given me any, and he died when I was seventeen. Then my mother went away, without even telling me where she was heading, leaving me completely alone.

I would have been in terrible difficulty, except that a very nice Chinese man in the town let me move in with him and work in his business. He was not married, and he and I became very close. He gave me enough money so that I could take a bookkeeping course. I was sorry I could not take the more advanced course. I had the money, but I had trouble with the language. All the books were written in Dutch. I learned Dutch, but my knowledge of the language was not good enough to read the books. So I dropped out of bookkeeping and became a barber.

I was baptized when I was eighteen years old. By this time, I felt I knew enough about Catholicism. I was determined and ready. I went to a priest and asked him to baptize me. The priest asked me what date I wanted to take the examination. He was very surprised when I told him that I was ready to take the examination that day. Of course, I was ready to be examined; I had learned the books by heart! Then the teacher who accompanied me explained everything to the priest, and he understood.

I worked as a barber, and though I was poor I got married and started having children. One day a Javanese friend of mine who was a Catholic priest asked me if I wanted to learn "magnetism." I did not know what that meant, so he explained that magnetism is a magical way of healing people. I don't know where the term came from or if this practice originally was Catholic. Some non-Catholic dukuns do it. He said that I might be able to learn how to do it for people in general, but if not I could at least heal my own family. I thought that this sounded interesting. After all, at some point in our lives we might get sick. I thought if I could cure my own wife and children, then we would not have to pay a doctor. It is a way to save money, isn't it? Because I was poor, I thought the priest was right, and I accepted his offer. However, the priest said that I had to meet one requirement: if I wanted to learn to be a dukun healer, then I had to leave all worldly things behind.

After thinking about it, I said I was ready. I left my job as a barber. A few days later, after I attended the mass on Sunday morning, I immediately went to see the priest to begin to learn magnetism. The church where the priest worked was about sixteen kilometers from my house. I pedaled there by bicycle. I always went with him whenever he had some healing work to do in other places. I spent every day there with him and did not leave to come home until ten o'clock in the evening.

The priest had many "students" then, and I belonged to the second class. There were four people in my class. My friends always brought their notebooks with them, but I did not. I just listened to the priest and noticed everything he did. We learned and practiced at the same time. Some time later one of my friends gave up. This was followed by another friend, and finally I was the only one left. It is very hard to learn magnetism. One has to have a strong brain. One has to be able to concentrate the mind and watch the movement of a pendulum for a long time. If one is not strong, brains will get dry, and this is very dangerous. Once a friend of mine who did magnetism was careless, and his mind went out. After that, he could not even add two plus two. It was years before he recovered.

After I completed the class I tried to cure one of my neighbors who was insane. I needed a few years because I was only beginning in my practice, but finally I was successful in curing her. Since then people have come to my house and asked me for help. Today I have so many visitors that sometimes I have no time to rest. They come even at night. Actually I learned magnetism only for my own family, but I have promised I would help others for no charge. Therefore, I do not ask my patients for anything. People come here with their burdens. They are in trouble. Should they pay me for my help? This healing ability is my gift, my mission on this earth, so I do not feel I should not give them additional financial burdens. They are already suffering because they are sick or have problems. I should help them without asking for pay.

Actually, when I was younger I wanted to be a priest. I never wanted to give troubles to others, but to help them. I was used to living alone, without a family. But I could not achieve my ideal of becoming a priest because I did not know that I had to go to seminary. Now I think it was best that I became a dukun healer instead. I can help people in my own way.

Once my priest friend visited my house. He acted shocked. He told me he was very surprised to see that I had left my barbershop. He got angry and asked me how I earned a living and supported my family. I said, "Don't worry. We will not die from starvation. I have given our lives to God, and I believe he will take care of us all." When the priest offered to teach me magnetism, he told me to leave any worldly things. Yet, now he got angry to know that I left my job. It sounds strange, but it is not. It turns out that this was his testing of my determination.

It is like a story about spiritual power from the wayang shadow-puppet show. In that story, Gatotkaca, a knight, got some spiritual power from his grandfather named Seto. But before he received the spiritual gift, Gatotkaca had to make some promises. One requirement was that Gatotkaca had to stay away from women for a certain period of time. After he got the spiritual power, Gatotkaca left his grandfather. Seto wanted to test his grandson, so he changed himself into a beautiful woman and tried to seduce Gatotkaca. When the grandson refused to marry this "woman," Seto was very pleased. That is what the priest was doing to me. When he saw that I remained steadfast in my determination to leave my job for the healing work, he was pleased.

This priest now works in another town, but he comes and visits us sometimes. When he comes, he brings things for us. He brings clothes for my five children. We have learned that God takes care of us. God gives enough food to the birds in the sky. Why should we be afraid of being starved? Sometimes it is hard to believe. It is human, but I do not worry. Though I am sixty years old, I am still strong and healthy and always have enough food for my family.

My Christian name is Peter. Jesus Christ examined Peter three times. God did the same thing to me several years ago. Once my wife told me she needed some money the following day. I told her that I did not have any money. Then I prayed. When night came I still did not get any money. I prayed again. I asked God if I should borrow some money, but I was not allowed. Morning came, and yet I did not get any money. I prayed again, and I asked God if I should borrow from someone. I got the same answer.

At about 10 o'clock I prayed again. I began to worry because my wife had to get the money at 12 o'clock. We only had two hours left. At 11 o'clock there was a knock at the door, and a woman came in. She had come to this small village, all the way from Jakarta, and gave me an envelope. She said that her aunt asked her to give the envelope to me. She told me that a long time before, her aunt came here and asked me to cure her son. I had long forgotten about that. The woman sent the envelope to thank me. I opened the envelope and found some money. It was the exact amount needed by my wife. On other occasions I had two other examinations. In the second examination, I got the money half an hour before the time limit, and in the third examination, I got the money only five minutes before the time limit!

After I had studied magnetism for about a year, the priest let me practice in my own house. However, I still had to show the "prescription" to him before I gave it to the patient. So, when a patient came to my house, I would concentrate my mind and pray. Then I made the diagnosis and the prescription. Then I went to the priest for consultation, telling the patient to wait in my house. After the consultation, I went home with the medicine. The prescription usually consists of leaves and seeds.

The priest told me to develop what I had learned. He also told me to look for a new teacher because my healing talents had developed beyond what he could do. He told me the teacher I had to find was not human. I read and reread the Bible, and at last I found the teacher. It was Jesus Christ himself!

Formerly I only cured sick people. Now, since I have become famous, people come here with different kinds of problems. Sometimes I refuse them. I do not want to help people who want to divorce or gamble. I do not want to help those who want to break our religious rules. At first the sick man or woman and the people who needed my help had to come here for me to cure them. Over the years, as my spiritual powers improved, I did not need the man or woman present. I only needed his or her photo. Now, I do not even need their photo. All I need is the name and address of the person. I do not give medicine any longer. I make the diagnosis and give the prescription; then they have to find the medicine for themselves. I do not have to show the prescription to the priest either.

Today, we live in a modern time. However, people still talk about black magic. You can believe it or not, but it is real. We were born free, free to do good things or free to do bad things. God did not create the sun for the good only, but for the bad as well. Magnetism can also be used for different purposes, good or bad. We can use magnetism to remove the underground natural power. So magnetism can help people, but it can also be very dangerous and destructive.

In learning to be a dukun, we are supposed to develop ourselves without the help of others. Some people want to learn magnetism from me. I never teach them. I just talk to them about common things. Those who are intelligent and sensitive understand what lies behind my words. I do not tell them to fast. We have to eat enough food to get the strength. I do not tell them to fast or avoid eating certain foods like the Muslims do. In my view, everything that comes from God is good, including food. I tell them that it is important that they learn to control their passions—especially their anger.

To my followers I emphasize that they should try not to sleep as long as other people. I think it is harder to control one's self and to have less sleep than to fast. I do not want them just to stay awake. They have to pray while they stay awake. Staying awake is useless if you do nothing. Once I tried to stay awake as long as I could. I managed to stay awake for seven months. Some time later I tried again, and this time I managed to stay awake for one year without any sleep.

An old saying from our ancestors says that we will not get good luck if we go to sleep early. We have to try to find what is behind that statement. I think it means that you accomplish nothing when you sleep. How can you get money if you just spend your time sleeping? I do not mean to say that you will get money if you stay awake. You will get nothing if you do nothing or think nothing when you stay awake. At least while you stay awake, think about what you have done and what you have achieved. Be introspective. Then you can plan what you will do and what you want to achieve. Also think how you will have it done. So, the statement given by our ancestors is logical. We have to realize that the ancestors have their own way of teaching and advising us.

Some people still go to quiet places today, looking for a good place to meditate. It is easy to concentrate our mind in quiet places. Actually we do not have to go to such places to meditate. We can do it in a busy marketplace if necessary. We have to remember that we can find God everywhere. We can meet and talk to him in any place at any time. Sometimes God seems "far" from us. I say the word "far" in quotation because actually he is not. We can find him everywhere. He is always close to us. We might feel that we are far from him and that we can stay away from him; that is, when we feel guilty and afraid.

Many people are afraid of death because they have sins. They are afraid of the hell with the great fire. The faithful, however, will smile when their time comes. They believe that, after their death, they will rise again and go to heaven to live in God's love. Death is nothing to be afraid of.

Some people keep certain weapons, like keris daggers, as their spiritual protection. Others try to have invulnerability. It is not bad to keep weapons, but we have to remember that they are just weapons. It is silly to make them the boss. We are the boss. It is even sinful to adore them. Only people who do not have self-confidence try to get invulnerability. They forget that God is always with us. They forget that God always protects and takes care of us.

Our ancestors managed to live a long time. Today our food contains chemical substances such as fertilizers, insecticide, and so on. Our ancestors used traditional medicine taken from plants. Today people go to the doctor immediately when they feel sick. The medicine the doctor gives is nothing but poison. Our factories are also cruel killers. Factories appear everywhere, especially in towns and cities. They cause air and water pollution, which endangers our lives. We cannot live at ease today. Our material desires have become our boss. We have so many problems, and we die young.

Some people say that God has determined our lives and that we should not try to change the problems we face. I do not agree. In my opinion, we were born to fight. We have to fight continually in our lives. Those who are strong will become the winners and live long, and those who are not strong will lose and die young. I do not like the words "destiny" and "fate." I prefer the phrase "God's plan." God's plan implies that we, human beings, are not passive. We also take an active part.

When people want to take an action to help themselves; they come to me. They can come here anytime they like. I will open the door for them even if they come in the middle of the night. We do not know when we might get trouble. If it is a big problem, people cannot wait for my "office hours" to come. Should I refuse my visitors, especially those who find their way to this isolated village on a long journey from other towns? I cannot. As a result, I spend most of my time helping others.

Because of this I do not have much time for my own family. However, I believe God takes good care of them. My wife and my children understand my role in life. I let my children make their own decisions. As a father, I give them advice, but they decide everything themselves. I do not tell them to learn magnetism. My oldest son seems to be interested in magnetism, but I never teach him. He just listens and notices everything I do. That is the best way to learn.

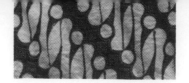

A Buddhist Temple Caretaker

Like the Hindu religion that preceded it, Buddhism spread into Java from India. For almost two thousand years both religions interacted with Javanese native animist religions to produce the distinctive elements of Javanese philosophy. However, with the spread of the militant religion of Islam, Buddhism as an organized religion practically disappeared as an indigenous form. As in India, persecution by expansionist Muslims helped wipe out Buddhist organization. After the various native kings and rulers converted to Islam, often to gain priviledged trade status with Arab traders, most common people followed suit. Those who did not conform no longer called themselves Buddhists; they merely claimed that they were following the teachings from the ancient times. The word for "ancient" in the Javanese language is *budo*. In this sense, much Buddhist thought continued to exert an influence on Javanese thought, even among those who identified themselves as Muslim. The idea of karma is especially common.

Buddhism as an organized religion in Indonesia was revived only in the nineteenth century, as Chinese immigrants brought their Mahayana form of Buddhism with them. Today the majority of Indonesians who call themselves Buddhists are of Chinese descent. In addition to the Mahayana sects, beginning in the 1930s Buddhist monks from Sri Lanka, Burma, and Thailand have traveled to Indonesia spreading the Theravada sect. Most recently, in the 1960s the Nichiren Shoshu sect spread into Indonesia from Japan. There are now officially seven sects of Buddhism in Indonesia, comprising about 2 percent of the population.

Buddhists are allowed freedom of religion under the sympathetic influence of the Indonesian nationalist philosophy of *Pancasila*. Expansionist Muslims wanted to make Islam the state religion, but

President Sukarno and other nationalist leaders instituted formal recognition of five major religions: Islam, Catholicism, Protestant Christianity, Hinduism, and Buddhism. In 1953, the first official celebration of *Waisak* (Buddha's date of birth, death, and date of enlightenment) was held at the ancient Buddhist monument at Borobudur. Thirty years later, the Buddhist organizations had gained such influence with the government that President Suharto declared Waisak Day a national holiday.

This woman, born in China in 1912, is a volunteer caretaker at one of the most active Chinese Mahayana Buddhist temples in Yogyakarta. Facts of this woman's life reveal larger trends facing the Chinese in Java. Like many other Chinese, she owned her own business and ran it successfully. But while economically prosperous, her family's life was politically perilous. In the early 1960s, People's Republic of China was actively supporting the Indonesian Communist party. The fact that many party members were Chinese meant that the anticommunist riots of 1965 inevitably took on an anti-Chinese tone. Economic resentments, religious rivalry, and political conflicts combined to make the Chinese a target for lower-class Muslim mobs. After these attacks, many Indonesian Chinese left the country or sent their children away. That was the case with this woman, half of whose children are now living abroad.

After 1965, the anticommunist Suharto government broke off diplomatic relations with China and took stern steps to prevent propaganda from being brought into the country. Any books written in Chinese characters became illegal to import. Thus, while Buddhism has not been suppressed because of its religious difference, its Chinese writings have sometimes been confiscated. Overall, though, Suharto has been rather friendly to the Chinese minority, especially wealthy business owners who have been active in promoting business/government cooperative programs for economic development.

This woman is seventy-six years old, yet she still actively works in helping to care for the temple. The first meeting with her took place after the celebration of the Chinese New Year feast and also the day following. She remains busy in her daily schedule; temple visitors often ask her for advice or assistance. She appears contented in her old age because she feels useful; through her prayers and temple activities she is doing something she believes is helpful to others. This is the Buddhist ideal of Bodhisattva. She was interviewed at a dining table in the temple, by Ratna Indriani (female, age twenty-nine), translating the Indonesian with questions by Walter L. Williams.

I was born in Kwang Tung, in China, but my family moved to Indonesia when I was eighteen years old [in 1930]. All eight of my children were born in Indonesia, and I have lived here all my adult life. Some of my children live here, and some presently live abroad. I have only been involved in helping at this Buddhist temple for the past fifteen years, after my children were long on their own. I am actually not an employee here, but only a volunteer to help out of my own free will. How I came to be involved with the temple is a long story. I used to be an atheist, a real fanatic. Neither my husband nor I believed in religion. At that time, if I looked at a prayer book or saw people praying, I just mimicked them rashly, without any reason.

My husband died when I was thirty-six years old. After that, I had to bring up my children by myself. I ran a shoe shop and was a modern woman. I just did my business and enjoyed myself. I swam, played tennis, and did other sports. At that time, it was rare for women to do all this. I did not waste my time and energy with men but focused on my business, which became quite successful. I did not want to remarry. I just wanted to take care of myself and my children. I went to the best hairdresser in the city; people always admired my hairstyle.

I followed the principle of always being in the right path, so that nobody could speak badly about me. I was not an educated woman and had only attended a common school—just enough to learn how to read and write. But I felt it important to educate my children. I sent them to Mandarin schools. When the government prohibited separate Chinese schools, I sent them to public schools even though they were not as rigorous.

When I was about fifty years old [in 1962], I had a turning point in my life. I experienced a vision. One day when I was alone in my house, my deceased brother, who had been dead for fifty years, appeared to me. He would have been ninety-five if he had still been alive. I saw clearly with my very own eyes as he knelt with his face to the earth. It was strange indeed, but I did not feel afraid at all. I saw him just like a real person. He did not move from his kneeling position at all, and I watched him for more than two hours. When he was alive he was a technocrat and was not religious. I thought maybe he wanted me to cleanse his soul from his earthly sins so that he could return to Nirvana. So I got a Buddhist Holy Book and then read the Parita from the Holy Book three times. I prayed beside him. After doing that, he vanished. I was very surprised. I felt like I had really been looking at an actual human being. I just did not feel afraid because he was my eldest brother. How can you explain an event like that with logic?

Another experience convinced me of the power of spirituality. On a visit to east Java I met a man I had never seen before. He was a dukun, a medium. I didn't believe in such things. But what was odd was that when he saw me, he called me to him and told me, "Your brother's spirit came to visit me. He had come to me because I can talk to the spirits. He told me I would see you and that I would recognize who you are. He said to say thank you to you because you lifted him to Nirvana by praying with him." I was completely shocked by his statement. Since I had seen my brother so clearly right beside me—saw him appear right out of nothingness—and prayed the words of Buddha, I became more and more convinced of the power of Buddhism.

There was another experience. Although I did not worship it, I had a statue of Kwan Yin, the Chinese Buddhist goddess of mercy, in my house at that time. I went to visit my sister-in-law who was a Buddhist. I saw her pray and read her Holy Book, so I followed her. In my heart I felt guilty because I was not actively following Buddha. My ability to read Chinese characters allowed me to read the prayers. Silently I prayed to Kwan Yin, asking her to appear in my dream. That night I had a dream of a big table, beautifully gilded in gold. The cups were made of jade and the chopsticks of ivory. There was a huge feast there, with many people around the table. The other people began to eat and drink merrily, and they all got their share. But I stayed away from the table and got nothing.

I woke up from this dream with regretful feelings, but I understood what the dream was telling me. I did not get to eat the feast because I had not accepted Buddhism. I wanted to be included in the happy feast, so from that moment I decided to try to pray to my statue of Kwan Yin. When I did this I saw another vision. This vision was Kwan Yin handing me a child. What I am telling you is the truth. I don't make up stories. With confusion I accepted the child. At that time I did not really understand what happened. After I finished praying, I went downstairs. As soon as I stepped onto the first floor, I heard one of my little grandsons cry painfully. He looked strange because his head was in a slanting position. I took the child upstairs at once. His head would not return to its normal position. I bowed three times in front of Kwan Yin and begged for her mercy. I prayed and sprayed the child three times with water, just as Kwan Yin holds a water urn to dispense her merciful gifts. The boy recovered at once. He is now sixteen years old, alive and very healthy.

I could tell you several other experiences of that sort, which cannot be explained by logic. All those have been enough to convince me. I regularly pray to the statues of the Buddha and Kwan Yin here in the temple. I do volunteer work to show my gratitude to them. Besides me, some servants work here who help to clean up and keep the fires burning. They sleep here, but I rarely do. I sleep at my own house. For the time being I live with my son's family. In three months, when my grandchildren have finished their school year, the family will move to another town in central Java. My son plans to sell the house, but I won't leave until Buddha gives me permission. When I am allowed to leave, Buddha will provide someone else to come along to take care of the temple. That is what I believe will happen. It is all planned; there are no accidents.

My experiences have proved my beliefs. What I have told you is the truth. Before I had those experiences, I was strictly an unbeliever. Had I not witnessed them with my very own eyes, I would not have believed Buddha. That is my character. Buddhism helped me get through the turmoil of the 1960s. At that time, all people in Indonesia experienced economic difficulties. That resulted in many attacks on Chinese people, which frightened us greatly. In my opinion, difficulty is common for the Chinese. I explained that to my children. Some Chinese left Indonesia, but I did not want to return to China because I thought my children would not like living there. They were used to living in comfort here. And yet, once they became grown, I let them choose their own future. Four of my children have remained here and become Indonesian citizens. They are all doing well. Two of my children decided to go to live in China, and two others live in Hong Kong.

I often receive their letters, but I don't want to visit them because I am too old to travel. They do not say anything important in their letters or anything about their choice to be in China or Hong Kong. They dare not complain because they have made their choices. If they are not happy, it is the result of their own actions. It is their karma, for which they made the cause. I don't want to listen to their complaints.

I always let my children make their own choices. I never even tried to force them to become Buddhists. They understood my experiences, but up to now they have not really been active Buddhists. Although our Buddha is generous, we do not try to influence other people to worship Buddha. We want them to come of their own free will. It is against the principles of Buddhism even to attempt to convert others to Buddhism. I myself had nobody to influence me. People make their own decisions in Buddhism. For example, three years after I accepted Buddha, I stopped swimming, playing sports, and going to the beauty salon. I do not know the reason I stopped all that because Buddhism does not prohibit those activities. It just seemed that I preferred spending my time praying. I don't know whether I am stable or not, but this is the reality for me since I have been a follower of Buddhism.

There are many Buddhas in Buddhism. When holy people achieve holiness, or enlightenment, they become Buddhas. They no longer participate in human affairs. Kwan Yin is a special case. She had almost achieved a state of holiness, but rather than become a Buddha she decided to keep her position as Bodhisattva. Bodhisattvas are persons who devote themselves to helping others. No one can become a Buddha without first becoming a Bodhisattva, but Kwan Yin gave up her chance to achieve Nirvana because of her immense compassion for the common people. That is why, when people come to the temple, they turn to Kwan Yin if they need help. She is in fact below Buddha, but she is the closest to the people. The purpose of Buddhism is to help people attain an enlightened life condition, but on their journey every Buddhist should try to help others as much as they can.

The temple is active all the time, but for young people who are busy with their job or schooling, there is a meeting on Sunday. They usually only come once a week. In this meeting, all the members take turns in presenting the sermon. They have an organization that decides which member will present the sermon on each date. Services are free for anybody to come. On Sunday mornings we have a service called the Holy Parita Ceremony, which is conducted in the Pali language.

In addition, on the first and fifteenth dates of each month we have another Parita ceremony conducted in the Mandarin language. On these occasions the *Pak Meis* usually attend. Pak Mei is an elderly woman, who has a special role and wears a yellow robe when she prays. A woman can become a priest if she wants to, but a Pak Mei is not a priest. She helps carry out the services and is closer to the congregation. For example, a Pak Mei carries out a "rice prayer," a prayer for poor people that they may receive enough rice to eat. There are many Pak Meis in this temple, more than I can count.

Old people have an important role at the temple. We have more time to pray than the young people do. The elderly usually give prayers at least twice a day, morning and evening. We always read our Holy Book regularly. By doing this, we benefit our relatives and our community, especially those who are so busy in their jobs that they do not have time to pray regularly. We elders help balance the cosmos.

The temple has a foundation to support it. The foundation takes care of setting policy. We never ask for money from people, but we have not experienced a shortage of money. I don't know how, but money just comes by itself. We open the donation box, and there we find just enough money to provide the needs of the temple. We always spend just what we need to get something started. For example, if we want to paint the temple, we only buy one gallon of paint. People ask the brand name and number, and then more paint shows up. That is also true of donations of oil to burn in the temple lamps. We often find bottles of oil left beside the altar of Kwan Yin.

In this world we are like people in the dark. When we pray to Kwan Yin, we ask for some light so that we may find happiness and an easier way of living. In one's darkness, a person cannot see things. If you are offered choices of things in life, you cannot choose if you do not use some light. You need lights to see your fortune. Just like people who want to find a lost diamond, they need a torch to clear their way. Thus, oil for the lamps comes without being asked. The same thing happens with incense. We never ask

9. Women carrying food offerings for the Waisak Buddhist ceremony at Borobudur. *Photo: Walter L. Williams*

temple visitors to pay for the incense they use for offerings. It is free. They voluntarily give money by placing it in the donation box as they leave.

In my opinion, it is totally wrong for people to come to the temple just to ask about their fortune or their future. Many people come here to ask for things such as wealth, happiness, success in their studies, business, or life. Buddha will not be happy to hear such things. We never promise or give such persons any encouragement. We just give them an opportunity to communicate with Buddha. We serve the people in serving Buddha. People can come to pray for their relatives who have died, but we do not hold funerals here at the temple. We do not want people's prayers to be disrupted by such things. The same thing applies to weddings. People will hire a special place for their wedding; that is not considered an appropriate activity to take place at a temple. One's connection to Buddha should be beyond earthly things like that. It does not matter to Buddha if you are married or not.

During my service in this temple, I have seen various kinds of people. There are always many people. I do not know them, but I recognize them. Most elderly visitors are women, but among the younger ones men predominate.

There are three kinds of religious activities in this temple. People who follow Confucianism, Taoism, and Buddhism all come here to pray, and every part of the temple is considered holy. The Taoists and Confucianists usually prefer to pray in the front porch. The altar of Kwan Yin is on the back porch, and at that place we allow no animal food because Kwan Yin is compassionate to the animals as well as to humans. All the Pak Meis here, including me, are vegetarians. Once someone said to me that if you eat animals, the spirits to whom you pray will not listen. Instead only evil spirits will pay attention. Since I became a vegetarian, I feel more healthy and patient.

I don't really know that much about the followers of Taoism and Confucianism. I believe that those who follow Taoism worship the spirits of their ancestors, while those who are Confucianists follow the teachings of the famous Chinese philosopher. The temple is just their medium of communication with their worship. We share the temple with them because they have nowhere else to meet. Society does not differentiate between us, and people always get confused and think that Buddhists, Taoists, and Confucianists are one and the same. I really do not mind because Buddhists feel that people are free to follow whatever religious activities they desire.

We cannot really separate our Chinese ethnic customs from our religious beliefs. Our services, for example, are based on the Chinese lunar calendar. We have services every full moon and every new moon. Most Buddhists in Indonesia are Chinese, so there is not much conflict. Unfortunately, we sometimes experience some problems from the government. We have complete freedom of religion, but if we ask for Chinese writings there can be difficulties. We often ask for more Buddhist books from abroad, but it is difficult to get them approved by the government censors. All imported books written in Chinese characters are suspected of being communist propaganda, even though we assure the government officials that they are religious books. Other than that, we do not experience any opposition from the government.

We cannot really separate this temple from the Chinese heritage. The walls are covered by paintings of famous Chinese legends. We have a feast to celebrate some Chinese holidays, like Chinese New Year. So when people equate Buddhism with Chinese identity, that is quite natural. Actually we are not exclusive. We want other people to see that we open our doors for anyone who needs the Buddha. We welcome the Javanese fruit and vegetable sellers from the nearby market, who often come to ask for a prophecy. If Javanese are uncertain in deciding something, even if they are Muslim or Christian, they can come and ask for help. We let them ask for anything because it is not our business to interfere. We give services to anyone.

I feel helpful to people who come to the temple and am contented with my life here. I never applied for Indonesian citizenship because it is expensive to do so. As long as there is no requirement, and I do not interfere with other people, I believe no one will harm me. I don't really care to become a citizen because I am old and have no more expectations than to live in peace. I don't mind renewing my noncitizen resident permit every month, which costs only a small amount. Yet, I don't want to leave Indonesia. This is my home. I want to die here. Even though I am not a citizen, I love this country.

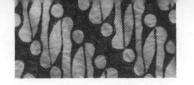

PART III

Looking toward the Future

Development, Education, and Youth

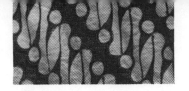

A Muslim Convert

This man, born in 1923, today lives quietly on his farm near Surakarta. One advantage for Indonesians is that landowning is more widely dispersed among the population than is true in many Third World nations. Despite the poverty of landless peasants, many of whom flee to the city in search of jobs, there is not the extreme concentration of landownership among a small elite as in Latin America, the Philippines, and other areas that inherited a colonial plantation system.

This man, a retired language teacher for the Indonesian armed forces, was interviewed in Indonesian by F. X. Andrianto (male, age thirty-three), and Walter L. Williams. He represents the moderate middle class, especially in terms of his approach to his Islamic religion. He diligently follows the daily rules of this faith and would be characterized as a *santri*, or strict Muslim, yet he has a critical perspective toward Muslim extremists. Like many nationalists, he is uneasy about the rise of Muslim fundamentalism. His opinions demonstrate that Muslims are not of one mind and that the religious factions with Islam are complex.

He has a broader perspective because of his own cross-cultural experiences. Unlike most Indonesians, who have never left their country, this man lived in the Soviet Union for three years through a development of Indonesian foreign policy of the early 1960s. Indonesian President Sukarno, one founder of the nonalignment movement among the new Third World nations, after 1960 became more anti-American. His shift had much to do with the British colony of Malaya. Sukarno favored the incorporation of Malaya into Indonesia and reacted negatively when Britain, with the support of the United States, created the separate independent nation of Malaysia. Sukarno tried to conquer Malaysia militarily and gained military support from the Soviet Union for his expansionist policy. The Russians saw Sukarno as an important potential ally, which they needed in Southeast Asia to counter American alliances with South Vietnam, Thailand, the Philippines, and Malaysia. As a result, they sent shipments of military equipment to Indonesia and took Indonesian armed forces personnel to train in Russia. This man was part of that training.

More conservative members of the military, as well as pious Muslims, did not like Sukarno's thrust in leading Indonesia into the arms of the atheistic and anticapitalist Russians. In 1965, amid general economic chaos and after some generals in the army were killed, the military used the destabilized situation to eliminate the Indonesian Communist party. Sukarno was eventually pressured to turn power to General Suharto. Not only did Suharto pursue an anticommunist policy domestically, but he also made peace with Malaysia and cancelled Indonesia's alliances with Russia and China. From that point, Indonesia became a firm American ally. This man, along with the other Indonesian personnel in Russia, was recalled. He certainly would not have gone to Russia if he were opposed to communism, but he demonstrates that major power propaganda did not always succeed. He had ended up a moderate—distrustful of both communism and Muslim fanaticism.

The current debate among nationalists, who wish to see Indonesia develop its economy along a Western model, and the fundamentalist Muslims, who oppose this model, is both social and economic. Socially, the fundamentalists are reacting against the massive changes in life-style that capitalism engenders. Just as with fundamentalist Muslims in Iran, or for that matter fundamentalist Christians in the United States, the fundamentalists in Indonesia feel threatened by all the rapid changes affecting the family, women, and children's declining respect for tradition. They lash back by trying to legislate one model of what families should be, what subservient roles women should take, and how to repress youth so that they will not be sexually or otherwise out of control. After seeing urban youth adopting Western clothing styles, dancing to Western music, and becoming more sexually open, it is all too clear to the fundamentalists that the next generation is changing in radically unfamiliar and alien ways.

Economically, the face of Westernization in Indonesia is often Chinese. Because the Chinese minority is so prominent in the business and manufacturing sector, as international trade expands, their businesses grow to truly big business proportions. The Chinese model of development, which the Indonesian government has been following in the 1980s, is for Indonesia to become a manufacturing center for world trade, like Japan and Taiwan have done. Muslim fundamentalists explicitly reject industrial development, as inevitably leading to moral corruption and the alienation of Western individualism. Fundamentalists do not clearly offer an alternative, but they have tended to favor financing the nation as the Middle Eastern countries have done: through exportation of oil and other natural resources. Because Indonesia has huge reserves of oil, timber, and other resources for trade, this is a possible alternative.

Straddled between the Pacific and the Indian Oceans, Indonesia is being pulled both culturally and economically, in two directions. Whether Indonesia will move more toward the Islamic world of the Indian Ocean, or whether it will continue to develop as a partner in the Pacific Rim, depends on explicit decisions made by the national leaders. At its base, the capitalist/fundamentalist debate is about the direction of Indonesia's future development.

Many questions remain. Will Indonesia remain a firm American ally, as it has become under Suharto, or will it attach itself more to the Middle East bloc? Will Indonesian business interests be as oppressive to their laborers as the first generation of capitalists in other countries have been, or will the government adequately protect workers before an antagonistic labor movement arises? Will the government be able to persuade more people to have fewer children by instituting rural development programs and comprehensive old-age support programs for the poor and by providing financial incentives for childless persons to adopt orphans rather than reproducing, or will the overpopulated rural areas continue to spew forth numberless peasants into the slums of the rapidly growing cities, only to fester in economic resentments against the prosperous Westernized classes? Will other religious options arise, as the spiritual emptiness of Western materialism becomes more manifest, or will the imposition of a theocratic Islamic state be the only alternative? Will the government institute courses in the schools on comparative religions, thus promoting tolerance of Indonesia's various spiritual traditions, or will Islam be a required course in all schools? Will society accept the reality of diversity, or will it degenerate into civil strife as one group attempts to impose its version of truth onto all others? These are the types of questions that face Indonesia, and indeed many nations, in the 1990s. For now, it seems that the pro-Western forces firmly control the government, but that may change as Indonesia's people confront the realities of even more rapid change in the future.

Islam derives from the Arabic word *aslam*, which means people who devote themselves completely to God. In this sense Muslims often say that being Catholic is Islam, Protestant is Islam, Judaism is Islam, and that therefore Islam existed long before those other religions. I personally do not agree with that idea because Islam was founded only after 500 C.E., long after Judaism and Christianity had become organized religions. I sometimes question the statements of dogmatic Muslims because my understanding of Islam came late in my life. As a child born into the Islamic tradition, I, of course, had learned to pray when I was very young. But my real comprehension of Islam came only in 1985, when I was almost sixty-three years old.

When I was five years old my parents sent me to an elderly Islamic teacher to learn to pray. In the Islamic school I had to pray five times a day, standard for observant Muslims. I did that every day until I graduated from high school. But to tell the truth I did it only because my parents and our Islamic tradition required it. I did not really enjoy doing it because I did not actually understand its meaning. That is why, when I moved away from my parents, I did not pray any more. I entered a secular university, and I became secular in my beliefs. I thought that science was the answer to everything. I devoted my life entirely to scientific learning until I graduated in 1959.

After finishing college I worked as a high school teacher, then as a lecturer teaching the Indonesian language. Later I entered the Indonesian armed forces and taught Arabic and Indonesian languages for them. During this time I completely forgot my five daily prayers. At that time, the government was receiving military assistance from the Soviet Union, including ships for the Indonesian navy. All the ships' manuals were written in Russian, so we needed translators. Because of my abilities in languages, I was sent to

Russia in 1963 to learn the Russian language and work as a translator. I lived in Russia for three years.

While there, my teachers also taught me Marxism, and I was almost converted to atheism. If only I had not been reminded of my happy childhood and its Islamic traditions, I might have become a communist. A lot about Russia was impressive. Everything was provided by the government: free health care, education, and support for the aged. The towns were kept very clean, in contrast to our dirty streets in Indonesia. The people there were hard working. But they did not like us foreigners, so I was not too impressed with their friendliness. Overall, it seemed to me that their lives were monotonous and not very cheerful.

I was glad to return to Indonesia in 1966. By this time, the political situation had changed a lot. All the Russian manuals and training were thrown out, and the new military materials were in English. Since that time the major foreign language in use is English. There was no longer any need for my Russian translation, so I went back to teaching Arabic and Indonesian.

I retired from the navy in 1972. Using my savings I had collected during my years in the navy, I bought a house and some land near Surakarta. I began farming and some part-time teaching, but I was not as busy as I had been earlier. Still, I did not go back to my five daily prayers. People said that I was *abangan*, a Javanese term meaning an atheist, but I did not care.[1] I would have remained abangan if a strange thing had not happened to me one day. It was a nice morning in 1985 when I was working in my farm. Suddenly I heard a voice saying, "You have to pray." I did not believe in superstitions, but anyhow I became very afraid after hearing this voice so distinctly. I thought that I was going to die and that God had given me one last chance to pray.

I went to my bedroom right away and tried to say the Islamic prayers, but I could not remember the words that I had learned as a child. I took out a book of prayers and tried to memorize the sentences line by line, but again I failed. During the night, that same strange voice came again. I woke up with a start at midnight, and I heard the voice say: "What are important are not the words you utter but what really comes from your heart." I was terrified. At once I began to pray silently. From that time on, I have done my prayers regularly, five times a day. It has really had an impact on my life. Since I have been praying regularly, I have been feeling more peaceful in my heart.

One year later the voice came to me again. This time it said, "You must fast during the fasting month, even if you can only do it for two days." I followed these instructions and was able to fast the whole month. Since then I have become a genuine Muslim: I pray every day, read the Holy Koran, fast during the fasting month every year, and try to live according to the teachings of the Prophet Mohammed. These are the basic principles of Islam.

When I talk about Islam and its development in Indonesia, I have to talk about it from the very beginning. The Prophet Mohammed was not only a religious leader but also the head of a government. The Koran not only tells how to devote oneself to God and obey his rules but also teaches how to govern a country. After the Prophet died he was replaced by his closest followers, who also became the heads of governments. Islam split into two groups: one was called Shia, and those who disagreed were called Sunni. The Shia is practiced in Iran today. They are quite fanatic and cruel because they believe that people outside their group are sinners and thus deserve to die. In Indonesia those who prevail are the Sunni.

Islam in Indonesia can be subdivided into several kinds of Sunni Muslims. The majority is the abangan, as I used to be. They are the people who claim to be Muslims but do not live according to the Koran. Traditionalists form the second group; they practice some of Mohammed's teachings but combine it with local forms of mysticism. They consider this mixture an appropriate adaptation of Islam for Indonesia, in accord with our native traditions. Fundamentalists make up the third group: they have arisen in this century. They want to purify Islam from the mystical and traditional elements. They are usually the younger Muslims who have gone to the Middle East to study Islam; in returning to their country they think that Islam in Indonesia is not really Islam, but a mixture between Islam and Hinduism, Buddhism, Animism, and mysticism. These young Muslims usually react aggressively, to the point of trying to force Indonesia to follow literally the teaching of the Koran as it is practiced both religiously and politically, in the Middle East.

Still another group, the highly educated and Westernized Muslims, feel that the fundamentalists are trying to impose a Middle Eastern cultural imperialism onto Indonesia. They are Muslim, but they favor the West over the Middle East. They always try to rationalize the teachings of the Koran and suit them to the modern way of living. In the colonial era, this group was led by those who had been educated in Dutch universities; since 1965 they have gone to American universities. They do not want Indonesia to be an Islamic state, and they are more sympathetic to the non-Muslim populations of the country—the Christian, Hindu, Buddhist, and Animist worshippers. Politically, this group of secular Muslims is called nationalists.

The abangan, who usually serve as the floating mass, do not take much active interest in these religious debates. But as far back as I can remember there has always been a conflict between the fundamentalists and the nationalists or between the fundamentalists and the traditionalists. In the 1930s, for example, there was a conflict in north Sumatra between the traditionalists and the fundamentalists, who learned Islam directly from the Arab merchants who sailed from Saudi Arabia to Sumatra. The traditionalists were supported by the Dutch, who did not like the militant Muslims. Before the rise of the secular nationalists, the Muslims always organized the anti-Dutch resistance.

A lot of people think that the revolution was a war between the nationalists and the Dutch, but in my opinion it was basically a conflict between the traditionalists and the fundamentalists. The small nationalist segment allied with the fundamentalists to defeat the Dutch, but those who did not actively support the revolution remained neutral because they feared the fundamentalists. In 1945, at the birth of the republic, there was a conflict between the fundamentalists and the nationalists over the national philosophy of *Pancasila*. The fundamentalists wanted to insert in that statement of the goals of the revolution, and in the Indonesian constitution, a declaration that Islam was the official state religion of Indonesia. The nationalists, led by Sukarno, wanted freedom of religion. They came up with the national motto of "Unity in Diversity" to promote this tolerant view of the different religions and cultures of the people.

The nationalists won, but to placate the fundamentalists they declared "Belief in God" as the first principle of Pancasila. The fundamentalists had to accept that compromise, but they continued to strive for the imposition of an Islamic state. Recently, under the influence of the revolution in Iran, some young Indonesian Muslims started to make some violent moves. They are mostly those who are dissatisfied with increasing Westernization in the social development of the country and jealous of the Chinese domination of the economy. Muslim mobs bombed some Chinese-owned banks, burned Chinese shops, and even bombed the famous Buddhist temple at Borobudur.

In my opinion, all these actions are not really Islamic. Islam never teaches people to kill or harm other people's belongings. Islam basically opposes violence. A case in point is what the Koran says about stoning. When the Prophet was alive a woman came to him and wanted to be punished for her adultery. In the Arabic tradition, a woman who committed adultery was supposed to be stoned to death. But what was Mohammed's reply? He asked her to wait until her baby was born. After the baby was born, the distraught woman came back to see Mohammed again. This time the Prophet asked her to wait until the child grew up. Don't you see— he hoped the woman would finally forget the whole thing. But years later, after the child had grown up, this woman stubbornly came to see Mohammed again. The Prophet asked the woman whether she really was willing to be stoned, and when she said that she was, Mohammed asked other people to do it. He did not want to stone her himself. In a country where the tradition of stoning people to death was commonly practiced, this shows that Mohammed actually did not agree with that tradition. He finally agreed because this woman felt that she could be freed from her sin only if she were punished. He agreed reluctantly.

I think that people who do not understand Islam thoroughly tend to oversimplify it according to their own ideas, to derive benefits for themselves. An example is the Muslim rule that men are permitted to have up to four wives. In the villages, many men take more than one wife, and they say they are doing this because it is a teaching in the Koran. However, if we read the Koran carefully we see that the rules for taking more than one wife are not easy at all. It is written that the man who wants to have more than one wife should have the permission of his previous wife or wives before marrying again. It is written that he must be able to divide his love, time, and attention equally among all his wives and children and that he should have enough wealth to support all of them adequately. Furthermore, the Koran itself states that even though it is permissable for a man to

10. Muslim women in white robes coming out of Islamic mosque after Friday prayers. *Photo: Martha Pardede*

take additional wives, it is better for him to be satisfied with only one woman.

Another issue that is often brought up, is the cruel punishment written in the Koran, such as cutting off one's hand for theft or cutting off one's head for murder. People frequently question whether this punishment really comes from God. We have to remember that the teachings in the Koran concerned not only heavenly things but also the day-to-day governing of society at that time. The fact is, at that time, the Middle Eastern people were quite barbaric. Thus Moses among the Hebrews, and the Prophet among the Arabs, had to make very harsh rules, otherwise those people would not obey. This is why I do not favor fundamentalism of any kind. I do not want to "purify" Islam to make it more Arabic. I don't especially like the Arabic society as a model for our Indonesian people.

If we have to apply those rules strictly as they were written in the Koran for the unruly Arab people over a thousand years ago, we will be barbaric ourselves. I personally think that the rules of the Koran should be adapted to our modern society today, to account for the development of human civilization. Among the advanced nations, I think only the United States and Russia still practice capital punishment. I think it is time we move beyond all those relics of the past. The basic message of religion should remain the same, but the practices should be adapted to modern life. Other Muslims might not agree with me, but that is my conviction.

The desire of the fundamentalists to make a state religion and to enforce the laws from ancient times is only a political ambition. As it failed at the beginning of the republic, so it will also fail today. These extremists certainly exist in Indonesia today, just like the Christian fundamentalists in America, but I believe their number is too small to overtake the government. The majority of Indonesian Muslims are peaceful and prefer to compromise with the non-Muslim people of the country. I do not fear that Indonesia will fall into the religious and political chaos such as that prevailing in Iran today. Iran is a good example of what happens when an intolerant religious group gets into power.

I may sound too optimistic for those who really are fearful about these fundamentalists, but why should I not be? Islam teaches me to be optimistic, kind, and nonviolent.

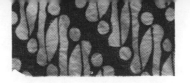

A Teacher

This seventy-year-old man is now teaching English at a secretarial school in the city of Semarang in central Java. He began as a teacher under the Dutch and continued during the Japanese occupation and the following independence. Although he was initially proud to teach in the independent public schools of the Republic of Indonesia, he has become disillusioned due to the Indonesian government's lack of support for public education. The government has decided to try to provide a basic education for larger numbers of people, rather than to focus on a more thorough education for an elite.

Faced with widespread unemployment, the government has also followed a deliberate policy of paying low salaries to civil servants in order to spread the money to more people. This policy has helped decrease unemployment, but it has led to widespread corruption; civil servants are tempted to take bribes to supplement their meager salaries. Although the government periodically conducts campaigns to attack corruption at the upper levels of the bureaucracy, it seems hopeless to reform the system without substantial increases in lower-level salaries.

In the 1980s, inflation has gradually eroded civil servant salaries even more. These low salaries have had a tremendous impact on the public education system because teachers do not have many opportunities to take bribes. Many have had to take a second job to make ends meet, and this has decreased the number of hours they can devote to their students. Many schools have gone to two sessions per day, as the overpopulated Javanese villages must accommodate larger numbers of students without any increases in their budgets. Even devoted teachers must now spread themselves so thin that many see their job as hopeless. The best students go into other career fields because teachers are so underpaid, and those who do teach often do so because they have been unable to get a better job elsewhere.

As the performance of teachers goes down, the reputation of public school teachers sinks ever lower. In contrast to the high degrees of respect offered to teachers during the Dutch colonial era, when education was a prized rarity, teachers today are given little respect. In Indonesia the problems that U.S. teachers faced in the 1980s are magnified ten times. Indonesia is an example of what happens when a government gives low priority to teacher salaries. As second-rate teachers are inadequately trained and as that training becomes more and more methodologically outdated, the quality of education falls further and further behind.

This teacher reflects the disillusionment and frustration that many educators feel in Indonesia today. Unless the Indonesian government changes its priorities to increase teachers' standards of living substantially, it is difficult to see how the country can advance educationally. Because the government claims that it has no money to do this, perhaps international development programs and First World foreign aid programs should attach higher priority to supplementing teacher salaries. Another possibility is for government to institute university scholarship programs for top students, in exchange for which the graduates would be required to teach for a certain number of years in public schools. Another idea would be for government to provide free housing for teachers and to supply servants to do the domestic chores. However improvements are made, it is the consensus of many Indonesians that their nation cannot continue to progress without substantial financial infusions into its public educational system.

This teacher was interviewed in English by F. X. Andrianto (male, age thirty-three) and Walter L. Williams, at his office at the secretarial school where he teaches.

In the the early part of this century, it was very difficult for Indonesians to go to school. Getting admitted into the Dutch school system was almost impossible for Indonesians. Fortunately, in 1920 the Liberal party came into power in the Netherlands, and they began to promote education in their colonies. My father was working for the Dutch as a civil servant, which helped me gain admission to the

Dutch elementary school and later to the Dutch teacher training school in East Java. After graduating from nine years of school, I decided to become a teacher. I really thought that being a teacher was the highest position an Indonesian could have at that time. All my teachers were Dutch, and they looked so clever, rich and respectable to me. I think that is why I wanted to be a teacher also.

It was not at all easy for an Indonesian to become a teacher. My schoolmaster was actually shocked when I said during my graduation ceremony that my intent was to become a teacher. He said to me privately that I would never be able to be a teacher as long as the Dutch were still in Indonesia. But I was lucky because the Liberal party was still in power, and they decided to accept a few Indonesians into the Teacher Training Institute. After passing the entrance test with high marks, I was admitted. There were only four Indonesians at that school. The Dutch students there treated me as a second-class citizen, but I did not care at all. I kept studying hard and competed to be better than them. I respected the teachers because they taught very well and were very strict in discipline. I had to speak Dutch all the time, and my grades in Dutch language were always very good. I think that was why my teachers liked me. They forced me to be loyal to the Dutch queen. I said I was loyal, but deep in my heart I did not respect the queen, maybe because I never met her.

I attended that Teacher Training Institute for three years, and a year after I graduated I began to teach the Dutch language. I was nineteen years old at the time. Actually, I wanted to teach in a Dutch school because the salary was much higher than the salary for teachers of Indonesians, but as an Indonesian I was not permitted to become a teacher in a Dutch school. It was not a matter of capability, but simply for racial and political reasons. Dutch students were simply unwilling to be taught by an Indonesian teacher, even though I was a graduate of the Dutch Institutes.

Everything changed when the world war broke out, since many of the Dutch men went back to the Netherlands to fight. With fewer Dutch teachers, the government began to invite the Indonesian teachers to teach in Dutch schools. But before being able to teach there the Indonesians had either to go to universities in the Netherlands or attend a higher teacher training institute in Jakarta. Those who went to the Netherlands were the children either of the sultans or from rich families. When they returned to Indonesia they usually became lawyers or politicians. As the son of a lowly Dutch civil servant, I decided that I should remain a teacher, so I decided to enter the advanced teacher training institute. I graduated from that school after two years of studying hard.

During those two years the situation changed quite drastically. A lot of the Dutch families left the East Indies, as they called Indonesia back then, in fear of a Japanese invasion. The school that had formerly taught Dutch children now was populated mostly by children of the native bureaucrats who worked in the Dutch colonial system. After graduating I became a teacher in that school. A lot of my students were the children of the Indonesian elite. I was quite happy because the students respected me and my salary was quite high. I received seventy guldens a month, which if compared to the present day [Indonesian money] Rupiah, is about Rp. 600,000. That is more than three times what public school teachers make in Indonesia today. I had married, and we could live comfortably on thirty guldens a month. We had two servants, lived in a comfortable house, and could afford to travel quite a bit during the holidays.

Looking back, I really think that those were the best years of my life. Unfortunately, this comfortable situation did not last long. The Japanese came to take Indonesia away from the Dutch. At the beginning the Indonesians welcomed the Japanese. They said that they were our Eastern brothers who would educate Indonesian people and liberate them from Western colonialism. It was true that the Japanese trained some of the young people to become good soldiers. More common people were permitted to enter schools, as Indonesian nationalists and moderate Muslims began to open Indonesian schools. But in their daily practices the Japanese turned out to be as cruel as the Dutch, or even more cruel.

For example, if the Japanese soldiers walked by on the streets, the people were not allowed to look at them. Indonesians were supposed to bow until the soldiers were out of sight. If an Indonesian dared to look directly at a Japanese, they would be severely punished. One of the cruelest punishments they did was to put people in small metal cages and keep them there day after day in the hot sun without giving them food or drink. A lot of our people died in this way. Food was very difficult to find. The best food was consumed by the Japanese soldiers, and our people ate whatever was left over. Finding a snail to eat was considered very precious, and many had to eat the branches of the banana tree.

I still taught at the same school in Jakarta during the Japanese occupation, but the Dutch language was strictly forbidden. We had to speak Indonesian or Japanese. My salary kept going down and down, but my family was luckier than most. We were still able to afford to buy rice and some vegetables, even though the rice was poor quality with a lot of gravel in it. Eating meat was only a dream for us during those years. Everyone was hungry. The Japanese era was really the hardest time in my life. Fortunately it lasted for only about three years.

Suddenly, in 1945, the Japanese surrendered, and we proclaimed our independence. The new government decreed that all schools should be run by Indonesians. There were not nearly enough teachers, of course. Most of the teachers were graduates of the Dutch Teacher Training Institute like me, but there were also some graduates who had attended the nationalists' and Muslims' schools. I was lucky enough to be appointed a school headmaster. I was now a government civil servant, working at last for my own government. Even though my salary was not as high as the one I received during the Dutch era, I was proud and happy to be the boss of our own school system.

We still taught students to speak the Dutch language, but we also added English, German, and French. In my opinion, at least as far as teaching foreign languages is concerned, that school was much superior to the present-day Indonesian high schools. Today, most students do not understand or speak any foreign language at all, even though English is still taught. Maybe the language teachers in the past were better than the younger language teachers today. A lot of my former high school students are today the leaders of Indonesia, and their foreign language skills are better than the new generation. The young people do not want to speak Dutch any more.

Ten years ago I retired from teaching in the public schools, and since then I have taught English correspondence in a secretarial school. But I actually do not enjoy teaching these young students today. They are stupid, lazy, and have no manners. Today teachers are demoralized; their monthly salary is not enough even to live on for a week!

I have six children, and all of them are married and graduates of a university. Five of them have senior positions in government offices, but the youngest is a teacher. I think my youngest son is not very wise in choosing teaching as a profession. He wants to be a teacher like his father, but he does not understand that being a teacher during the Dutch era was very much different from being a teacher now. At that time, I was quite rich and respected as a teacher, but being a teacher nowadays . . . [laughs]. If I were a young man now, I would certainly not decide to be a teacher. I would probably study management or be an engineer to get the same standard of living that I had as a teacher under the Dutch. I do not need to be a very wise man for it to become clear enough that a teacher in this present situation is no good. For most Indonesians today, they do not respect teachers or show their gratitude as they used to do. I may sound unpatriotic, but I believe this is true.

A Catholic Teacher

This fifty-seven-year-old man teaches Indonesian and French languages at a Catholic school in Yogyakarta. Sometimes Indonesians have converted to Christianity in opposition to the dominance of the Muslims. In the case of non-Muslim minority ethnic groups, they may feel better able to defend their cultural heritage from Javanese cultural imperialism as well as Islam. However, in Java, as this man points out, the acceptance of Javanese cultural elements in Catholic church services is an important means for the abangan people to react against the fundamentalist Muslim attempts to "purify" Islam of its unique Javanese elements.

Beyond those factors, the most important catalyst for the spread of Catholic and Protestant religions in Indonesia has been the emphasis on education. Christian groups tend to pay their teachers salaries significantly higher than those of teachers in the public schools, and some Christian teachers, especially European or American missionaries, are generally better at teaching their own languages. Public schools do not have foreign teachers or sources of foreign financial support. Today Catholic and Protestant schools are widely viewed as the best schools in the country. Upper middle- and upper-class families, even if not Christian, often pay to send their children to Christian schools because of this reputation; moreover, it is socially prestigious for a family to say that its children attend Christian schools. Many of these children accept the religious instruction they receive in school and become Christian when they mature.

This teacher was interviewed in English by Robertus Widjojo (male, age thirty-three) and Walter L. Williams, at the Alliance Française center in Yogyakarta, where he often goes to read French periodicals and books. He spoke of his Catholic faith, his family, and his concerns for the educational development of Indonesia's future generation.

When I was born in 1931, I was the oldest child. Later my mother had three other boys and five girls. We were all baptized as Catholics while we were babies. My father was baptized by a Dutch missionary when he was in secondary school. My mother was baptized because she married my father. He was a good Catholic, but the thing I most remember about him was his self-assurance. My father worked in a sugar factory. During the Dutch colonialism only a few Indonesians had been trained in the technical skills to work in the processing department of the sugar factory. My father was considered an expert because he was a graduate from a technical academy. He used to move from one sugar factory to another in central Java, which is where the sugar plantations were concentrated. The economic condition of our family was good under the Dutch, but it got worse during the Japanese occupation, and later during the revolution.

Although my father worked with the Dutch, his nationalism was strong. He did not let the white people intimidate him. For instance, he told his bosses: "If you have given this job to me, let me do it. It's my responsibility. I don't want anybody to interfere, including the Dutch people. I don't care if you're white or not." And my father always kept this principle. He was not afraid of his white manager; he was not a flatterer. He knew that there were only a few people who had the skills that he had. On his level, there were no other Indonesians. They were all Dutch, but my father did not feel inferior to any of them. He showed his nationalistic self-assurance, without force but always being aware that he was a role model for other Indonesians.

Still, he knew that he had to face the risk of being fired. He said it would be an honor if he were fired for standing up for himself. He used to say, "Are colored people worse than the white people?" Once there was a kind of coup in the factory. There were some workers who supported the communists. They spread anti-Dutch feeling. Then they overthrew my father since they saw him as simply the manager for the Dutch. He was opposed to colonialism, too, but he realized you have to have training. The people who overthrew my father did not have the skills to run the factory. It was a chaotic time.

About that time the Japanese came, and the Dutch people were sent into exile. The Japanese made my father director of two sugar factories because there were not enough skilled technicians. During the Japanese occupation, of course he worked with the Japanese. You see, everybody had to stay in his own post. This also happened with the people who worked in the bank. At his factory, and in the villages, my father was well respected. No one blamed him for working with the Japanese.

Then during the revolution, he was needed by the Indonesian government. I think he was put under the Department of Industry then. Meanwhile, my mother worked with the villagers, preparing food for the guerrillas. They sent the food to the rebel base-camp, which was not too far away. Since there were only a few vehicles, they had to carry the food on foot or go by horsecart.

We survived those hard years because of the close relationship between the members of the family. My youngest sister's husband says that we are too intimate. I think this comment reflects the fact that he is an outsider. When we were still living in the same house, we quarreled sometimes. That is usually true when a family lives together. Our parents played a very important role here. We are different, but at the same time we are one. We all have the same religion as Catholics, but it doesn't mean that we have to have the same opinions. So, we are like Indonesia in miniature—we are a kind of "unity in diversity."

The same Dutchman who built the sugar factory in Ganjuran, where I grew up, also built the hospital and the Catholic church there. Some people felt that Catholicism survived in Indonesia only because the Dutch supported it. However, the years since we got our independence have shown that Christianity in Ganjuran did not depend on the Dutch. Catholicism grows very well there even without colonialism. There is a village in that district whose residents today are mostly Catholics. They were not Catholics during the colonial era. So, the conclusion is that Christianity had nothing to do with colonialism. The people became Catholics because they wanted to.

The truth is that Catholicism began to grow more rapidly after the revolution than before. The prophecy of our Indonesian bishop,

Monsignor Sugiyopranoto, came true. Once this bishop had a quarrel with the Dutch manager of the sugar factory. The manager said that if the nationalists took over Indonesia, they would destroy the Catholic churches. Our bishop replied, "Just wait and see. All your Dutch buildings will be damaged, but my Church with all its institutions—the schools and the hospital—will grow quickly." And it is true! The Dutch left, and Christianity grew even faster. Their being Christians had nothing to do with Dutch economic prosperity. If the economic condition had had something to do with the religion, it would have gotten worse after the Dutch left. The church people would not have any jobs. However, this did not happen.

Another reason that Christianity grew even faster after the revolution is that, once the Dutch left, the churches started incorporating gamelan music into their services. The Muslims do not do this; so in some ways the Catholics are becoming more Javanese while the Muslims are becoming more Arabic. In my opinion, that is the biggest influence in Catholicism's spread. The people implement their Catholic creed in accordance with their Javanese vision. Nowadays we feel that our Javaneseness is accepted by the Church. Once I met a French priest who had visited in our villages. He said that we have a high Indonesian culture which we should contribute to enrich Christianity but that the Indonesian priests do not have the courage to take up this potential. Well, I said, "Father, you are talking about Javanese culture, not Indonesian culture. It is the Indonesian culture that we still have to develop. Javanese is not the same thing as Indonesian!" The priest then understood and agreed with me, but his encouragement was still important.

I think my brothers, my sisters, and I have never had the thought of changing to a different religion. I don't know why. I think it is because of the education given by our parents. We have to respect our parents. Father knew Dutch culture extremely well. He was able to use Dutch idioms when he spoke. He spoke that language as well as a native speaker does. According to him, European children do not respect their parents as well as we do; we Javanese respect and love our parents with all our hearts. We do not just pretend to respect and love them; we really do it sincerely. We have to admit, however, that Europeans are emotionally more open and closer to their children. We should take that good characteristic as well.

We think that religious matters are more important than worldly ones. We have to love others as our Heavenly Father loves us all. That is the basic teaching of our religion. As a consequence, we are devoted to our parents. For example, when my mother became seriously ill, all my brothers, my sisters, and their husbands and wives came. However, my mother told them to leave. She said [in Dutch], "Een diest is boven alles." It means duty comes first. So, my brothers and sisters left, going to Jakarta by night train. As soon as they got to Jakarta the next morning, they got the news stating that my mother had died. So, they immediately went to the station and took the morning train back to central Java.

I try to encourage the same ideas of duty and family loyalty to my two children. My boy is in the fifth grade, and the girl is in the second grade of elementary school. My wife used to teach in a kindergarten. Now the children want her to stay at home. I think an outside job makes a woman "more human." My wife is the queen of this house. I do not blame her when she does something wrong. I just say "better next time." The most important thing is that we should understand each other.

I am Catholic through and through. I went to a Catholic elementary school. Then I continued my study in seminary. Actually I wanted to be a priest, but failed, so I went instead to a Catholic senior high school for those who want to be elementary school teachers. My father suggested I should study there for two reasons. First, a teacher's job or duty is close to that of a priest. Second, since I have many younger brothers and sisters, my father wanted me to get a job as soon as possible. He allowed me to go to Gadjah Mada University, but on condition that I had to finance my own study. He let me stay and eat in the house. At the time there were no television sets. We did not go to the movies. So, we could concentrate our minds on our schoolwork. Most students stayed with their parents. It means that the parents could control their children.

Students were afraid of their teachers. Teachers often beat their students—something that we don't do now. Students tended to be afraid of the teachers rather than loving them. That does not seem to be so good, yet if you had gone to school during the Dutch colonialism, you would have gotten a better education than the present graduates. That's true for several reasons. First, we did not have so many students in each class then. As a result, the teachers could pay more attention to the students and their progress. Second, the facilities were relatively better then. Third, the teachers required us to do a lot of reading. We had to go to the library very frequently. Students do not go to the library now. Chairil Anwar, one of our greatest poets, for instance, was only a junior high school graduate, but he read books on philosophy. He read a lot of books!

Today, children are uprooted from their local societies. The educational system should be decentralized. All students are required to be taught the same material on Indonesian national history and civics. That is good for creating a sense of nationality, but it ignores the local culture. Some subjects should be left to each province to decide. The officials at the grass-roots levels know best what is needed. The curriculum should develop the "self" of the students. Teachers do not pay enough attention to their students nowadays, which is not surprising given their low salary levels. Formerly the status of teachers was very good, but today it is not. Teachers should also encourage their students to read a lot more. There need to be many changes.

For example, science education needs to be vastly upgraded. The government should also encourage scientists to do research. Research is very important for our nation's future. The government should provide the funds, and researchers should be well-paid. Scientists do not want to do much original research because there is not adequate financial backing.

Another form of education that is increasingly important is foreign language. As Indonesia takes its place in the world and more international people come here, we need more people who can communicate. Yet our schools do not do as good a job at language training as formerly. I speak fluent Javanese, Indonesian, English, and French. I also understand Dutch and German. Not many young people are multilingual like that. Today I teach Indonesian and French. It was a kind of coincidence that I learned French. You see, I studied in the Indonesian language department at the university. One of the books we had to study was in French. It was about Indonesian, but it was written in French. I decided that this must be an important language, so I took a French course. We do not have many French teachers here in Yogyakarta. I am a rarity. The time allotted for French classes is very, very limited. I encourage my students to take a French course. I feel I am successful if they take just one. My knowledge of Indonesian and French support each other. When I teach, I often use comparisons. Once, a while back, I spent my spare time working as a guide for French tourists and as a translator.

For the sake of our nation's future, we should be giving a lot more attention to education. We must also depend on our schools to teach proper values. As Indonesia modernizes and industrializes, there is a danger that we can lose our traditional values. Europeans were quite ready economically and technologically to face industrialization, but their problem is that they lost their values. They became materialistic. Americans are even more so, because they did not have much of a cultural heritage. Here in Indonesia, we need to learn from those mistakes. If we do not prepare our mental attitude, what will happen to our country and our people in the future? We might end up being even more materialistic than the Americans!

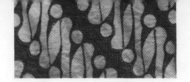

A Homosexual Principal

When the Europeans colonized the Third World, sixteenth- to twentieth-century documents reveal that homophobia (hatred of homosexuals) was part of the cultural imperialism that they imposed on the indigenous cultures. Ironically, because of antihomosexual prejudice in Europe, many homosexually inclined men gravitated toward the colonies as a means of escaping discovery at home. Some of them established same-sex relationships with Asians in native societies that were more tolerant of homosexuality. Perhaps research in the records of Christian missionary groups and colonial government archives will yield more information on this subject, but probably the most valuable source is the personal narrative of homosexuals.

Indonesia shares with other Southeast Asian nations a heritage of accepting homosexual behavior in many of its traditional cultures. The best known examples are among the Bugis of Sulawesi, the Dayak of Kalimantan, and in the Ponorogo area of east Java. In Javanese popular culture, there is often a relaxed acceptance of homosexuals and gender nonconformity. For example, one popular entertainment is *ludruk*, a form of theatre in which female roles are traditionally played by transvestite males. The actors in these troupes are often homosexual and serve as sexual partners for married men. With traditions like this, it is not surprising that transvestite homosexuals are well known in modern Indonesia. The term for such individuals is *banci*, similar in meaning to the "drag queen" of America and Europe. Bancis often make their living by either prostitution or employment in beauty salons and the fashion industry. They commonly organize fashion shows, sometimes with government sponsorship, that are attended by the general population.

Non-cross-dressing gay men in Indonesia are a separate group, distinct from banci. Gays are most noted as models, dancers, tour guides, hair stylists, and fashion designers, but they are also active in other types of jobs. An open gay scene exists in all Indonesian cities, but many homosexuals remain secretive. Lesbians are quite secretive, even from gay men. Those in hiding mainly fear that their families will discover their inclinations, though many others do not make much effort to restrict their social life. Employment discrimination against homosexual or violence against them is rare. Government policy is generally nondiscriminatory; it is an open secret that some top ministers in the government are gay. Indonesian values—social harmony, peacefulness, and the national motto "unity in diversity"—seem to protect gays from mistreatment more completely than Western notions of individual rights.

As a result of the lack of discrimination, there has not been much in the way of a Western-style politicized gay and lesbian liberation movement; thus, a separate gay community has not developed its own institutions to care for its members. Yet, even though the general society is tolerant, some families are not. Some young people, especially those from Christian or fundamentalist Muslim families, are even thrown out by their families when their homosexuality is discovered. They often have nowhere to go, unless they can find an older sympathetic homosexual to help them.

The man interviewed here is a good example of this phenomenon. He was born in central Java in 1914, of Chinese descent, and has been aware of his erotic attractions toward men since he was twelve years old. When he was a teacher and later the principal of a school, he carefully hid his homosexuality. In 1965, during the anticommunist purges, he was accused of being a communist and fired from his job. Although his dismissal had nothing to do with his homosexuality, after that he has taken a more relaxed and open life-style. Today he makes no attempt to hide from his neighbors or friends. He identifies himself by the English term "gay."

His experiences reveal the crushing impact that Dutch homophobia has had on Indonesians, yet his story also reflects the strength of character that many gay men and lesbians build in the process of finding their own self-respect as unique individuals. His relaxed outlook on life provides an important role model for younger gay people. He is "successfully aging," as gerontologists define that term, by developing a strong sense of family responsibility toward younger gay males. By helping others he feels a strong sense of purpose in his life. The self-respect that results leads to his happiness with his life.

Walter L. Williams interviewed this man in English at the man's spotlessly clean and comfortable house, where his large collection of books and artworks adorn the walls. He lives quietly on a typical middle-class residential street in the city of Magelang in central Java, along with four young gay men for whom he is currently caring. They eat their meals together, as a family. The boys often have their friends over for visits, and the house is alive with the conversations and laughter of a number of adolescents and young men. A second visit coincided with the birthday of one young man, and the house was covered with brightly colored decorations.

Two months later, on a subsequent visit for the principal's seventy-third birthday party, the house was packed with many people—his former coteachers and students plus about forty gay men. He had helped many of these men, who now came back to honor him, in the past. In private conversations, several of these young men who had formerly lived there expressed gratitude for the generosity and love he showed them. In his role as a mentor to the young men and in the genuine feeling of family he has created within these intergenerational relationships, this older gay man has performed a socially useful act in caring for homeless youth.

The struggle to overcome homophobia, if successful, often brings with it the gift of self-respect. It took the tragedy of unjustly losing his job for this man to realize that self-respect is more important than outside approval. Yet by going his own route in life, he has created intense feelings of respect from the youths he has helped. In his old age he has learned that by benefiting others he has also benefited himself.

My family originally came from China, but has been in Indonesia for eight generations. I feel more Javanese than Chinese in my background and personality. Though my father was educated in a Chinese school, he saw that Dutch education would be of more advantage to his children because the Dutch were the ones in power in Indonesia. So he sent me and my brothers and sisters to Dutch schools. My grandmother was a Catholic, a very severe woman. She demanded of my parents that we children become

Catholic, and so I was baptized as a Christian. I was a very good Catholic.

In recent decades, however, I do not feel at home with the Catholics any more. There are so many changes in the church, which I could never accept. In addition, the priests today are Indonesian, and I do not think that they are as good as the Dutch priests used to be.

I do not recall the Catholics ever mentioning homosexuality. They were very repressed about anything sexual. Yet, when I was twelve years old I realized that I was sexually attracted to boys. One day a friend of mine, he was a Chinese man about twenty years old, opened his trousers and let me enjoy myself. I felt this was very nice. He appreciated it, and it was enjoyable for me, so I visited him often.

One of my uncles, who was divorced from his wife, was attractive to me. I would visit him and cautiously began to touch his body. When he did not object I got bolder; though I was only fourteen, I was quite assertive. But later, he tried to have anal intercourse, and I did not like that, so I stopped visiting him. I wanted to be the active one.

Shortly after then, I became a lover to a classmate of mine at my school. We were both Chinese boys of the same age and shared a special friendship. We used to go to the seashore to watch the sunrise together. It was romantic in all the ways you can imagine. He touched me, and I loved his physical presence so much that I could get so excited just from his touch. We became lovers and were very happy together when we were fourteen and fifteen years old. I have photographs of us in our happy times together. But then one day, after we had been together for over a year, we were swimming, and he dove into a pool. He hit his head, and it killed him immediately. It was a terrible shock. I went into a severe depression after that. Even after all these years, I still remember his kisses. So gentle and nice. . . . He was a great one for kissing.

Later, after I finished high school, I went to Jakarta to attend a teacher's college. I had always wanted to be a teacher. Though I was aware of my sexual attractions to males, I was very much afraid of scandal. At the student dormitory, four of us would sleep together in the same bed, so it was very difficult. We could only kiss in bed secretly.

The Dutch were extremely hostile to homosexuality, and in 1933–1934 there was a big controversy when a high Dutch colonial official was kicked out of job because he was gay. Several other men, both Dutch and Indonesians, were implicated. It was in all the newspapers. That had a big impact on making me afraid to do anything sexual with another man, and so I went into a long period when I hardly did anything sexual.

Antihomosexual feelings in Indonesia today are a result of the influence of the Dutch and also the Arabs. Unfortunately, the Arabs have had a big influence here due to the impact of Islam. There are many Islamic men who will go to bed with you. It is so easy to get them to do it. I had a gay nephew who has since died, but he had a preference for Arab males. He claimed that 90 percent of them were sexually available. Yet, even though they are engaging in homosexual behavior, they say that it is wrong and that Islam forbids it. They are hypocrites, pure and simple.

What I have found in my life, and that of other gays I have talked with, is that it is much more difficult to get a Chinese boy to engage in sex but pretty easy to get an Arab or an Islamic Javanese to do it.

I graduated from college in 1935, excelling in both academics and sports. As a young man I wanted to show people that I was more masculine, so they would not suspect that I was gay. So I did all the athletics. I put so much effort into it, and I became a star in basketball, swimming, tennis—oh, so many fields. I enjoyed these activities very much, but I was also motivated for appearances' sake.

My chief motivation was to gain community respect. I did not want wealth or power, but I did want the respect of people. I was able to accomplish this goal, first as a teacher and later as I became the most well-known headmaster in my city. In this circumstance, I was extremely concerned about the community finding out I was gay. If it had been known, I would have lost their respect and maybe my job. Losing the job would have been the least of it, but the respect of the community was very important to me.

I did eventually lose my job, but it had nothing to do with homosexuality. In the mid-1960s there was much turmoil in Indonesia, and many people were accused of communism and lost their jobs. I was one of those. I knew I was not a communist, yet I was still thrown out, despite my years of dedicated service. This had a big impact on making me realize that respect had to come primarily from myself rather than just from others. I gained the gift of self-respect, by which I was able to survive that difficult time.

Another thing that helped me become more self-respecting was the influence of my nephew, who was openly gay to our whole family. He was a very nice person, and all our relatives liked him. The family was not ashamed of him. That is because our family is not so strictly Chinese in their attitudes. The more strictly Chinese a family is in outlook, the more condemnatory they are likely to be if a family member is gay. They always expect sons to get married and have children. Luckily, my family did not put that kind of pressure on me or on my nephew. I always said that I was married to my career, and they accepted that.

In recent decades, what I have observed is that both my family and my former students continued to respect me. In the 1970s a group of my former students got together and attempted to give me an automobile as a present. I told them that I did not need an automobile, that it would only be a nusiance and an added expense for me to maintain. So I thankfully declined their gift. Then they asked me what I did want. I thought about it and decided that what I really wanted to do was to travel abroad. I had spent years reading books about other lands, but I had never left Indonesia. So they raised the money to buy me a trip to Europe. It was a great experience for me, even though I got homesick after two months abroad and returned home early. Now I can truly say that I have done the things I have wanted to do in my life. Now I am content to stay at home, with my friends and my books, and enjoy my retirement years.

It has really only been since my retirement that I have taken a more relaxed approach to life and decided that people must accept me as I am. I do not advertize my preferences, but I take no pains to hide or cover up my feelings. I have had many young men living with me and visiting here, and I have no hesitation about them being seen coming and going to my house. I will even give them a kiss in the yard and do not feel tense about showing my feelings. I feel much more accepting of myself than I used to be.

When I was a headmaster and had been able to buy a seven-bedroom house, I took in boarders to help pay the bills. They were high school students whose parents entrusted them to my care so they could live close to the school. I liked having them around, but I did not dare to do anything sexual with them. Then about fifteen years ago I became close to a young man in his early twenties. He worked in a beauty salon, shampooing hair. That is a common occupation for gays here. He wanted to go to school, but he had to spend all his money to pay rent for his boarding house, so he had none left over for tuition. I liked him very much, so I told him, "Why don't you stay with me, and I will not charge you rent. That way you can work less hours, and can afford to pay for a school." He moved in, and I taught him to speak good English so he could get a good job. Later, I helped him get a job at a hotel, working for a former boarder of mine who is gay. Today he is still working there and is doing very well in his career.

After he left, I met another good-looking boy. We just started talking one day at the post office, and he asked if he could come visit me. We had sex sometimes and got along well and later he moved into my house. Then another one moved in as well. I felt a need to help these gay boys, so I let them live here for free. Eventually, the nongay paying boarders started asking prying questions, so I decided to have only homos living here. I really did not need the rental money anyway since my house is paid for and I have a teacher's pension.

After a while I became worried that I was only helping them in an immediate way, providing free room and board, so I decided to start pay for their schooling as well. That has been difficult sometimes to collect that much money, but it has been worth it. I have supported twelve boys in all. The youngest was fifteen years old when he came here, and the oldest was twenty-six when he moved out. There were a couple of bad ones, who did some stealing but 80 percent of them turned out well. My best successes have been with those I sent to hairdressing school; all of them have good jobs today.

I was educated by the Dutch, so I am very strict with rules for them. Each one is responsible for some household chore, which I assign and expect them to do. They cannot go out after 9:00 p.m. so they will be forced to stay home where they can do their studies or reading. I do allow them to have their friends come here as visitors, however, and sometimes I rent videotapes that we watch on the tv.

They have usually had some problem in their family background, so many of them are wild and undisciplined. I set firm rules for their benefit in learning. If they break a rule, I scold them and tell them I am very disappointed after all I've done for them. They know they can leave any time they want to if they don't like it, but the discipline is good for them. Those who are older now, and off on their own, tell me that they recognize the rules were for their benefit. I make sure they say that to the young ones here.

Some of them have very sad stories in their backgrounds. One Chinese boy named Chang lived with his mother after his father had been killed in an accident at this job. Neighbors told him that he had been adopted as a baby, and he asked his mother if this were true. She would not tell him. Later, she confronted him about stories she had heard that he was having sex with other boys. Hoping to get his mother to tell him if he were adopted, Chang told her that he would tell her the truth if she would tell him the real story about his background. She told him that he was adopted, that his biological parents had died, but that he had a brother who had been adopted by another family. Fulfilling his promise, he told the truth about his sexual affairs. She reacted very badly and told him he must leave immediately. So, at age eighteen, he was kicked out of home with nowhere to go.

Another gay boy brought him to me, and Chang asked if he could stay here. He wanted to go to hairdressing school. I said ok, I would do it, so I got him admitted to the best hairdressing school in the city. It was directed by a former student of mine, and he gave me a big discount, but it was still expensive. However, Chang was a good student, diligent in his work, and so sweet to me.

Later, he wanted to visit his adopted mother again. I encouraged him to do it, to try to make up with her. But when he went there she was cool toward him. She would not even tell him how to locate his real brother. He did not try to go back to her after that, and he decided that his real home was with me.

Now Chang is twenty-five years old, and he has a good job in one of Jakarta's leading salons. He calls me regularly from Jakarta, even though the long-distance rates are expensive, and he visits me regularly. He always brings me a present on my birthday. He calls me Daddy. I don't insist on that, but that is what he and the other boys want to call me. He and the others cut my hair, do little things for me, give me stylish clothes, and bring me gifts. Last year he and I went on a vacation to Bali together, and as I getting ready to return home he gave a large sum of money. I said, "What is this for?" But he just smiled and told me it was for me.

For all these past years Chang has wanted to find his brother. After much effort, he located the boarding house where his brother was staying. When he got there, however, the landlord sadly told him that the young man had recently committed suicide. The landlord gave Chang his brother's belongings, and when he looked through them he found photographs of the boy. From these photographs Chang discovered that this boy was one of his close friends and a sexual partner when he had been a teenager, but neither one of them knew they were really brothers.

Tono is another one, who is still living here now. He is sixteen years old and was brought here by a gay friend of mine. All the gays in the city know about my home, and if they find a homeless gay they send him to me. I never look for these boys; they always come to me. This boy was found wandering on the city square, dressed in rags. They fed him and found out that he had been kicked out of home by his stepfather.

Tono moved in here, but later he stole Rp. 10,000 from my bedside table. He used the money to rent videotapes for the boys to watch when I was gone. I cannot tolerate a thief, so I got mad and ordered him to leave. He left, but I found out that he was suffering with no good place to live. His father had died, and the mother remarried. The stepfather was cruel and did not give money for her children. Tono was very ashamed of his stealing, so I let him come back after his mother begged me to let him come back. The mother badly wants to leave but has no money for a divorce, so she is forced to continue living with that beast of a man. The other kids went to a foster home, but Tono wanted to come back to me. So she begged me, and I let him. I realized that I acted too rashly because since he came back he has been great. Now I am sending him to hairdressing school.

Another young man who is living here now comes from a very wealthy Javanese family. They were sending him to law school. But when they found out he was gay, they stopped sending him any money and would not even answer his letters. He had to drop out of law school. He had known me formerly, as friend to one of the boys here, so he came to me and asked me to live here. Unfortunately I cannot afford the high costs of law school, so he has now gotten a job. Regrettably, it is not the best job to match his intelligence.

I provide these boys a free place to stay; I pay for their food and give them a little spending money sometimes. I wish I were rich so I could do more. If I have trouble with my finances, I pray to God, and I always manage to get some money from the most unexpected places. I pray to the Chinese Buddhist goddess Kwan Yen to be my intermediate god. Former students will drop by sometimes and give me money. I never have to ask them for money, but they send it because they know I try to help others. These younger homeless boys cannot, of course, yet afford much, but they will give me gifts of clothes for the boys and whatever they can afford. I want to try to build among them a sense of responsibility toward the younger ones coming along so they can help others as they themselves were helped. I hope that some of them will continue this tradition after I am gone.

I try to imprint into my boys that there is no wrong in being gay, if they are living right and helping other people. What they do in their love lives is their own business. I always tell these youngsters that living as a gay is very hard because many people in the community do not approve of them. If living as a gay is hard, I tell them, it gets harder if you are gay and poor. So I advise them to study and work hard so as to get a good job and to be very careful with money so they can afford to live well. And then later, when they are mature, if they want a boy they can afford to help him financially also.

I always advise them not to be afraid to help people, to help those in need, otherwise they will become very lonely men. Alone with their money. I know some gays who have much money and much more beautiful houses than I can afford, but it is not a home because they are there alone. They try to buy love, and I don't want to do that. They may throw expensive jewelry and clothes at their current sexual interest; but they are not really helping this person, and they are not helping themselves. Those who don't help people always end up worried that they will be alone. I have seen this occur often in the decades I have been observing gay men.

We gays do not automatically have a family to fall back on, so we have to work hard to create our own sense of family. Helping others, especially the young, gives a reward later on—when, I never know, but I am sure there will be. I have my reward already, and the major reward for me is that I like my life and I like my home. I read my books, watch tv with the boys, advise them with their problems. My boys and my friends and my books are my companions. I don't mind being by myself when they go out, and I don't mind getting old.

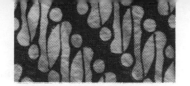

A Matron of a Christian Orphanage

If a Javanese family has too many children, or the parents die, traditionally some of their relatives adopt the children. In an agrarian
society that prized children for their economic contributions as farm
workers and supporters of the parents in their old age, there was
seldom such thing as an unwanted child. With overpopulation and
migration to the cities, that attitude has now changed. The Indonesian government and Islamic and Christian religious groups have
responded by creating orphanages for the increasing numbers of
homeless children. In the 1970s, Indonesian social workers were
negotiating arrangements through the United Nations to have some
of these homeless children adopted by wealthy Western families, but
in the 1980s the government rejected this program. Government
leaders felt it was insulting for Indonesia to unload its children to
other nations.

The result has been an ever-growing number of children packed
into overcrowded orphanges. Many of these children are not actually
homeless, but their poverty-stricken parents cannot afford to feed
them. They send a child to an orphanage, where the child will be
fed, until such time as they can afford to feed the child at home.
Others of the children are illegitimate. Due to the tenets of Islam, it
is socially unacceptable for a woman to have a child before marriage.
Although birth control is widely available, abortion is not; therefore,
the choice for an unmarried young woman who gets pregnant is
either to get married, to give the baby to a relative, or to send it to an
orphanage.

This woman is fifty-one years old. She and her husband live at
the Protestant orphanage in the central Java town of Purwodadi,
where she was interviewed by Ratna Indriani (female, age twenty-
nine). Like the other persons in this collection who demonstrate a

heightened life condition, this woman gives meaning to her life by caring for others—creating a sense of family among the orphan boys for whom she cares.

I am a teacher and the mother of three children. My eldest child is now also a teacher, and the other two are university students. I work as a teacher at the neighborhood public elementary school. My husband directs a boy's orphanage that is operated by a Protestant Christian foundation; I am his assistant. Being the matron of this orphanage is my side job, even though it is a full-time responsibility. We have been living here at the orphanage since 1982, but actually we have been taking care of the orphan children much much longer. Just after the 1965 coup, when the orphanage was handed over to us, it was in another very rundown building. There were many children there, and my husband and I had to do much work just to keep everything going. My own children were still small, but I was fortunate that some male high school students agreed to watch over my kids in the evenings while we were at the orphanage.

Children at that time were different from today. They were easier to handle because problems were not as complicated as nowadays. That is how I was able to handle them, even though more children were packed into the orphanage. Today, at least, there are other orphanages in this area. At this orphanage, we only take boys above age six. It only makes trouble if you try to mix boys and girls. Besides, there is more need for orphanages to keep boys because girls can be more useful helping their mother at the market. As far as age, they have to be old enough to look after themselves, in going to the bathroom, for example.

We usually are able to limit the number of children we agree to admit, based on our capacity. Sometimes we have to take in more children than we should, during the time of scarcity before the harvest season. Many children are delivered to us by their own parents because, for farmers without many resources, it is a very hard time before their crops mature. When the harvest begins, the children go back to help the family gather the crops. After that, the number of children staying here returns to normal. In recent years, we have usually had about fifty boys.

We give different kinds of help to different children, depending on their situation. We have only four boys who are without mother, father and other relatives to take them. For those, and for those where the mother has died or abandoned the family, the child lives here and receives free food and lodging from the foundation. Single fathers cannot really care for a family, unless they have a daughter old enough to take on the motherly role for the younger brothers and sisters. In the case of a father dying or leaving the family, we usually try to have them stay at home with the mother. In Indonesia it is always a problem for a woman to rear a son without male help, so she usually remarries and takes her children with her. Those families without a father need more financial help than otherwise. Until she remarries we help the mother by providing rice and clothing for the children and paying their school fees. They come here once a month to collect their rice. We do the same thing for very poor families, even if both parents are present.

For some other poor families, who have a few more resources, we pay only the fees for the child's school. They do not need to come here because we pay their school fees directly to the school. We expect those parents to keep their children and pay for the child's textbooks, food, and clothing. In addition to all this, we give another type of aid to families involved in running a small business. If they experience a temporary economic problem, we loan them capital; of course, we cannot help much, but we do what we can. We only choose those whom we predict will be able to repay it later. If there are serious problems with the business, we cannot provide funds. Because we do not charge interest, we cannot risk losing our loan money. This program has worked well, and those we have chosen have always returned the money to us.

The foundation does not have a standard amount of money to give because we always base our aid on their necessities. We do not discriminate on the basis of religion in choosing which people are most in need, whether they are Christians or Muslims or whatever. The foundation usually trusts my husband and me to decide which persons we will help. Most children are Javanese, but sometimes we take in children from other islands. Several years ago, after a terrible explosion of a volcano on Bali, we took in a number of orphaned Balinese Hindu children. One of them is now working in a big hospital in Semarang. He often visits us here. We are like his family because all his relatives were killed by the volcano.

The source of the foundation's money is varied. We get private donations from Christians who live in Semarang, and also the government provides us with a monthly subsidy. We raise our other income through two sources: we rent out rooms to rural students who come into town to attend high school, and we operate a cafeteria that is open to the public. The cafeteria is quite popular in town, and it provides some spending money to the boys who stay here. We hire adult cooks, but the boys help run the cafeteria—washing the dishes, sweeping the floor, wiping the tables, and serving. Everybody is involved. We make a profit, which then goes into the general operating budget of the foundation. On holidays the cafeteria is extra busy, and we give the kids extra money for this work so that they can enjoy themselves.

Our biggest problem in running the orphanage is always money. Now, for example, is a hard time for us. According to regulation, each child needs to have his school fee paid in advance. Those who have to take the entrance exams must pay all expenses before they are accepted into classes. We get a regular monthly subsidy from the government, so there is no extra money allotted at the beginning of the school term to pay for additional expense like that. At least for the Christian schools, we can get the administrators to postpone the fees for our kids until we have enough money to pay. During these past few years, we have managed to get by each time. Thank God!

The foundation does not seek out orphans. We have more people trying to get us to take their children than we have space. We usually only accept children who come with papers of recommendation from a church. We need assurances that they truly are destitute because there are so few honest people nowadays. When we have depended on a recommendation from a governmental official it has often turned out to be false; the official was given a bribe by a family that just wants free lodging for its children. We have to take precautions about this.

Unfortunately, none of our genuinely homeless kids has ever been adopted. Once there was a childless couple who came to us looking for a boy to adopt. That is not too common because childless couples usually adopt one of their relatives' children. In this case, though, everything was arranged for the adoption. But at the last moment the boy refused to leave the orphanage. He cried and would not leave his room. He preferred living here to living with a family he had never known before. Of course, I could not force him to leave. Finally, he ended up staying with us. Those boys who have parents usually leave the orphanage whenever the parents feel that they can afford to keep them at home or when the single parent remarries. When the economic situation improves at home, they usually wish to have their children come home, but sometimes there are problems between the new stepparent and the children.

On holidays, we allow the children to go home if they wish. In the case of those boys who have neither parent, they go visit their grandparents, uncles, aunts, or cousins. There once was a boy whose parents had died, and he was brought here when he was four years old. After two years some people came here and claimed him as their nephew. They wanted to take him home with them, but he refused. Later, when he had grown bigger, he even refused to visit them. I gave him money for transportation, but I learned from the other boys that he had not really gone there.

Some others, like that boy, seem seem reluctant to go home, but I encourage them to leave because I think they need a change of atmosphere. I am a devoted mother, but I know I cannot share my love among so many children. I hope they realize that I love them, but my love cannot represent the love of a real mother. Still, some of them refuse to go; I don't exactly know why. I often ask them why they do not feel homesick or why they don't long for their family. Often my questions are left unanswered. Maybe they are not happy at home. Maybe their mother has remarried, and they do not get along with their stepfather. Maybe their room here is nicer than their house in the village. Who knows?

Every year we give the children three uniforms for school, plus one boy scout uniform. For their daily casual clothing, people often donate secondhand clothes. Unfortunately, most clothing donations are adult sizes, and we don't know what to do with these. For Christmas celebration, the foundation usually gives special clothes as a present. We encourage the family to give presents to the children as well, even if it is only a little bit. Sometimes they give a used bicycle, or extra clothes, or special homemade foods. I don't think the other boys feel jealous over this because we encourage them to share their happiness together. It is important for the family to keep in touch with the child. The parents do not pay us for rearing the child, and if they give us money we put it in a special account to use later for that child.

We give the children different amounts of pocket money. The small children get a little extra if they have done something useful. The older boys get more money because they are expected to do more. The small ones are not jealous because they realize that they will get more as they get older. We devise the living arrangements in the rooms in such a way that children will mix with different ages. This is important for the little ones. In this way, older children can help. The big boys help in taking care of the small ones in their residential group. They need to learn responsibility and must realize that my husband and I are busy people and cannot do everything ourselves.

We change these residential groups once a year so that each boy can get used to a variety of people. Older boys are more difficult to rearrange because they usually form their own gangs. They share their secret jokes and discussions. However, we encourage the multiage residential groups to do things together. For example, every residential group raises its own coop of chickens. The money they get from selling their chickens goes into a fund, and the group decides what they want to buy with it. For example, they might decide to buy a radio for their room—something they can enjoy together.

We prefer, though, that they develop their own musical skills rather than just listening to the radio. We recently bought a set of gamelan instruments, which they play in turn. They enjoy this and often play until late at night. I have to warn them not to play too loudly because of our neighbors. Usually my warning is enough.

Because this is a Christian boy's home, we usually have some sort of spiritual meeting every evening. My husband and I used to lead these meetings ourselves, but now we let the older boys lead them. I always try to attend at least twice a week. On Sundays they go to a Sunday school nearby, and the big ones attend church services. For those older than age sixteen, Christian teachings classes are held with the older girls from the Christian Girls Orphanage. Those who go to the Christian classes are usually from Christian families and baptized as babies. These classes prepare those who are going to confess their faith.

We never punish the boys physically by beating them. My husband and I agree that he disciplines the older boys and I deal with the small ones. The older ones are more difficult to control. They sometimes break the rules by staying up at night or sleeping late. My husband usually takes care of it by privately talking to the boy he considers the leader; he takes a walk with him or goes to restaurant where they can talk alone. Talking in a friendly atmosphere somewhere else is one of his successful methods. The boy is not hurt by this advice.

My husband used dialogue as his technique, but I am a little bit different. Some of the younger boys are really naughty, but I never find it difficult to solve the problem. Once we had a boy who kept stealing his friend's food. We always serve the food in one big bowl and plate to a residential group, and this boy often took someone's share besides his own. After observing for some time, finally we knew who the thief was. I called him into my room and warned him. But he kept stealing food. Finally I lost my patience. I told him that he had lost the right to share his meals with his group and would have to eat by himself in the kitchen. I told him I would order the cook for one week not to give him anything to eat except vegetable soup. At first he was very angry and refused to eat anything. Later, another boy told me that he went into the kitchen by himself and ate his vegetable soup. It was a good sign that he was ashamed and accepted his punishment. After that time, he was a good-natured boy and never gave us any more trouble.

We rarely have to deal with any serious issue like crime. Once we had a boy who kept stealing money. We talked with him and warned him not to repeat this crime, but he still did it. After this, I discussed it with the foundation's board and consulted the reverend at the church. Finally, we decided to send him home. It was a bitter decision, but we felt there were so many other boys who needed our attention. If we let this boy stay, instead of admitting another boy, he might influence the others. We would not risk that. His family took him, and I have never seen him since then. We had to send a few other children home, but not many.

We have never experienced a really serious problem, like murder or drug abuse, though one boy got drunk. He returned to the orphanage late one night, and his friends informed that he was delirious. They found an empty bottle of cheap alcohol beside his bed. We took him to the hospital, where he was very rude to the doctors and nurses. He spoke in low Javanese to them, as if we had never taught him how to behave like a real Javanese. We were quite ashamed to have such a boy in our orphange. The next day, after he had recovered, he did not seem regretful. Since we saw no repentance in his attitude, we called his relatives. When his father came to take the boy home, he was very ashamed to have such a son. I never saw that boy after that. I think we have been fortunate that most of our boys have been nice children.

We try hard to give the children a proper education. We encourage some of them to learn vocational training and others to go to the normal high school if they want to become nurses, soldiers, or clergymen. We also allow the most intelligent boys to continue their study in the university, especially if they show good manners and high dedication to their studies. Those who are not too bright we encourage to try again and again; we tell them that their hard efforts will eventually be rewarded. Those who do this always become serious students. Most of our boys, I am proud to say, complete their field of study and have important jobs in society. Those who succeed in obtaining good jobs often offer their "brothers" here a job at their work place if there is an opportunity.

Some fail in their studies. We try our best to locate jobs for them somewhere. One boy could not do his studies because he had a cataract in his eye, but he refused to be operated on. We tried to get him a job as a janitor in my school, yet he could not even do that well because his eyesight got worse. Finally, he had the operation and then got a good job. Later, I learned that he returned to his village and was married. I am happy when I hear that our children are successful and happy.

Working in this orphanage, I witness many touching incidents. Many children develop self-conscious feelings about being orphans. One of our boys who had succeeded in winning a prestigious scholarship to a university in Semarang was ashamed to tell his friends he had been raised in an orphanage. There is a kind of shamefulness in this because having relatives is so highly valued by Javanese. This boy would sneak out of his university boarding house to come back and visit us. I feel great pity for him, but I know that I cannot fight against fate.

I always treat the children like my own. My love is limited, but I am touched by their love. We often have reunions. The boys come, sometimes with their own families now that they are married, and we have a wonderful time together. There is a time for happiness, and there is a time for sadness. It is hard when one boy is ill and we have to sit beside his bed all night long worrying about him. To do this job one needs courage, patience, and a willingness to be human. I think working in an orphanage is a noble job. I learn a lot from living with the boys. I feel God's love as portrayed in the boy's happiness. They enrich my soul.

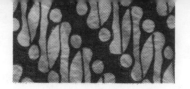

A Mother

In Java gender interestingly combines rigid role ideals and flexible practicality. Especially due to the strict influences of Islam, with its unbending rules, the father is seen as the head of the family. Areas are clearly designated men's work and women's work. Yet in traditional village life women have significant economic power. In their control of the family finances, especially through their own income in marketplace selling, women offer significant economic support to the family. As a result, they have decision-making power, to which men often defer.

Men often participate in child rearing. Men even do domestic work around the house, clearly the area of the women, if it is necessary. This is the case with the woman interviewed here. She was born in 1923, in a village near where she now lives. Unlike many Javanese, she speaks bluntly, in short, to-the-point sentences. Although completely uneducated, she thinks independently, questioning the common Javanese belief in fate. This demonstrates that village peasants do not necessarily merely accept the values in which they have been enculturated.

When she became so busy having more children, her husband willingly assumed the housework and cooking. He was flexible because having more children was worth it. In his case, the traditional Javanese value of children is stronger than the rigidity of men's gender roles. This husband evidently continues to value having lots of children, though his wife clearly recognizes from her own experience that there is a need for population control. She strongly supports the government's family-planning program for her children and for Indonesia in general. Although uneducated, she expresses a sophisticated understanding of the need for limiting births and encouraging education for the future generation.

A Mother

She and her husband live in their small house in the central Java town of Sukoharjo, where she was interviewed in Javanese by Robertus Widjojo (male, age thirty-three), with questions by Walter L. Williams. Some of their grandchildren, who stay with them, interrupted the interview several times. She gave the impression that she did not have time to talk further about these topics because she had to put the grandchildren to bed.

My parents were peasants. I am their youngest child and have two brothers and two sisters. We are all Muslims. I did not go to school. When I was small, only a few people sent their children to school. They were the rich—the government officials and the nobility. People thought that it was no use for girls to go to school because we should be "in the kitchen." Actually my parents had the money. It was the Dutch who did not give us the chance. As a result, I'm sixty-five years old and illiterate. I'm one of the victims of the Dutch policy. I think people should have sent their children to school. Now we have so many schools, and they are open for everybody. I think that education is very important. That's why I always try my best to get money for the education of my children—so they will be clever and get a job.

I was seventeen years old when I got married, and my husband was twenty-one. My husband worked part-time in the Railway Company, and he spent his spare time working as a barber. My parents chose the man for me, as was the custom at the time. My father liked him very much and said he was a good man. So we got married, and within a year I gave a birth to a baby boy. Everything has changed now. Parents do not choose the man for their daughter and the girl for their son. I think it is good to get to know each other before two people get married. Be close friends first. But I don't want my children to go "too far" before marriage. [Laughs]. What's important is to know their personality and how they get along with our family and relatives.

Anyway, three years after my husband and I got married I had my second child, and there were approximately two years between the rest. We had no plan for how many children we wanted to have before we got married, but we had fourteen. We lost two of our sons. So now we have only eight sons and four daughters.

After I had three children, I began to feel that I had too much work to do. I complained to my husband and often let the work go undone. I hoped my husband would get angry when he came home from work. But he didn't. He never got angry. Instead of being angry, he did all the housework, including the cooking. And, when the food was ready, he came to me and told me to feed the children. How could I be angry? When I gave birth to my fourth child, I began to lose a lot of blood, and I always fainted. So, I always prepared ten eggs to eat. I couldn't tell my husband to stop having children. I couldn't do that. Otherwise, he would leave me! When the government began the family-planning program, it was no use. We were already too old.

Actually I had tried some kinds of fruit and drugs to prevent pregnancy, but failed. People say we have to be very careful when we are pregnant to avoid miscarriage. Well, I don't believe that a bit. I used drugs. Once I fell down in the bathroom when my pregnancy was eight months old. I always worked hard when I was pregnant, and I never experienced one miscarriage. If God wants us to have children, then it will happen!

Some people think every person already has his own fate before he is born. Well, that's nonsense! What we ourselves do makes things happen. If we have many children, we will be very busy. Then we don't have the time to work for money. Money doesn't come by itself, does it? We have to work for it. I think you will be surprised if suddenly you see money appear on the table. Some of my children send me money. They don't do this regularly. I never asked my children for money. You see, I always feel disappointed if I don't get what I want. So, I don't ask for money because I don't want to be disappointed.

I tell my children not to have many children. I tell them to learn from my experience. My son who lives in east Java has now got two children. When I visited him, he said he was already busy. My children now realize how hard I had to work and how busy I was raising them. I think it would have been better if the family-planning program had come earlier. I wish we had not had all these. [Interviewer: Why did you have so many children then?] [Woman:] Well, ask him! [She pointed at her husband, who was sitting meekly in the corner with a rather self-satisfied look on his face].

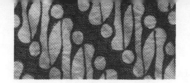

A Mother and Revolutionary

Like many people interviewed for this volume, this woman was active in the revolution. Although privileged as a child, she still resisted the Dutch colonial system. She hated the Japanese occupation even more than she did the Dutch. She recognizes the inadequacies of the Indonesian government—the corruption and excessive bureaucracy—but remains a strong patriot. Indonesia's changes, not only political but also social and economic, can be seen in this woman's life. Clearly the modern nuclear family is most important to her. As Indonesia is being transformed into an urban capitalist society, husbands and wives are becoming more intimate: partly because stressful jobs are increasing and partly because the stable village neighborhood is disappearing in big city life. Same-sex friendship networks become less important than in the village, while the companionate marriage is becoming more important. People turn to their spouses, rather than their close friends, for emotional support.

This woman is considered by her community to embody the Javanese ideal of a successful mother. She raised ten children, all of whom have graduated from universities. Now sixty-five years old, in her retirement she spends much of her time as a volunteer marriage counselor helping young women. Like the other people in this volume who have voiced the most positive outlook on their lives, this woman has found a sense of happiness and accomplishment in her efforts to help others. By feeling that she is doing something useful, for her children and grandchildren as well as for the women who come to her for counseling, she has created a purpose for her life. Her sense of accomplishment in the revolution is matched by her sense of accomplishment in her personal life. By helping others, she helps herself.

The other element of this woman's strength is her spiritual tenacity. She is a *hajah*, a devout Muslim who has made the pilgrimage to Mecca. Yet, as with many Javanese, her intense religious beliefs actually mix the ideas of several different religions. She is active in a religious movement among the educated elite, referred to here as Javanese Mental Health, which attempts to integrate Javanese mystical ideas with Islam, Buddhism, Christianity, and the concepts of Western science. Her attitudes reflect the Buddhist-Hindu concept of karma, and her favorite song is the Christian hymn "Ave Maria." She played this song on the organ in her living room before she was interviewed in Javanese by S. M. Darmastuti (female, age thirty-three). The interview took place at her home in Yogyakarta on Friday, the Muslim holy day, when she was not engaged in her volunteer work.

I am always lonely on Fridays because this is the day I have nothing to do. On the other days of the week, I am a volunteer social worker for a mental health organization. I work without pay as a consultant for people, especially women, who are having trouble with their marriages. I give them advice because most such women need someone to help them distinguish which of their feelings are valid and which are invalid. By far their most common problem is when a wife discovers that her husband is having a love affair with someone else. So many women believe that old Javanese saying "love comes from the stomach," which means that a husband will be satisfied if the wife provides him with good food. When I was young, that saying was true, but nowadays men need women who can do more than cook. Today a person needs a spouse who can be a friend.

Today, men have more problems with their businesses, and they need wives who can understand their difficulties. I have six sons and four daughters. Four of my sons are engineers and very busy in their jobs. Three of them have no problems with their marriages because their wives also have jobs. But the wife of my oldest son is an ordinary housewife. She had some troubles when my son came home and wanted to share his stressful issues from work. Because she did not have a job herself, she could not really understand what he was talking about. In the early years of their marriage this was not a problem, but later on he felt that his wife's attention was more focused on their children instead of on him. This is a dangerous thing for a wife to do. I know for certain that his wife is a very good woman. She is a good wife and obedient, but she became too occupied with her routine at home. She was so concerned with rearing her four children that she never paid attention to her husband.

I advised my son to encourage his wife to take up a daily activity outside their home and to hire a servant to handle the housework. Thanks be to God, he agreed. He rented a little store in the market, and his wife runs it every day except Saturday and Sunday. At two o'clock in the afternoon the children come home from school, my son comes home from his office, and now his wife comes from her shop. Well, you know what, it works! Now, they try to understand each other's problems and try to help each other. Before, I think she seemed to be ignoring her husband's stressful issues not because she did not care, but because she could not imagine the problems her husband had. Now that she is busy in her own job, she can better understand that the issues affecting people are not just "home" problems.

Frankly speaking, I once faced a similar problem, but my late husband was a very understanding man. He encouraged me to join a woman's club to get me out of the house. Once a week I would meet with the other ladies, and that was enough for me to get some fresh air after a whole week in the household. I use my own experience as a guide to help other people who have similar troubles in their married life. There is a saying, "Every family had its own cross to bear," meaning that all people have their problems to face. For example, my youngest son was the most difficult one to raise. He was naughty. I say naughty, and that is really what I mean. Even though he was quite smart, he had many difficulties around the time he hit puberty. I think he was even more intelligent than his sister, who is now a lecturer at the university in the faculty of psychology. I am so proud of her; she recently won a Fulbright Scholarship to do additional graduate study in America.

As a mother, I feel a great sense of success that I was able to put all my children through college and graduate school. They have all become educated persons and have good positions in their careers. I feel the secret of their success is that I pray a lot. I have faith that God will lead those who pray. I realize that I am just a humble woman with limited ability and education. When I was widowed, I did not think that I would be able to do all this. My husband died when my eldest son was beginning college, and the youngest child was still in kindergarten. My youngest son grew up without a father. His older brothers and sisters helped him very much, but still he lost something he will never find again. That is why he became so naughty. He was like an untamed lion. Well, I prayed to God to lead him, and God did what I asked. That boy is now an aeronautical engineer and a director in an airline company. Oh, if only my husband were still alive now. . . he would be so proud.

Sometimes I have to admit that I do not understand God's will—why he seized my husband so early. I have twice faced this loss of someone I loved who died young. Besides my husband, my first daughter was thirty-seven years old when God asked her to come to his eternal house. She was mother to an eleven-year-old son, and she died while delivering her second child. Oh, you can imagine how I felt, to watch my own child die. I was right beside her when she breathed her last breath. She was a medical doctor, and her husband is a physician. He is a specialist in babies, and her brother-in-law is an expert gynecologist. Both of them were there when she was delivering her second child, and there was not a thing they could do. Both she and the baby died together. It is a tragic story.

When I face trouble I always remember my husband. He steadfastly encouraged me to be strong. He was a teacher in a high school. Right after we got married, Indonesia was occupied by the Japanese. It was difficult even to find enough money to barely live. It was completely forbidden to have any sort of party or enjoyment. We got through our years of marriage on nothing but love.

Neither my husband nor I are reserved in our personality, but my children are. They were all so serious with their lessons at school. My husband became an engineer, and they wanted to be educated to be like him. He was forty-eight years old when he left us. We had a very hard life after he passed away. The money I got from his office was not enough to pay the children's school fees. I tried to work as well as I could. I also sold all my jewelry. Whenever I would find a good bargain in jewelry, I would buy it and then sell it at a retail price. My oldest sons took jobs while they were in college to pay their own school fees and to help me pay for the younger children's educational expenses. Oh, I still remember when my fourth son was able to buy a new pair of pants with his own earnings. He walked back and forth in front of me; he was so proud. Now both he and his wife are economists and work in the same bank.

Maybe you look at me today and think that my life has been easy. Well, that is not true. I remember only a week after my husband died: a man came to my house and told me that his office would offer me inexpensive rice as a benefit to me because I was a widow. I was very appreciative of this. He asked me for some money and asked one of my sons to accompany him to carry home the rice. My son agreed, and he brought along a big sack to carry it in. They went to an office, and the man told my son to wait outside until he negotiated the deal. My son waited here for more than three hours, but the man never came out. Finally he went into the office, and they said the man had simply walked through the office and immediately went out the back door. They did not know anything about the rice. I remember how disappointed my son was when he realized the man had cheated him. I just do not understand how that man could do that to a family in the midst of mourning.

I wanted to tell the police, but my sons reminded me that if we asked the police to search for the man it would just cost us more money. The police were facing financial difficulties at that time also, and it was common knowledge that most of them would charge the people who asked for their help. This never happened when the Dutch occupied Indonesia. Frankly speaking, the Dutch police were much more disciplined than has been true since independence. When I was young I had never heard of a crime done by a policeman. I always held the police in high respect because they were really guards to help the people. There were not pickpockets in the marketplace like today. No gambling was allowed. We trusted the police deeply. They were holders of the law, not law breakers of today. The police department is one thing that the Dutch did better than the Indonesian government.

My father worked for the Dutch. He came from a rich aristocratic family and managed a government equipment shop. The Dutch were expert administrators. There was no corruption in the government as far as I knew. If an offical was dishonest, the government promptly fired the violator. Today there is much more bureaucracy and corruption, and the violators go unpunished.

The main thing I disliked about the Dutch administration was its system of education. There were many different kinds of schools, and those who applied to become students were strictly selected according to the social class of their family. The Dutch did this to keep the loyalty of Java's leadership class, by giving them extra privileges and turning them against the peasants. They then used the educated high class to help administer their colony. You can imagine how proud and haughty were those admitted to the high-class school. Those snobbish high-class students treated the lower classes quite badly.

Those students who got into the high-class school had all their needs taken care of, and they got a very good education. Even today, you can see how the educated older generation have a better education than the younger ones. Most of us who went to Dutch schools can speak several languages—Dutch, English, French— quite fluently. Today's students, even at the university level, do not speak good English even though that is required in the schools. Hardly any of them speak Dutch or other languages any more. Most young people who have learned foreign languages did not learn them in the public schools; instead they have paid for additional lessons at private language institutes. That is what I did with my children.

Still, even though my own education was good and my life as a young girl was easy, I did not like the way the Dutch treated the Javanese. They acted like they were better, and anyone who opposed them was wrong. I still remember when I was in the third grade of elementary school, my history teacher, a Dutchmen, told us that Pangeran Diponegoro, a nineteenth-century prince of the Yogyakarta kingdom, was a troublemaker. The teacher said he was a rebel who had been captured and died in exile. Fortunately at home my elder brother told me that Pangeran Diponegoro was in fact a hero who had resisted the Dutch takeover of our independent country. He said that the Dutch were our true enemy and that they should be chased out of Indonesia. This was the first time I heard about the Dutch "occupation." Before that, I thought the Dutch had always been here. I learned from the patriotic example of Diponegoro about my loyalty, pride, and idealism to help make our country free. Hatred toward the Dutch existed among my people long before I was born, but I got that feeling by the time I was eleven years old [in 1934]. Even though my own family had a good position in the colonial government, I wanted the Dutch out of Indonesia.

I have to admit that we Indonesians have not shown the expertise in handling our educational systems and governmental bureaucracy that the Dutch had. Sometimes I think the public order was destroyed for Indonesia by the Japanese occupation. I think they planned to occupy Indonesia long before the war broke out. The Japanese had many big shops and companies here during the 1930s. There were many Japanese people here, and later we realized that they were serving as spies and detectives for Japan. Two years before the Dutch left, I remember my friend told me one day that she saw two Japanese unloading a big crate from a truck near the market in downtown Yogyakarta. They were delivering that crate to a large shop run by a Japanese man. One Japanese man stumbled, and the crate fell. When the crate broke open, my friend clearly saw that it was full of rifles. My friend was surprised, but she pretended not to see—not because she was afraid of the Japanese, but because she was afraid that she would be called as a witness if the police found out about it. Later, when the Japanese troops arrived in Yogyakarta [in 1942], these Japanese shops became army posts. The shopkeepers put on officers' uniforms. They were in fact members of the army during the previous years.

The Japanese occupied Indonesia only three and a half years, but our suffering in that time was more than the three centuries of occupation by the Dutch. I hated the Japanese. They were skillful soldiers, but cruel administrators. Their greed was felt by all Indonesian people, from the highest to the lowest classes. They forced Indonesian people, even the educated, to work for them. They robbed the wealth of the uppper-class families and forced the peasants into their labor gangs.

The Japanese changed the educational system drastically, making only one kind of school for everybody. Speaking Dutch was forbidden. The new languages were Indonesian and Japanese. Many people from the higher classes had difficulty in speaking Indonesian because they had never been taught that language. I was working as a teacher at that time, and I took an evening course to learn the new Indonesian language. I also took a part-time job sewing clothes for convicted criminals in the jails.

One day I had to take the clothes to the manager at the jail. I saw the prisoners, some of whom were young Dutch men. They had not seen a woman in a long time. Wow, most of them looked at me with their wild eyes, whistling and shouting while reaching their hands through the bars of their cages. I remember being so afraid. That was the first and last time I went to the jail. The manager said that they had not had any chance to touch a woman since they were in prison; he said that some became homosexuals, and they had a better temperament and a better survival rate than those who became depressed, agressive, or destructive. After my experience seeing those poor prisoners, I did not work again. My husband had to work hard while I stayed home as a houswife. He was afraid that I would be attacked if I worked outside the house because sometimes the Japanese soldiers raped women.

There were many changes in my life when the Japanese occupied Indonesia. The biggest change occurred when my husband was ordered to move to Bogor, in west Java. He had a new post as a lecturer in the Agricultural Academy. We moved there, and life was much easier. When we first arrived, the Japanese officer in command there thought my husband was Dutch. He was tall, light-skinned, and with a Dutch-looking nose. He was interrogated by the Japanese, and if they suspected him they would have thrown him in prison. But at last my husband convinced them that he was a real Javanese.

We lived in Bogor for one and a half years, until August 1945 when the atomic bomb was dropped on Japan. My husband felt this would mean the defeat of the Japanese, so without the permission of my husband's boss we moved to Yogyakarta to join the People's Independence Army. The atomic bomb was the cruelest weapon men ever invented, but it was a benefit for Indonesia. The Japanese were forced to surrender. It was important for us Indonesians to act fast because we knew the Dutch wanted to come back into their former colony. By the time British troops arrived to get the Japanese, the Indonesians had already succeeded in capturing the remaining Japanese soldiers and proclaiming our independence.

Behind the British troops came the Dutch. They wanted things to be just like before the war. But now the condition was different. We were ready to fight against them. Even though the Japanese had been so cruel, we still have to thank them because they encouraged our belief that we were strong enough to oppose the Dutch. Their coming to Indonesia was a kind of blessing in disguise. By the time the Dutch returned, we considered that Indonesia was already a free country. We totally refused their coming here, and war began again. This time Indonesian people fought against the Dutch, their British allies, and the Gurkha Commonwealth troops from India. After a time, the British and Gurkha pulled out, and our only enemies were the Dutch.

When the independence of Indonesia was proclaimed, there was a shock among most Indonesian people. It seemed to me that they did not know the real meaning of freedom. They thought that freedom meant they could be free to do anything. There were many roberies, and many local militias followed only their own rule. Fortunately, in this anarchical situation our leader Sukarno managed to handle the problem well. His fatherly voice tamed the youngsters' emotion. Thank God he was able to stop the rioting. He was aware that the Dutch would come and that we had to have a strong and united army to face our enemy. I don't know what would have happened if we did not have Sukarno at that time. He was the only person who could inspire the people to courage, enthusiasm, and pride in being Indonesian. He was not only the proclaimer of independence but also, we should admit, the greatest hero and the greatest orator Indonesia has ever had. We have to remember that, even when we recognize his shortcomings and his mistakes as president.

One thing that we should learn from the entire experience of occupation and our war of independence is the importance of unity. Without unity, Indonesia could not have reached its goal of nationhood. I have witnessed many kinds of rioting by Indonesians, both before and after independence. I think those bad things would never have happened if we genuinely had unity and a consciousness of being one. That doesn't mean everything should be "one," like only one political party. Not at all! I mean we need to be "one," while retaining our diversity. As long as we cannot manifest that feeling of our national motto, "unity in diversity," we will not be able to genuinely make progress as "one" Indonesia.

During the revolution my husband and I joined the guerrillas to chase away the Dutch. We went to the place where the guerrillas built their camp near Yogyakarta and volunteered. My husband became a soldier, and I became a cook. I worked in a moving kitchen, following the guerrillas wherever they went. It was a really terrific experience. It is hard for someone born after independence to imagine how we felt. But if you were there at the time, you would have joined the guerrillas also. I saw my friends die in the fighting. I saw many people suffer in the war. Every time my husband went out to the front, I prayed that he would return alive. Having seen the fighting firsthand, I can say strongly that I don't want war to happen again. In the minds of my children, they think I am a heroine of Indonesian independence. But I just did what I thought was right.

Before the war my husband had gone to a school in the Netherlands, and he developed some good friends there. We were not against the Dutch people, just against their government trying to rule our country. When he was living in the Netherlands, one of my husband's Dutch friends became as close as his own brother. When the Dutch troops came to Indonesia after the Japanese surrender, this friend was a soldier. He tried to find our address. He finally found it, at great danger to himself, but our house was empty because we were away at the front. He left a letter, explaining that he knew nothing about the mission of the Dutch army. He wrote that he and his soldier friends had been deceived by their own government, which had told them that they were coming to Indonesia to protect us from the Japanese. They had no idea that they would be fighting to prevent Indonesian people from gaining their own freedom.

He wrote that he was sorry to be here as an enemy and that he and many of his Dutch friends hoped that the Indonesians would be victorious. Later, when we returned home, we found that letter. Thank God, he never met my husband in battle. Years later, he came back to Indonesia as a tourist. He came here with his wife and two children to honor my husband and to beg our forgiveness for his government's colonialism. That was such a nice meeting! I just cannot imagine what would have happened if he had met my husband in the war.

During the revolution the Dutch tried to use local people as spies. One time when I was back in Yogyakarta I witnessed a friend of mine discover a young Javanese woman who was spying for the Dutch. I saw him shoot her dead, right behind my house. I was very afraid because the dead body was buried there for three months. Stories of ghosts were very popular at that time, especially about people who had been killed in the war. Usually such stories were told from mouth to mouth, but sometimes articles about ghosts would appear in the newspapers. After the war was over, I was relieved that her family dug up the body and buried her in the cemetery.

During the war the Dutch also brought in mercenary fighters, called the Green Berets. They were from the Molucan Islands east of Java. Their ferocity was more frightening than the Dutch troops. The Green Berets killed many Javanese people, not only adults but also children. They conducted horrible massacres. Four years ago my daughter visited the Netherlands, and while she was there she saw the Molucan neighborhood. She talked with a former member of the Green Berets, who were taken there after the Dutch evacuated. He said that life was hard there, and most Molucans felt badly treated by the Dutch. Of course, they could not come back to their home because the Molucan Islands are now part of Indonesia, and they would be considered traitors.

I think they got what they deserved. In the Netherlands, they were never treated as first-class citizens and now their descendants are suffering for what their fathers did. My daughter told me about the prejudice that grew up against them, that if there was a crime the first ones the Dutch people suspected were the Molucans. I'll bet they would be as happy as I would have been if they had never joined the Dutch side. I once read in a newspaper article that they wanted to come back to live in Indonesia but were afraid.

It is not easy to gain happiness in one's life if you do things just for your own profit. That is the mistake of the Green Beret mercenaries, who thought they were going to profit but only ended up miserable. In contrast, those of us who fought with the guerrillas fought only to end colonialism. We wanted to create freedom for the Indonesian people—that is all we wanted. Most of those who joined the guerrillas felt the same way we did. Only a few did it for their own gain, in hopes of winning a powerful post in the government after independence. Those who felt this way were either killed in battle or have ended up unhappy in their old age. I can name them one by one, and you can see what I mean, but what good would that be? Everyone gets what they truly deserve.

I also see some people who I know never joined the army, yet today they claim veterans' pensions. They have cheated the government for their own benefit. I could easily expose their deception by testifying what they did during the war. But when I see their poor lives my heart is really touched. I think they would never have lied if their lives had been easy.

The people who should be most greatly honored are members of the Students Army. At the time of independence these youngsters were intelligent students who demonstrated their bravery and became highly respected by the people as well as the enemy. Their group was very disciplined, and they always had perfect timing when attacking the enemy. They were the favorite group of President Sukarno. When the war was over they were given first choice of becoming officers in the Indonesian army or getting scholarships to continue their studies at first-class universities. Today many are high-ranking officers in the armed forces or ministers in the government. When they were fighting, I believe they never did that with the goal of becoming a general or a government leader. I am sure they fought with a pure heart to free Indonesia from oppression. That is why, afterwards, God gave them what they should have.

Because of my activities in the revolution, my children think I am a superwoman, but I think *they* are super. I chose all of my children's names to begin with the letters "Su," which means "super." If I succeeded in making them super, I think it was because God heard my prayers. I told you I pray often for them. I love them, and never leave them alone when they have a problem to solve. I think they had the courage to continue their education because they did not want to be left behind by their friends. I cannot educate them myself, but I encourage them to gain a better life, and I tell them the only way they can do that is to go to school diligently. I just give them a lot of attention and try to be their friend.

I had to give that encouragement to my husband also. In 1969 he had a chance to do graduate study in America to get his degree in agricultural engineering. He went by himself so that he could concentrate on his studies, without having to worry about the children and helping me with the housework. My children were very proud of that event, although his twelve-month absence from home was very hard on the whole family. He left me with my ten children, including the youngest who was still an infant. He always wrote long letters to us, and he sent us his pictures that he took there. Life in America seemed very different from here.

His trip to America inspired me to learn English. A very good English teacher taught me how to speak grammatically and how to pronounce English well. I enjoyed very much being a member of a women's English Conversation Club. I am not an active member anymore because now I prefer to devote my time to the public mental health organization. I am also a member of the Javanese Mental Health Organization, which concentrates on gaining mental and moral health. This is not a competing religion to Islam, and we are far from what people call occult mysticism. Javanese Mental Health focuses and concentrates on how we can lead our lives happily, close to God and loved by others.

This club is open for anyone who wants to have happiness. Usually we meet three times a month, discussing our actual problems and trying solve those problems by using our Holy Books. We call our books Holy Books because they were compiled by a Javanese holy man who wrote them after heard God's message. He was not a holy man who wrote them after he heard God's message. He was not a dukun, or a witch doctor, but just an ordinary man from Solo. He found it difficult to try to gain religious insight through foreign languages. Rather than trying to find God's word through Arabic or English, he wanted to know whether God would let him pray in Javanese. He wanted to know whether God would accept his prayer. Because this man asked so devotedly and because he had a pure heart, God let this man hear his teachings directly. He was taught by God about higher morals and the way to be close to spirituality. This man wrote what he had heard. Those writings have been published as our Holy Books.

These teachings do not contradict my religion of Islam. In fact, since I have joined the Javanese Mental Health Organization, I have been able to better understand Islamic teachings. After learning these teachings, I know for certain how people should act toward others and toward God. I can now truly see the message behind the Koran and the meaning of the pilgrimage to Mecca. I will even say that I hold to these teachings with fanatical zeal because I know what is written is these books is true not only dogmatically but also intellectually. Once an Indonesian medical doctor studying at the University of Leiden in the Netherlands wrote his doctoral dissertation on Javanese Mental Health. His dissertation, based on these Holy Books, has been praised as being equal in importance to the philosophies of scholars like Freud, Adler, and Jung.

Because of Javanese Mental Health I can face my big problems in life. Please don't think that I have no problems in my old age now. All people have their own troubles and their own fates. As I said before, every family has its own cross to bear. Solving our problems differs in every case. But we should always know and believe one thing deeply: every prayer will be heard by God. Our deeds are also our prayers. That's why if we do bad things, then that means we are praying for bad things to happen to us. On the contrary, if we always do good things, that means we are sending forth prayers for good things to happen to us. Prayer is not only what we speak but also what we do in our daily lives.

Believe it or not, I can free myself from worry by putting my life and problem solving to God. I have learned from the Javanese Holy Books that if we have big problems that we cannot solve it is better that we give those problems to God to solve. This does not mean that we should run away from our problems. No! We should first try as hard as we can to solve them before we give them to God. We only turn them over to God when our hands cannot handle them. God will then solve our problems easily, if we will just try to do God's tasks in the world. You know what God's tasks I am talking about? Those tasks are doing good things to others.

I have been using this approach to life, and you know what? It always works. Every time I have a problem that I cannot solve, I simply say: "God, you are an expert on solving problems. I believe you can do this one better than I. Please solve this problem, and I will do your tasks in return." After saying this, I try especially hard to do my work diligently, to contribute more to my organization, and I donate my money to the poor and to those who need it. Then guess what? Maybe you think this is riduculous, but it works! I can see actual proof, which I can know intellectually as well as by faith. I always say that intellectual knowledge without religious faith is crippled, and religion without intelligence is blind.

Now I have my memories of my wonderful husband, my devoted children provide me with everything I need, I have fifteen grandchildren, and I have the good feelings from the many people whom I have been able to help. God gives love to those who give love and happiness to those who act to make others happy. I am very happy with what I have. This is what I call Javanese Mental Health.

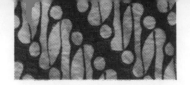

A Father Concerned about Education

In the opinions of many, one great failing in contemporary Indonesia is the education system. The government has done a good job of ensuring that practically every child has access to at least a basic elementary schooling; beyond that it has not given youths the training necessary to lead the nation into the twenty-first century. Plagued by inadequate salaries for teachers, outdated methods of teacher training, poor library facilities, and reduced equipment budgets, the schools are bursting at the seams without accomplishing their basic goals of education.

Indonesia's first decades as an independent nation were marked by divisive forces that almost pulled the nation apart. University campuses were often so politicized that education was impossible. The Suharto government has tried, above all, to create stability in the country. The government's interest has been more concerned with keeping the peace in the schools and employing loyal teachers than in the quality of education in the classrooms. Many Indonesians agree that this stabilizing enforcement was necessary, in the context of the near chaotic conditions that existed under Sukarno. Yet, now that the nation has experienced two decades of stability, more and more Indonesians are calling for a shift in focus.

This necessary shift applies particularly to schooling. Many educated people think that the current educational system turns out docile conformists rather than creative thinkers. Teachers' unquestioning support for the status quo is considered more important than their critical abilities. Schools and universities seem more concerned about those in the hierarchy maintaining their own status and power networks than in helping the students learn the new skills required in the future. Parents who can afford it send their children to private schools and then to universities abroad for a better education. Others are beginning to speak up and expect a better quality of schooling for the children. Often the Dutch-educated elders, who received a more thorough education than is available today, can supply the necessary perspective for evaluating the present educational system. This man's attitudes are typical of the critique one hears in private conversations, though seldom in public speeches or in print.

Born in 1928, this man is old enough to remember the traditional ways. Although he sees the need to adapt to modern times, he does not want to lose the valuable aspects of traditional Javanese culture. He has a sophisticated understanding of the ways in which an urban wage-labor economy pulls families and communities apart, in contrast to the agrarian village where the family worked together and neighbors helped one another. Now, as people pursue their individual employments, away from family and neighborhood, there is not as much social glue to hold relationships together. He further understands the impact of increasing contact between Indonesians and outsiders, as more Indonesians travel abroad and more tourists come to Java. He expressed his opinions while being interviewed at his home in the town of Purworejo, speaking in Indonesian to Martha Pardede (female, age thirty) and Walter L. Williams.

There are many differences between education under the Dutch government and nowadays. Not all the people could enter school back then. The Dutch made regulations to limit the number of people who could be admitted to schools, and they only allowed children of their government employees to attend. Actually they didn't really want to educate the natives. They only set up schools for the children of aristocratic families and the children of their government employees because they needed them. It was a part of their political attitude. They wanted to influence the aristocratic families to be loyal, and they needed some natives to do administrative work for them.

Besides the colonial government schools, other schools were sponsored by the Christian missionaries. I studied at this kind of school, one that anyone could enter. The missionaries even tried hard to inspire more people to join the schools, but sometimes the missionaries were disappointed. Back then, there was a great distance between the common people and the aristocrats, the upper-class natives who worked for the Dutch government. The aristocrats did not want to encourage the common people to enter the school because they wanted to keep their exalted status. It was a kind of feudalism.

Most common people, meanwhile, considered it useless to send their children to school. According to their opinions schools were not for them. They thought it was enough for the children to be trained as farmers. The common people thought schools were just for the upper class. They didn't understand the advantage of school. Especially for girls, they thought it was enough for a young woman to be trained as a future wife and mother. Girls were trained to do the work in the market, while helping their mother. It was considered useless to send girls to schools.

Today our Indonesian government has tried hard to make people realize the advantage of education. And I think most of the people now understand it. Still, sometimes poor people face obstacles in sending their children to the higher levels of school because the students must pay their fees and expenses. But I think, in general, our government has made some good progress in getting basic education to the common people.

In some aspects, however, education today is not as good as it was in the past. A very significant difference in the system of education today, versus in the Dutch time, is the role of the teacher. When I was a student, a teacher took a great role in educating a child or a student. The role of a teacher was very important. The profession of teaching was considered noble, a respectable duty. A teacher was seen as having a great role in building the student's character and the student's future career. At that time, teachers devoted most of their time and their mind to the progress of the students. A teacher tried to lead and develop the students' talents.

Today, it is difficult to find such a teacher. The usual teacher today knows nothing about the students. A teacher today just tries to supply knowledge, not educate. Teachers try to teach the students to memorize facts, without educating them either to see the relationship between facts or to solve the problems of real life. In my time, a teacher tried hard to arrange the method of education so as to put the student as close as possible to the realities of life. They gave students a basis to solve real problems as a basic approach to learning. Nowadays, a student who graduates from a technical school commonly doesn't even know how to use a hammer.

Today's students are not trained to think creatively with sharp analytic capability. Then if they face problems that differ from the one their teacher has explained, they become nervous and confused. And they are not taught to be workers, I mean, to accomplish tasks on their own. Actually that should be the goal of education. It is clear why most graduates try to become office workers or government employees; they are not trained to be practical or entrepreneurial.

I have many experiences dealing with such persons. I just try to understand them and show them the right way to handle a problem. It is not easy being a teacher. Teaching is not an easy duty. When I was young, not all students could become qualified as teachers. There were many requirements. Besides intellect, talent and motivation were the most important things. Then, a person who wanted to be a teacher had to face many hard tests and very strict selection. And he had to get some recommendations. Only the top students could become teachers.

For most graduates nowadays, becoming teachers is the last of their alternatives. I mean, a person takes a job as a teacher because he or she doesn't have any other alternative, because he or she is not accepted in another field. We have to admit that most teachers, now, are actually not well-qualified persons for such duty. I think we have to be very careful in choosing who we are going to allow to mold the minds of our next generation. In my opinion our government has to be much more careful in handling this issue. Teaching is different from any other kind of job. We are dealing with people and their lives.

Teachers in the junior high school are especially important; that is the most important time for building the students' character. This needs great patience and attention. The children get their basic learning in that time, and the success of their later education depends on the foundations laid in junior high school. In part, teaching is so unattractive for graduates because of the low salaries, but if a person has good motivation and idealism, then actually one does not pay attention to money. Teaching is a kind of idealism. Someone who becomes a teacher should do so because he or she wants to help people to stand on their own feet, to share knowledge, so the students can face life and realize their dignity as humans. I realize it is not easy to do this. That is why our government has to carry out a strict selection, to decide who will be the best teachers. The future of our country and generation depends on it.

Today, parents have a heavier burden and responsibility than sixty years ago, when I was born. At that time, it was not difficult for parents to lead their children. Although they didn't send their children to school, at home they tried to train their children with traditional teachings and values. At the time, it was not difficult for us to understand and accept such teaching. We obeyed them. Parents at the time were very responsible. Then we respected them. Parents and teachers were the only persons to follow and to imitate.

Today, being a parent is difficult. Besides economic aspects, we face some other problems dealing with time factors. My activities are different from my father's activities fifty years ago. Today, we haven't enough time for children. When I was young, parents and children had a lot of time and activities to share. For example, we used to work together in the fields or when we were feeding the cattle. Such activities drew us closer to each other. In such situations, parents usually trained us with practical knowledge, values, and ideas and told us their hopes concerning their children. They told us what they wanted us to do. Now, the situation is different. Many activities demand a lot of the family members' time away from home. As a consequence, parents do not have sufficient time for their children. The time is just barely enough for them to know each other, to understand each other, or to share feelings and experiences. There is not enough time for fathers to share values with them or to strengthen them in facing life.

Another cause for the difficulties today is the development of every aspect of life. You know, it is easier for children to adapt to the new situation than it is for the adults. Then, according to the young people, parents or the old persons are no longer right to ask for help in solving their problems. Parents do not understand their problems, for they came from a different era. Parents with their traditional values are not the right people to talk to about today's problems and situations.

You know, sometimes we old people feel lonely and useless. There is a psychological effect. I kept busy in my job with the government Department of Public Works, but since I retired there is not as much for me to do. My wife feels this effect even more strongly because now our five children have moved away to different cities where they got jobs and are living independently. Sometimes she feels valueless. And teachers, as I said, do not try to understand the young generation and do not make any effort to lead it. In such situations, a child goes to friends for advice, believing they are right to help. There is no problem with this if those friends have good character and intention. If not, it can become a great problem, for sometimes those other kids are in the same confused situation.

Many young people fall flat on their faces for many reasons. They come to an unfamiliar problem that they have never dealt with before, and because they do not consult enough with an older more experienced person who has already faced that problem, they do not know what to do. Sometimes, a friend just shows a shortcut way to handle the pressure, such as drinking, smoking, and gambling. I prayed for God to help me, and I tried hard to guide each of my children wisely and to keep a good communication with them then and now.

But the young generation often does not want to be interfered with. They want to be independent persons too soon. They want to make up their own minds in decisions. There is a positive aspect to that, and I admire that about my children because I don't know much about the type of work they are doing. But they still have to be careful. Even the adult person, sometimes, needs other people's advice. The young generation, I think, are too brave. It is too risky.

Today there is a tendency for us to lose our traditional values. That is understandable, considering how the times have changed. Some traditional values are not suitable anymore to the modern times. To mention one of them, just take arranged marriage. It used to be a common thing among Javanese, especially among the aristocratic families, but today's young people want to choose their own spouses. However, many other traditional values are still relevant. For example, our ideals of cooperation and mutual aid and values about good manners. Javanese people used to be well known as familiar and friendly people, who would always help others. But today, it is different. I think it is one result of mass communication and transportation. As you know, during the last decade people from everywhere have started coming to Indonesia, as students or tourists. I see this whenever I go into Yogyakarta. These foreigners bring with them their ways of life, their ways of talking and thinking. And the native young generation, exactly like horses just coming out of their stables, try to imitate it. They follow their ways of talking, their ways of dressing, even their ways of life.

In the small towns there are still some of the old ways, but in the big cities they are all going away. There is no difference any more between young people in Yogyakarta and young people in Jakarta. Just the same. It is due to their milieu. And milieu is a difficult thing to escape. Just take language as an example. It is difficult to find a young person in the cities who can speak good Javanese fluently.

According to my opinion, we do not need to forget our good traditional values and ways of life if we want to adapt to future progress. We have to keep our arts, language, and culture. We just try to make it suitable, in such a way, to the current situation. Don't just finish it off. To develop national unity, we do not need to kill off our local cultures, languages, arts, and ways of life. Just let them grow and develop, as part of our larger Indonesia. I think they will brighten up our identity as Indonesians.

Some traditional values are still relevant to our current problems. Just take our values of good manners. That would be good to apply to any society. But sometimes, you know, we feel inferior. We respect another country's values, just because we think that Western technology is better than ours. If we see a Westerner acting a certain way, for example being impolite, we want to act the same way even if it might hurt someone else. We feel inferior. We neither respect our values nor feel that we have things to offer the West. The Western way of life, with its rushed and stressful life-style, with its spiritually empty pursuit of money, also has its own problems. In their worship of the West, many of our young people don't adequately appreciate their own cultural heritage. Such feelings are the result of too long a time under colonialism and feudalism. I hope you understand that. If what I have said to you has anything worth passing along to others, it is that the young generation should not lose knowledge and appreciation of our traditional ways, while it strives to adapt to the world of the future.

Notes

Preface

1.   There is a growing literature on Indonesia, and no attempt will be made to cite all of the major scholarly works. An excellent beginning, however, is James L. Peacock, *Indonesia: An Anthropological Perspective* (Pacific Palisades, Calif.: Goodyear Press, 1973); and M. C. Ricklefs, *A History of Modern Indonesia* (Bloomington: Indiana University Press, 1981). Other important overall studies are Ruth T. McVey, *Indonesia* (New Haven, Conn.: Human Relations Area Files Press, 1963), and James J. Fox, ed., *Indonesia: The Making of a Culture* (Canberra, Australia: Research School of Pacific Studies, Australian National University, 1980).

For a study of Javanese culture, the best introductions are Clifford Geertz, *Religion of Java* (Chicago: University of Chicago Press, 1960); R. M. Koentjaraningrat, *Javanese Culture* (Singapore: Institute for Southeast Asian Studies and Oxford University Press, 1985); Hildred Geertz, *The Javanese Family* (New York: Free Press of Glencoe, 1961); and Robert Jay, *The Javanese Villagers* (Cambridge, Mass.: M.I.T. Press, 1969). More specialized treatments include Ward Keeler, *Javanese Shadow Plays, Javanese Selves* (Princeton, N.J.: Princeton University Press, 1987); Joseph Errington, *Structure and Style in Javanese* (Philadelphia: University of Pennsylvania Press, 1982); Robert Hefner, *Hindu Javanese* (Princeton: Princeton University Press, 1987); W. H. R. Rassers, *Panji, the Culture Hero* (The Hague: Martinus Nijhoff, 1959). For concepts of political authority, see Benedict Anderson, "The Concept of Power in Java," in *Culture and Politics in Indonesia*, ed. Claire Holt, (Ithaca, N.Y.: Cornell University Press, 1972); and A. Milner, *Kerajaan: Malay Political Culture on the Eve of Colonial Rule* (Tucson: University of Arizona Press, 1982).

2.   There is a large literature on life-history methodology, which is well analyzed in an important survey of its history, methods, structure, and ethics: L. L. Langness and Gelya Frank, *Lives: An Anthropological Approach to Biography* (Novato, Calif.: Chandler and Sharp, 1981). This book updates and supplements L. L. Langness, *The Life History in Anthropological Science* (New York: Holt, Rinehart and Winston, 1965). Lawrence C. Watson and Maria Barbara Watson-Franke, *Interpreting Life Histories: An Anthropological Inquiry* (New Brunswick, N.J.: Rutgers University Press, 1985) offers an insightful critique of past life histories but makes a plea for their more extensive use. The revival of popularity of life history is noted in

Dorothy Holland and James Peacock, "The Narrated Self," a paper presented at the 1988 annual meeting of the American Anthropological Association.

See also David G. Mandelbaum, "The Study of Life History: Gandhi," *Current Anthropology* 14 (June 1973): 177–206; Barbara Myerhoff, "Life History among the Elderly: Performance, Visibility, and Re-Membering," in *A Crack in the Mirror: Reflexive Perspectives in Anthropology*, ed. Jay Ruby, (Philadelphia: University of Pennsylvania Press, 1982); and Paul Ticoeur, *Time and Narrative* (Chicago: University of Chicago Press, 1984). For an interdisciplinary review, see Daniel Bertaux and Martin Kohli, "The Life Story Approach: A Continental View," *American Review of Sociology* 10 (1984): 215–237; Daniel Bertaux, ed., *Biography and Society: The Life-History Approach in the Social Sciences* (Beverly Hills, Calif.: Sage, 1981); G. H. Elder, *The Course of Life* (Ithaca, N.Y.: Cornell University Press, 1984); Kenneth Plummer, *Documents of Life* (London: Allen & Unwin, 1983); P. Thompson, *The Voice of the Past: Oral History*, 2nd ed. (New York: Oxford University Press, 1988) and many articles in *Oral History* and *The International Journal of Oral History*.

3.   George Marcus and Michael Fischer, *Anthropology as Cultural Critique: An Experimental Moment in the Human Sciences* (Chicago: University of Chicago Press, 1986); and James Clifford and George Marcus, eds., *Writing Culture: The Poetics and Politics of Ethnography* (Berkeley: University of California Press, 1986). For a trenchant critique of this new approach, see Frances Mascia-Lees, Patricia Sharpe, and Colleen Cohen, "The Postmodernist Turn in Anthropology: Cautions from a Feminist Perspective," *Signs* 15 (Autumn 1989): 7–33.

4.   Feminist scholars have played an important role in reviving attention to life histories in the 1980s. See *Interpreting Women's Lives: Feminist Theory and Personal Narratives*, ed. The Personal Narratives Group (Bloomington: Indiana University Press, 1989); see especially Marjorie Shostak's article in that anthology, which describes the interviewing that led to her book, *Nisa: The Life and Words of a !Kung Woman* (Cambridge, Mass.: Harvard University Press, 1981). see also Susan Geiger, "Women's Life Histories: Method and Content," *Signs* 11 (1986): 336; and the chapter on women's life histories in Lawrence C. Watson and Maria Barbara Watson-Franke, *Interpreting Life Histories: An Anthropological Inquiry* (New Brunswick, N.J.: Rutgers University Press, 1985). Particularly important recent life histories of women in non-Western cultures, which also included valuable introductions, are Daphne Patai, *Brazilian Women Speak: Contemporary Life Stories* (New Brunswick, N.J.: Rutgers University Press, 1988); and Fatima Mernissi, *Doing Daily Battle: Interviews with Moroccan Women* (New Brunswick, N.J.: Rutgers University Press, 1989).

5.   Mandelbaum, "Study of Life History," 193–194.

6.   A consideration of some special features of Javanese narration of life stories is in James L. Peacock, "Religion and Life History: An Exploration in Cultural Psychology," in *Text, Play, and Story*, ed. Edward Bruner, (Washington, D.C.: American Ethnological Society, 1984). See also the writings of Pramadya Ananta Tur and Alton L. Becker, "Text-Building, Epistemology, and Aesthetics in Javanese Shadow Theater," in *The Imagination of Reality*, ed. A. L. Becker and

A. Yengoyan (Norwood, N.J.: Ablex, 1979), 221–243. Extensive discussion of the Malayo-Indonesian way of narrating life histories is in A. Milner, "Post-Modern Perspectives on Malay Biography" (paper presented at the Seminar Biografi Malaysia, University of Malaysia, April 1986); and in Wung Gungwu, *Self and Biography* (Sydney: Sydney University Press, 1976).

7. As is obvious in this and following paragraphs, for my approach I am greatly indebted to the ideas expressed by Barbara Myerhoff, my former colleague at the University of Southern California, and to the participants in the panel of life histories, organized by James Peacock, that was held at the 1989 annual meeting of the American Anthropological Association. See Myerhoff, "Life History," and Riv-Ellen Press, "The Double Frame of Life History in the Work of Barbara Myerhoff," in *Interpreting Women's Lives*.

A Market Woman

1. In the Dutch colonial era, very little education was available for the masses of Javanese peasants. It was especially rare for a girl to be sent to school, and as a consequence most elderly Javanese women today are illiterate. Since independence, however, the Indonesian government has made widespread efforts to provide at least a basic education for youths of both sexes.

2. Javanese, even more than most agrarian cultures, value children highly. They have traditionally given birth to many children. This was necessary in premodern times, when a high mortality rate meant that people needed to have large numbers of children in order to insure at least one surviving child to care for them in their old age. But in the nineteenth century the Dutch instituted sanitation programs, and with a decline in infant mortality the population of Java began to grow sharply. After Indonesian independence more food became available to the peasants because the Dutch were no longer taking all the profits from the land. In response to this increased availability of resources Javanese families had more food for their children, more of whom grew into healthy adults. With improved medical care becoming more widely accessible through programs sponsored by the United Nations and international development programs, the mortality rate declined still further. These trends combined to produce even more massive population growth in Java in the 1950s and early 1960s.

The nationalist leader Sukarno encouraged this population explosion because it fit with his expansionist dreams for Indonesia's future. However, after 1965 Sukarno was eased out of power, and the Suharto regime renounced military expansionism and confrontation with neighboring Malaysia. There was no longer a political reason to justify population growth, and by the late 1960s the international population control movement convinced the Indonesian government to begin family-planning programs. Initially, population agencies tried to get people to "stop at three" children; they were only minimally persuasive. By the 1980s effectiveness had improved, and the goal has been reduced to two children per family.

Although government policy has changed, cultural values promoting reproduction have been slow to change. Many families still have more than two children, and every adult feels social pressure to marry and become a parent. The respected term of address for any adult man is "Bapak" (father) and for an adult woman is "Ibu" (mother). It is just assumed that an adult will be a parent. A childless adult is looked upon with pity because without social security programs and pensions for the elderly most people still depend upon their children to care for them in their old age.

Parenthood is thus a major social concern. One of the first questions that Javanese people ask upon introduction to a stranger is "How many children do you have?" If one replies "None," the next question asked is a direct "Why not?" As long as people are so dependent upon children for their retirement, and as long as there exists such strong social pressure that every person should reproduce, population reduction efforts can have only limited success.

3.   The traditional Javanese calendar is very complex, consisting of intersecting cycles of five-day weeks and seven-day weeks.

4.   It is not possible to get most Javanese to discuss the events of the 1964–1965 anticommunist upheavals because they are still such politically sensitive topics. In this interview, the woman would say no more than this, even though she had been promised anonymity.

5.   Traditional Javanese music is performed at a wayang shadow-puppet play by a gamelan orchestra. Because gamelan requires a large number of musicians, it is not often that the masses could hear it before the coming of audio tape recordings and radio. Having a radio or tape player thus marks a major improvement for villagers. The government radio station devotes much of its airtime to wayang music.

A Farmer and Village Leader

1.   While marriages were traditionally arranged by the parents, it was not necessarily expected that an arranged marriage would be set for life. If a man or woman followed their parents' wish and sincerely tried to make the arranged marriage work, there was no dishonor if either spouse deserted the marriage after a year or so. Combined with higher mortality rates, this marriage desertion meant that an adult of either sex would have more than one spouse during his or her lifetime.

2.   Faced with severe overpopulation in Java by the 1960s, the Indonesian government developed a "transmigration" plan to encourage Javanese to resettle in Indonesian sparsely populated islands. Although inspired by the American western movement, most of these programs have not been successful. In the 1980s the government gradually backed away from population resettlement and began to emphasize reduction of the birthrate.

3.   These schools were designed by the Dutch to train bookkeepers and clerical workers for the colonial government, hence the emphasis on clear writing, following orders, and neatness of dress and comportment.

4.   The speaker is implicitly criticizing Indonesia's current underfunded public school system, where students must pay for their own books and supplies. For many poor families, these expenses make it difficult or impossible for their children to stay in school.

5.   Malay was the language favored by the anti-Dutch nationalists. As a gesture of respect for other ethnic groups, as well as the people of Malaysia, the Javanese-dominated nationalist party decided to use Malay instead of the difficult Javanese language. Malay, adapted to become *Bahasa Indonesia*, remains the national language of the nation, even though Sukarno's dream of unification with Malaysia is no longer being asserted.

6.   By 1943, Japan had decided to impound Indonesian crops to feed its armed forces in the South Pacific. More than anything else, this action alienated the Javanese from their would-be liberators.

7.   A sarong is a traditional Javanese man's dress. One long piece of cloth sewn together at the end, a sarong is wrapped around the body and rolled downward so that it covers the body from the waist to the ankles. A versatile garment, it can be unrolled to use as a shoulder covering or head covering in the rain and also as bedding for sleeping.

8.   From the earliest European invasions, Muslim fighting forces like the Hizbullah have been the primary organizations for military resistance to foreign domination. In some respects, the spread of the militant religion of Islam in Southeast Asia can be seen as a reaction against imperialism.

A Soldier in the Revolution

1.   This statement is, in essence, the Hindu-Buddhist concept of karma. The basic idea of karma is that, when someone does something bad to another person, there will inevitably be a tragic result for the perpetrator later on—either in this lifetime or in a future lifetime. Every action is both cause and effect, for either good or ill. Before Islam spread into Java, Hinduism and Buddhism were the dominant religions. Though most twentieth-century Javanese people consider themselves Muslim, many Buddhist and Hindu ideas continue to exert a powerful influence on popular attitudes.

A Seamstress

1.   It is common for university lecturers to have some kind of secondary employment because their teaching salaries are generally so low. Education in Indonesia has been greatly hampered because of the meager salaries paid to teachers at all levels. As a result, the teaching field does not often attract the top students. Those teachers who try to approach their job professionally are often overburdened.

2.   By the late 1950s there was a multiplicity of political parties in Indonesia, each vying with the others to capture more attention and support. As with many

successful entrepreneurs, this woman happened to be at the right place at the right time, and she quickly took her opportunity to build a business around this political activity. Her political neutrality served the business well. After the post-1965 decline of Indonesia's multiple political parties, she switched to making uniforms for the military as well as social groups and boy and girl scouts. Thus, in an era when politics has been kept subdued, this businesswoman has retained her flexibility, the secret of her economic success.

A Policeman

1.   A keris dagger is a symbol of power in Javanese society. Not only is it a deadly weapon signifying physical power, but it also represents one's spiritual power. Javanese authorities traditionally wore their keris on their back, inserted in their belt, as a symbol of their power and authority.

A Writer

1.   Among the status-conscious Javanese, a priyayi is considered an upper-class person educated in the refined ways of the Javanese elite. Traditionally, priyayi were officials in the sultan's courts. When the Dutch came to Java, they used the priyayi as native office holders and petty officials to administer the colonial system. Their descendents, plus those making false claims, sometimes use the title of priyayi, even if they are not government officials themselves.

2.   Reyog is a theatrical folk dance of east Java. Because of its lower-class circuslike atmosphere and also possibly because of the association of its all-male performers with homosexual behavior, participation in a reyog group by a priyayi might be looked down upon. In the Ponorogo district of east Java, however, where reyog first developed, all classes of men participate in a reyog troupe. There, participation in a reyog troupe is a mark of high status.

3.   The Mataram kingdom was one of the earliest Hindu kingdoms of Java, but the name Mataram was taken by a new dynasty in the 1600s. This dynasty later divided, and both branches continue in power as the sultans of Yogyakarta and Surakarta.

A Dalang Shadow-Puppet Teacher

1.   Actually, this dalang is boasting. Most dalangs also do not have a set fee, but they usually negotiate a suitable fee before agreeing to do a performance. His statements, although not strictly true, indicate the Javanese value of not appearing to be greedy for money.

A Muslim Convert

1. The term *abangan* does not really mean "atheist." Rather, it means persons who identify themselves as Muslim but who do not follow the daily precepts of the religion. In contrast to the strict Muslims, called *santri*, the more numerous abangan Javanese tend casually to mix tenets of Islam with elements of Hindu and Buddhist thought as well as the native Javanese religions represented by the dukun and the wayang traditions.

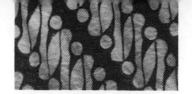

Index